Liverpool
A People's History

by Peter Aughton

Carnegie Publishing, 1993

Liverpool: A People's History
by Peter Aughton

Copyright © Peter Aughton, 1990

Published by Carnegie Publishing Ltd, 18 Maynard Street, Ashton, Preston PR2 2AL.
Typeset in 10pt Times and Plantin Medium by Carnegie Publishing.
Layout and design by Carnegie Publishing.
Printed by Redwood Books, Trowbridge, Wiltshire

First published in hardback, March 1990. This edition published September 1993,
Reprinted 1999

ISBN 0 948789-96-4

Liverpool

A People's History

by Peter Aughton

Author's preface

IT IS impossible to write a single-volume history of Liverpool without leaving out many things and many people who deserve to be mentioned. James Picton came closest to achieving a full and comprehensive history, drawing on original sources and on the work of men like Enfield, Troughton and Baines, who lived before him. It took two heavy volumes to write his *Memorials of Liverpool* and he had to follow these a few years later with two further volumes of municipal records, which were even heavier.

It is now over a hundred years since Picton's work was published and the tempo of change has increased so rapidly since that time that, although his work will always comprise an excellent set of reference books, a modern history must also cover not only the main events of the late-nineteenth century but nearly all the twentieth century as well.

This century we have Muir and Platt (1906) and Chandler (1957) to fall back on, and many valuable specialised works on Liverpool have been published in the last two decades. A sound economic study has been written by Francis Hyde and a very readable book by on *Old Liverpool* by Eric Midwinter. The Historic Society of Lancashire and Cheshire has published a valuable collection of papers on the slave trade, edited by R. Anstey and P. E. H. Hair; the Merseyside Archaeological Society has produced some fascinating books with detailed mapwork; the Liverpool Heritage Bureau has published an excellent volume on the buildings of Liverpool; Brian Walker and Ann Hinchcliffe have produced a well-researched volume of old photographs; and Countyvise, Editions Ltd., the Scouse Press and the Gallery Press have produced interesting and popular publications within easy reach of every pocket. There are specialist publications for those who believe that the history of Liverpool began with the formation of two football clubs, and other volumes for those who maintain that Liverpool's greatest era was the Mersey Sound of the 1960s.

In spite of all these publications, however, there seemed to be a crying need for a new general history, a people's history that breaks away from the more formal academic traditions and tells the stories of old Liverpool as they happened and, wherever possible, in the words of the people who were there to witness the events.

It has been an immense pleasure researching and writing about Liverpool. Its history is so rich, so varied and so interesting that I was sorely tempted to write far more, thus coming close to defeating one of the main objectives – to produce a book of manageable length, accessible to all.

Contents

Introduction

N he midst of the town rose the massive stone pile of the castle. It had known better days and its ancient, crumbling walls were overgrown with moss and ivy, but the four tall corner towers were still intact and the castle dominated the whole town, which spread out below in about two dozen narrow streets. A goodly number of vessels lay at anchor in the river, some riding out the tide in the middle of the estuary, others moored by hawsers to the river bank. But the central point of where the shipping lay was a small natural harbour known as the Pool. It was little more than a small tidal creek fed by a thin trickle of a stream which ran down from the green hills in the neighbourhood of the village of Everton. The Pool was a hive of activity, however, with wooden walled vessels from many distant parts busily loading and unloading their wares.

When Thomas Bulman and his wife arrived at the ancient chapel of St Nicholas, it had recently been elevated to the status of a parish church; they had brought their infant child Robert with them to be baptised. The young couple lived in Dale Street, the most populous street in town, where Tom shared a workshop with his brother, John, who was courting Ellen Rowson.

After the Plague and the Great Fire a number of merchants had left London to set up business in 'Leverpoole', a small market town on the Lancashire bank of the river Mersey where the shipping trade was growing very rapidly. A few skilled artisans like the Bulmans followed the merchants to the expanding town where they hoped to escape the overcrowded and rat-infested streets of the capital city to find a better life in the provinces. The Bulmans were a very old family of clockmakers who originated in Nürnberg, where Jacob and Caspar Bulman were making clocks in the sixteenth century and Thomas had a workshop at Swan Alley near London Bridge in the late-seventeenth century. Their chosen town was growing so rapidly that trade was said to rival even that of the great city of Bristol and some were already describing it as a London in miniature.

Although it had great pretensions as a sea port, the town still retained much of the character of a country market town. To the north was the medieval town field, and the townsfolk worked their strips of land within a stone's throw of the Exchange where the merchants conducted their business. On market days a steady, gossiping stream of ruddy-faced country yokels descended with their pigs and sheep along the approach roads, leading carts of farm produce from the nearby villages of Lancashire. Others came by ferry across the river from the Cheshire villages on the Wirral. Boats arrived precariously loaded with grunting pigs and cackling hens and sometimes even horses and cows. Fishermen from the coastal parishes moored their smacks by the river bank to bring their catch to add to the sights and smells of the market.

WE had been looking at antique clocks for over a year, with only rather vague ideas of what we wanted to buy. We were agreed on a long case clock but the problem was that most of them were too tall for a modern house and the smaller grandmother clocks did not quite have the age and character which we were looking for. It was still a rewarding exercise, however, and we had become quite knowledgeable on the prices and we could even recognise styles from the different periods.

One day we arrived at a market town in the valley of the Severn. An old house in the High Street had been converted for use as a showroom and on entering the building we were greeted by a fantastic collection of tall clocks standing like sentinels around the walls. They were all in reasonable agreement about the time of day but when a new hour arrived they all proclaimed the fact in different voices amid a great display of jangling disharmony which echoed through the building. We were greeted by the proprietor, who was a kindly, honest and elderly man, very much at home among his stock of ancient timepieces.

'Did you have anything particular in mind, sir?'

'Not especially. I would like a north-country clock by preference, eighteenth-century if I can afford it.'

He showed me a huge Yorkshire clock, which he assured me would keep excellent time. It was so big that I didn't think it would fit through the front door. He then showed me a very expensive clock by a well-known London maker who, he assured me, was 'in the book'. The clock might have tempted me, had I been a great deal wealthier.

In the meantime my wife had wandered off into a second, smaller showroom and she now returned with an excited look of discovery on her face.

'There's one in here I want you to see,' she said.

We walked across to the other room. There stood a clock, not as grand as the London clock, and only half the size of the Yorkshire clock, but somehow prettier and more homely than either of them. Our quest was over. Here was just the clock we had been searching for, but could we afford to buy him?

He, for I could not refer to an object with so much character as 'it', stood about six-foot-three and would fit our house extremely well. He was made of dark oak, with a slim case and a round lenticle where a brass pendulum oscillated busily to and fro. His dial was of bright polished brass, and I could tell from the style and the chapter ring that he was from the early-eighteenth century. He was the oldest clock in the shop, older than the London clock by a good fifty years.

'How much?' I asked the proprietor, waiting to hear the worst.

'This one is very difficult to value, sir.'

'Is he in the book?'

'No. But its a very fine clock. We only got it in a few days ago and we're not sure how to value it. You see, it was originally made as a thirty-hour clock but the movement was replaced soon afterwards with an eight-day movement.'

'It doesn't look like a conversion.'

'No sir. It's been expertly done by an eighteenth-century clock-maker, and we would never have known if we hadn't taken the movement apart to service it.'

I liked his honesty. I let him continue.

'Also, you can see that the case has been debased. These carvings are not original. They were probably added in Victorian times.'

For the first time I noticed that in the panels of the clock case were some unobtrusive carved spiral designs. I liked the designs. I found them very artistic and quite within character, but I accepted his point that they were not original.

'How old do you think he is?'

'Ten-inch dials are very early sir. It could be seventeenth-century. But we have chosen to be cautious and we have dated it at around 1700.'

He was nearly three hundred years old. I was impressed. He was older than I thought possible.

'So what do you think he's worth?' I asked again.

He quoted a figure about twice as much as I wanted to pay but substantially less than I imagined the clock to be worth. I unworthily blessed the person who had done the carvings and had put the clock within my price range.

The clock had a scent of polished wood and beeswax. The dial was of polished brass with cherubs' faces in the spandrels at the four corners and a beautiful scrolled pattern of foliage inscribed inside a chapter ring of white metal. Beneath the chapter ring, at the bottom of the dial near the thirty second mark, a most important piece of information was engraved in a beautiful lettering with artistic flourishes on the longer characters. It described the name and place of the clockmaker. He was so old that even the spelling of the placename had not evolved to its final form. The inscription read 'Tho. Bulman, Leverpoole'.

Longcase clock by Thomas Bulman of Liverpool.

Clockmaking was a prominent industry in Liverpool from the late-seventeenth century. The clock pictured here is probably the oldest surviving Liverpool clock, dating from around 1700. In style it is a good example of a Lancashire clock of the period, with oak case and round lenticle, an engraved brass dial with white metal chapter ring and cherubed spandrels. Even at this period the clockmaking industry was highly organised, and the clockmaker could purchase gears, spindles, springs, clock-cases and other items from specialised manufacturers.

In my subsequent search to find Tom Bulman I came to know Queen Anne's Liverpool well enough to give a conducted tour of the place. But this was not the only period of Liverpool's history which fascinated me. I quickly determined to undertake a journey in time from 1207 to 1989, to discover the story of how the twentieth-century city grew from its humble beginnings before the time of Magna Carta, to meet and gossip with characters from every century on the way, to explore and fill in the gaps between. Unless you have studied Liverpool for many years, empty your minds of any preconceived notions. There are many surprises in store, for the history of Liverpool is a great story and it deserves to be better known.

Peter Aughton
October 1989

Chapter One

The Pool

HE RIVER rose in the millstone grit of the Pennines. It was not a long river and it was not a particularly large one, but it drained an area with an above average English rainfall and it had grown to a wide and powerful stream by the time it neared the sea. On its approach to the coast the river widened out until the banks were three miles apart; then it seemed to change its mind and the banks came closer together and approached to within a mile of each other, forming a narrow and fast-flowing estuary before finally making its entrance to the sea.

The boulder clay on the east bank supported a lush green carpet of vegetation. To the north lay a narrow deposit of alluvium and beyond was a golden beach backed by wild hills of blown sand which reached to the horizon as far as the eye could see. Inland to the east was a wooded ridge rising to about five hundred feet and with outcrops of red sandstone showing bare through the trees and undergrowth. A small stream splashed down from the ridge and flowed through a dark peat bog to the table land where it found a way to the wide river below. When it reached the levels near the shore the stream opened out to form a large pool which expanded and contracted with the ebb and flow of the tide.

There was no human habitation near the pool but there was some evidence of cultivation, and a casual traveller might descry a peasant in the distance, following a team of oxen with his wooden plough and turning the clay soil to prepare the ground to sow his crop. It was well over a hundred years since the Norman Conquest and the Anglo-Saxon people had grown accustomed to the new feudal order in which, for the most part, they were subservient to their French-speaking Norman overlords.

The people were born to a brief hard life of labour. They thought themselves fortunate if they lived long enough to raise another generation to work the lord's land. The villein was not quite a slave. He had a holding of land at the will of his lord, but he was still the property of his master and in return for his holding he had to perform a variety of services. He was not allowed to leave the land, and if he did then he could be brought back by force. His daughter could not marry

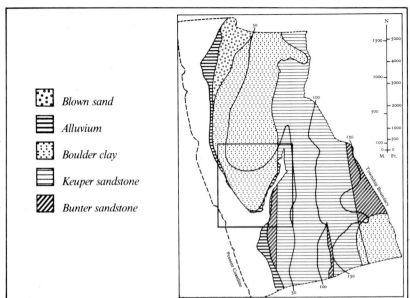

The geology of Liverpool township, showing the thirteenth-century coastline. The square area outlined is that shown on pages 22-3. With a shallow tidal pool offering a relatively safe anchorage and with an area of elevated land at least partially protected by a small peninsula, this site was an obvious choice for King John when he decided to create the new borough of Liverpool in 1207.

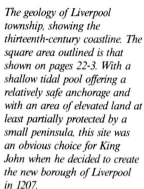

without the payment of a fine. He could not even die without his lord demanding his best cow or the equivalent as 'heriot' payment. The folklore spoke of a supposedly free England under the Anglo-Saxon kings – a distant arcadia of memories handed down through the generations of the people. How much of this was true is difficult to assess but the legend lived on for many centuries, suggesting it had more than a grain of truth about it.

It was rare for a monarch to visit this remote part of the kingdom, but when King John was travelling through the northern counties his journey took him from Lancaster to the port of Chester, where travellers could embark for the passage to Ireland. The crossing of the Mersey was at Warrington, and it is unlikely that the king ventured far from the trodden path, but John was planning a great expedition to Ireland and he was seeking another place of embarkation to supplement Chester in the north-west counties. King John's advisors explored the coastline around the Mersey Estuary. They discovered the ancient coastal settlements at Aigburth, Toxteth, Kirkdale and Crosby. Inland were Croxteth, Roby, West Derby with its old Norman castle and Walton-on-the-Hill with its parish church. They also discovered a small tidal inlet on the banks of the Mersey.

The inlet, or pool, lay in the parish of Walton. It had been granted to Warine of Lancaster by Henry II and had devolved to Henry, the son of Warine. The place was known locally as the 'liver' or the 'lever' pool, a description which referred to thick or sluggish water, possibly because of the growth of seaweed round the edges of the little creek. With its natural sheltered harbour, it seemed a suitable spot for a port, and the king was advised to acquire the land to assist him with his Irish campaigns.

But John did a great deal more than acquire the land. The following year he decided to create there a new town with a royal charter, with free men, certain trading rights and other royal privileges:

John by the grace of God King of England, Lord of Ireland, Duke of

Normandy and Aquitaine, Count of Anjou, to all his loyal subjects who
may wish to have burgages in the township of Liverpul, greeting. Know ye
that we have granted to all our loyal subjects who shall take burgages in
Liverpul that they shall have all the liberties and free customs in the
township of Liverpul which any free borough on the sea has in our land.
And therefore we command you that in safety and in our peace ye come
thither to receive and occupy our burgages. And in testimony hereof we
transmit to you these our letters patent. Witness Simon de Pateshill. At
Winchester the 28th day of August in the 9th year of our reign [1207].[1]

At first sight it appears a very generous charter. In fact the liberties
and free customs were no more than those already granted to other
ports and 'boroughs on the sea'. As always in such matters, moreover,
the rights were at the king's discretion. They did not hold for all time
and the 'charter' was strictly speaking little more than an invitation for
interested parties to purchase a burgage in the new town. But the word
'free' meant far more in the Middle Ages than it came to mean in later
centuries. The town would be populated by free men, and John's
charter was very unusual in that, although there might have been a
handful of primitive dwellings between the Pool and the Mersey, there
was no existing town, no church or chapel, not even a hamlet on the
site. The royal borough had effectively been created from nothing.

This apparently desolate and unpeopled site consisted of a broad
promontory between the Pool and the Mersey, with a small hillock
rising to a height of about fifty feet and commanding a view of the
entrance to the harbour with grand vistas of the whole river estuary
and a fine view out to the Welsh mountains on the western horizon.
This was the place where the town was to be founded. Fields were
cleared from the woodlands to the north. Some may already have
existed as part of the manor; they became known as the Oldfields, the
Dalefield and the Heathy Lands.

Planned towns were favoured places, with rights, privileges and
royal patronage to attract new residents. The burgages were small plots
of land within the town boundaries, and the holders were called
burgesses. The plots were large enough to accommodate a house and
premises for trade, and they were accompanied by two strips in the
town fields, amounting to between one or two acres of land. The
package on offer was enticing and many people did 'come thither' to
claim the burgages. Most of them were men local to Lancashire and
Cheshire, but some came from Ireland, Wales and further afield to
stake a claim in the royal borough.

Some came to farm the land; some to trade in the new town; others
still were attracted by the opportunity to work on building the town
and its castle. The Benedictine monks from the Priory at Birkenhead
claimed an early interest and it is just possible that the original
peasants of Liverpool Manor were allowed a burgage in the town
which was founded on the land which they worked. The quality of life
in a royal borough was little better than in the country, but if a villein
could escape to a town then he could not be retaken by his master
within the boundaries of that town – if he had friends and a trade with
which to make his living then escape was a way to win his freedom. It
is likely that a few of the earliest residents of Liverpool arrived by this
unorthodox route.

A simple pattern of streets developed. The plan was like the letter 'H'

Saxton's map shows 'Lerpoole Haven', where some Tudor travellers claimed that up to three hundred vessels could lie at anchor, a deep bay to the north of the small town. Villages such as Kirkdale, West Derby, Roby and Childwall are easily recognised, but the early spellings, such as Everton and Wavertree, make some places harder to identify. Note also the River Alt, Simonswood Forest and several deer parks, including Knowsley and Toxteth.

with the bar at the centre extending in both directions to give a total of seven streets. The street names were not recorded until the following century but it is likely that their names were acquired very soon after the streets were formed. Castle Street, the southern-most of the seven, met Juggler Street at one of the crossroads where Bank Street ran down to the Mersey on the left and Dale Street ran inland to the right. Proceeding along Juggler Street to the second crossroads was Chapel Street on the left and Moore Street on the right. To the north Juggler Street changed again to Whiteacre Street. These seven streets were for many years the total complement of the town of Liverpool. All seven streets survive, albeit in greatly modified forms, though only Castle Street, Dale Street and Chapel Street retain their original names.

The right to hold a weekly market every Saturday was granted from the outset, and an annual fair was held on St Martin's Day. As early as 1227 Liverpool had outstripped West Derby in terms of the volume of its trade. The tallage for Liverpool rose from £3 6s 8d in 1222 to over £7 in 1227, compared with figures of 13s 4d and £4 13s 4d for the same years at West Derby. It also compared very favourably with the far older and better established Lancashire towns of Preston and Lancaster, which in 1227 paid tallage of £10 0s 6d and £8 15s 4d respectively.

When it came to caring for the souls, however, Walton remained firmly in control of the new borough and it was nearly five centuries before Liverpool had its own parish church. The prosperity of the town was such that in Henry III's reign the Crown granted a new charter which cost the burgesses ten marks but which effectively remained the governing charter for the next four hundred years, all the intervening charters being little more than confirmations of the charter of 1229. The Crown conceded that Liverpool should be a free borough for ever; the burgesses were given the right to hold their own court and to deal out their own local justice; certain trading rights were given which placed the traders on the same level as the burgesses of other royal boroughs; but, most important, the charter gave them the right to have 'a gild merchant with a hansa and all the liberties and free customs pertaining to that gild'. The formation of a guild was a great step forward for the rights of the merchants and traders.

In Liverpool's early years the most impressive and important building to be erected was the great stone castle built by William de Ferrers, the Sheriff of Lancaster. It was built of solid sandstone on the prime site at the highest point on the promontory between the Pool and the Mersey. It was completed in 1235, from which it is reasonable to deduce that construction began soon after King John's original charter of 1207. The building was a good source of employment for many of the new trades and skills which the town was hoping to attract. An earlier timber-built castle existed at West Derby but it was allowed to fall into ruins after the completion of the stone castle at Liverpool.

The new fortress was heavy and solid, built out of local stone on a site about fifty yards square, and surrounded by a moat which was twenty yards wide in places and hewn out of solid rock. On the north-east corner of the castle was a large fortified gatehouse or barbican flanked by two small square towers, where entrance to the interior was gained through a vaulted passage and guarded by a portcullis. At the other corners of the square were tall rounded towers connected by thick curtain walls which rose high and sheer above the rock sides of the moat.

The castle was designed to be self supporting in case of siege and it therefore acquired a hall for dining, sleeping and general living, a brewhouse to supply ale, a bakehouse to supply bread, a covered well to draw water, and a chapel to cater for all spiritual needs. An underground passage ran from the north side of the castle to the shore, designed most probably as a channel to supply the moat with water. A stone dovecote was built against the south wall and under the shadow of the east wall an orchard was planted with apple trees growing down to the banks of the Pool.

Later in the thirteenth century the Moores, an important family of burgage holders, built their own substantial manor house on the outskirts of the town. Among other prominent local families were those of Cross and Norris. The Cross family were much later than the Moores in building themselves a town house, and the Norrises preferred to retain their main residence some miles to the south at Speke.

A horse mill ground malt for the Moore tenants and there was a water mill to grind the corn, driven by the small stream which ran down from the hills towards the head of the Pool. The earliest place of worship was probably the chapel within the castle walls, but soon afterwards the tiny chapel of St Mary del Key was built at the end of the street which became known as Chapel Street. It stood hard by the grassy banks of the Mersey and was built on a rock just above the sea shore. For a hundred years St Mary del Key served as the only place of worship outside the castle. Like the Chapel of St. Nicholas, which was built just to the east in the following century, St. Mary del Key was not a church, merely a chapel of Walton-on-the-Hill. It was used by the monks of Birkenhead Priory who built a granary to store their grain and who also operated the ferry to the Cheshire shore which is first

Ferrers
'Vairy or and gules'.

The Ferrers were the first Earls of Derby. William de Ferrers built Liverpool Castle between 1207 and 1235 and the Ferrers lived there until 1266. Mary de Ferrers, niece of Henry III, was ordered to surrender the castle to the Crown when her husband, Robert, was declared a rebel.

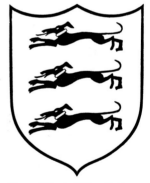

Moore (More) of More Hall
An early influential family in Liverpool, whose name may well come from the moorish ground that once lay to the north of the Pool. More Hall was built in the thirteenth century and Bank Hall in Kirkdale was built by Thomas Moore in 1388-89. Several new streets were laid out by Edward Moore in the seventeenth century, some of which still survive.

Crosse (Cross)
'Quarterly gules and or a cross potent argent in the first and fourth quarters'
The Crosse family inherited much of the property of the Liverpool family and were related to them by marriage (note the similarity in the coats of arms, see page 19). Cross Hall, on the south side of Dale Street, was built in the early-sixteenth century and John Cross bequeathed a building for the first town hall in 1515.

mentioned in 1256. Boundary stones were set to mark the limits of the market and the fair.

The castle, as might be expected, became a centre of violence and turmoil whenever war or rebellion spread to the north west of England and sometimes because of petty local jealousies. In the 1260s the Ferrers family, who lived in the castle for most of the thirteenth century, attempted to gain control of the borough and to deny the burgesses their legal rights under the royal charter. Robert de Ferrers, the main protagonist, carried his ambitions too far – he rebelled against the Crown and his lands and rights were forfeited.

This was not the end of the problems, however, for Robert de Ferrer's possessions became the property of his son Edmund, the next Earl of Lancaster, and Edmund also attempted to interfere with the rights of the townspeople. Edmund's henchmen tried to squeeze the maximum possible rents out of the burgesses and they put up the market tolls. The burgesses resisted. They had two royal charters in their possession. They knew their rights and they eventually took the matter to the crown court at Lancaster. Edmund was issued with a summons to appear before the court:

> And certain men of the Borough of Lyverpol came . . . And they say that the lord John the King . . . by his charter which they showed, granted to all his lieges who should take burgages there, that they should have all the liberties and free customs in the vill of Lyverpol, which any free borough on the sea has in the king's land . . . And because it is clear from their evidence that the aforesaid Edmund has usurped and occupied the aforesaid liberties, the sheriff is ordered to cause him to come here . . . And the community is ordered to be here then to prosecute on behalf of our lord the king . . . And the community put in their place John More, Adam son of Richard, Alan Walseman and Richard de Lyverpol.[2]

In this instance there is no record of the court's decision, but it seems to have gone against the town, for we discover that it was several decades before Liverpool was again able to exercise its full rights as a free borough, not, in fact, until a new charter was issued at the beginning of the reign of Edward III.

The rebellion of Robert de Ferrers took place in 1266 and when his wife Mary de Ferrers was ordered to surrender the castle she appears to have done so without putting up any form of resistance. Early in the following century, however, the castle was under siege for the first time in its history. In 1315 there broke out a rising known as the Banastre Revolt when Adam Banastre, supported by Henry Lea and William Bradshaw, attempted to wrest control of the county of Lancashire from the powerful Holland family. The Banastre Revolt was little more than a family feud, but a great many people were drawn into it and the feud developed into what was essentially a local civil war, with many of the leading Lancashire families involved in the fighting. It was a terrifying time for the people of the small fishing village when the rebels advanced with an army of followers to attack the castle, but the gatehouse and the great walls held out against the siege. The besiegers were driven back to take the defenceless town of West Derby where they easily took the old ruined Norman castle which could not possibly hold out against them.

Liverpool Castle probably suffered some damage from the siege. It was thoroughly repaired and strengthened only a few years later, but the reason for the repairs was not so much because of the war damage but rather the occasion of Liverpool's first royal visit. In the Middle Ages, Liverpool was a relatively small and unimportant example of the hundreds of royal boroughs that existed throughout the country, but in a few exceptional cases, usually when the perpetual wars with the Irish reached the centre stage, the King took a personal interest in Liverpool. In 1323 Edward II undertook a tour of Lancashire to try and restore order after the chaos which had been generated by the Banastre Revolt and the invasions of the Scots from over the border. He decided he would stay for a week at Liverpool Castle and the local residents were thrown into a great state of turmoil, for nobody had the slightest idea of what a royal visit entailed. The walls and towers of the castle were restored, as were the gates and buildings within the walls. The roof of the great hall needed repairs which amounted to the princely sum of 1s 8d. There was a great purchasing of victuals and provisions to wine and dine the King and his Majesty's extensive retinue in something approaching the manner to which they were accustomed.

The dates of Edward II's visit were from the 24th to the 30th of October 1323. His stay seems to have been largely uneventful, except that, after having seen Liverpool and met the people, he spent the next few years issuing them with all kinds of feverish orders to assist with his endless war preparations. First the bailiffs were instructed to warn all mariners to beware of pirates, then every person entering and leaving the port was to be searched in case he or she carried letters which might be prejudicial to the king. The bailiffs were also ordered to prevent the export of any horses, armour, or large amounts of money – but wealthy Flemings seem to have been excepted and were to be treated with the greatest respect and kindness. Any ship which was large enough to carry forty tuns of wine was to be apprehended and held in readiness for the King's service and any ship of fifty tuns burthen or greater was to be given instructions to sail directly for Plymouth where it would be made available for use of the King.

In the fourteenth century there was little peace for the English people as their rulers found fault with the Welsh, Scots, Irish, French, and each of their neighbours in turn. The Liverpool bailiffs were given instructions to detain any vessel which might be useful to the Crown's perennial military preparations. In 1333 they were ordered to retain vessels of fifty tons and over to assist with the wars against the Scots and two years later six of 'the largest ships to be found on the west coast between Liverpool and Skymburnesse' were armed and manned to do battle against our warlike northern neighbours. In the same year two fully-armed ships sailed from the Mersey in pursuit of a great foreign ship which was sailing for Dumbarton with a cargo of wine and arms destined to aid the Scots in their wars against the English.

In the north of England the impact of the interminable Hundred Years War against the French was less immediate than the effect of the wars with the Scots, but on more than one occasion ships were ordered to find their way to the south coast to assist with the defence of the realm. Early in the French war the bailiffs were instructed not to allow any vessel to leave for foreign parts except as a member of a large fleet with an armed escort and in 1328 the bailiffs were ordered to hold any vessels of forty tons burthen in readiness to resist the King's enemies from Normandy and Poitou.

Sometimes Liverpool served the purpose which King John had envisaged and became an embarkation point for troops travelling to Ireland. In 1372 we find mention of vessels as large as two hundred tons ordered to assemble at Liverpool for the transportation of William de Windsor, governor of Ireland, and his retinue.

The largest scene of activity which the port witnessed, however, was in 1361 when 'the whole navy of the land, completely armed', was ordered to transport Lionel of Clarence and his army to Ireland, with fleets sailing from both Liverpool and Chester.

Less is known about the humbler fishing vessels belonging to the local community which played an important part in the local economy of the Middle Ages, but there is occasional mention of the Mersey ferry and by the end of the thirteenth century there seem to have been at least three boats plying across the river for this purpose.

The earliest estimate of the population comes from the returns of 1296, when the number of burgages was given as 168, from which a total population of around 800 can be estimated. Some sources quote a figure of only 106 burgages in 1336, which implies a sudden decrease of population early in the fourteenth century. The population certainly did vary a great deal. Liverpool suffered badly from the Black Death of 1349 and also from another serious outbreak of the bubonic plague a decade later; in fact one of the first records of the Chapel of St Nicholas is the mass burial of plague victims in the year 1360. The burgess roll of 1346 shows 196 householders, so that allowing five people per household the population might just have reached the thousand mark before it was savagely cut back again by the ubiquitous horror of the Black Death.

The earliest list to give actual names of Liverpool residents is that of the 109 contributers to the poll tax for 1379. This fascinating return not only gives the names of the earliest local families, but it also gives the occupations of the tax payers and some idea of their relative wealth and status. The following is an extract:

POLL TAX RETURNS 1379[3]
Villa de Lyverpull

William de Lyverpull	— mayor	6s 8d
Richard de Aynesargh	—drapour	6s 8d
John Travers	—franklayn	40d
John de Hull	— fishmonger	2s
John de Eccleston of Lyverpull	— heringemonger	12d
Stephen le Walsh	— braciator	6d
Adam le Fourbour	— heringemonger	6s 8d
John de Wolleton	— braciator	6d
Simon de Kirkedale	— braciator	6d
Richard de Angrom	— drapour	12d
Richard Tipup	— drapor	12d
John Mercer and his wife	— cultores	4d
Henry Blakleg	— heryngmonger	12d
William de Roby	— draper	12d
Nicholas le Clerk and wife	— cultores	4d
Thomas le Fleshewer	— carnifax	6d
Henry Bushell	— braciator	6d
Emma de Sydgreves	— braciator	6d
Richard le Mustardman	— braciator	6d
Robert de Mawdesley	— cissor	6d
John de Longwro and wife	— cultores	4d

Walton of Walton
'Sable three swans argent'
  The Waltons were lords of the manor of Walton and held the sergeantry of the wapentake of Derby. They therefore had influence in Liverpool because the borough lay within the parish of Walton. In 1346 Richard de Walton held four burgages in the town and the family provided at least one constable of the castle.

Robert de Whalley — braciator 6d
Richard le Fermon and wife — cultores 4d
John le Somenour and wife — cultores 4d
Simon le Gardoner — pistor 6d
Thomas le Harpour and wife — cultores 4d
William le Herbirgh — fabor 12d
Patrick de Irlond — souter 6d
Richard de Blaken and wife — cultores 4d
Alexander le Ferour — faber 12d
John de Lynacre and wife — cultores 4d
Adam le Korker — huster 6d
Peter de Wilton and wife — cultores 4d
William de Litster and wife — cultores 4d
Adam de Ditton — serviens 4d
Henry de Whitby — serviens 4d
Roger de Ditton and wife — cultores 4d
Richard de Sefton and wife — cultores 4d
Robert le Shephird — serviens 4d
Richard de Heley —. serviens 4d
John servant of William de Roby — [serviens] 4d
Roger Walker — serviens 4d
John Passmyche — serviens 4d

Looking firstly at the occupations, the 'drapours' were drapers or cloth merchants. Adam le Korker was a retailer (huster). The fishmongers and herringmongers are seen to be very numerous and they indicate the extent of the local fishing industry. The 'braciators' were brewers and included a woman amongst their number, the alewife Emma de Sydgreves. Robert de Mawdesley was a tailor (cissor), Patrick de Irlond was a cobbler (souter). William de Herbirgh and Alexandr le Ferour were smiths (fabers). Simon le Gardoner, in spite of his name, was a baker (pistor). Those named as 'serviens' were servants, mostly in the households of the gentry, and those named as 'cultores' were agricultural workers of some kind. The relative wealth of the various occupations can be judged from the amount of tax paid. Servants and labourers rarely paid more than the minimum tax of fourpence, whereas the brewers were taxed at sixpence and some of the herringmongers appear to be among the wealthiest residents – in one case paying up to 6s 8d tax, as much as the mayor himself.

The family names of the great landowners, such as the Moores and Molyneuxs, had been in use for at least two centuries, but at this point in time the names of the common people had in most cases only been in existence for one or two generations. Family names were only just being finalised and passed on from father to son, and we are therefore witnessing not only some of the earliest family names in Liverpool but also names which originate in the town and which have since spread to other parts of the country. It is interesting to comment on a few of them.

Many of the names indicate places. William de Lyverpull, the mayor, was quite entitled to call himself after his place of residence by virtue of his position in the community. The first record of a mayor appears in 1351 when William the son of Adam held the office, an indication that only one generation earlier the mayor did not presume to have a fixed surname. Other placenames in the Merseyside area are represented by the names of Wolleton, Kirkedale, Mawdesley, Sefton

Liverpool of Liverpool
'Quarterly gules and or a cross formy argent'
  Richard de Liverpool married Margaret de Garston between 1212 and 1226. William, son of Adam de Liverpool, was the first recorded Mayor of the town, in 1351. The family of Liverpool existed for several generations but was extinct, at least in this area, by the fifteenth century.

Clafs.	No.	Claffic Name.	Common Name.	Price.
1. Fifh that breath by the Lungs.	1	Phocæna,	The Porpoife, *common*.	non efculent.
2. Such as breath by the Gills.	2	Raia,	Skate, or Ray, *c.*	1d. to 3d. *per* lb.
	3	Rana Pifcatrix,	Sea Frog, *c.*	non efc.
3. Offeous Fifh.	4	Rhombus Maxs.	Turbot, *rare.*	10d. to 18d. *per* lb.
	5	Solea,	Sole, *c.*	3d. to 4d. *per* lb.
	6	Paffer Bellonii,	Plaife, *c.*	3d. to 1s. *per* ½ doz.
	7	Paffer Fluviatilis,	Flounder or Fluke, *c.*	3d. to 1s. *per* ½ doz.
	8	Paffer,	Garbin, *c.*	4d. to 10d. *per* ½ doz.
4. The Eel-kind.	9	Lampetra,	Lamprey, *r.*	3d. to 6d. *per* lb.
	10	Anguilla,	Eel, (Silver) *c.*	4d. to 6d.
	11	Conger,	Conger Eel, *c.*	2d. to 3d.
	12	Ammodytes,	Sand Eels, *c.*	3d. *per* lb.
5. Fifh with foft Back-fins.	13	Salmo,	Salmon, *c.*	3d. to 1s.
	14	Afellus major,	Cod Fifh, *c.*	4d. to 8d.
	15	Afellus minor,	Whiting, *c.*	4d. to 6d.
	16	Afellus Pollachus,	Whiting Polluck, *r.*	2d. to 4d.
	17	Onus, five Afinus,	Haddock, *r.*	2d. to 4d.
6. Soft Fins, with fmall ones near the Tail.	18	Scomber,	Mackrel, *r.*	2d. to 1s. each.
	19	Eperlanus,	Smelt or Sparling, *c.*	4d. *per* lb. to 3s. *per* fc.
	20	Encraficolus,	Anchovies, *r.*	2d. *per* fcore.
7. Fifh with a Back-Fins, the firft prickly, the other fmooth.	21	Mugil,	Mullett, *r.*	6d. to 8d.
	22	Perca fluviatilis,	Perch, *r.*	6d. to 8d.
8. One foft Back-Fin.	23	Harengus,	The Herring, *c.*	1s. *per* 100 to 1d. each.
	24	Pilchardus,	Pilchard, *c.*	12d. to 3s. *per* 100.
	25	Spratti,	Spratts, *r.*	1d. to 2d. *per* fcore.
	26	Alofa,	Shad, *c.*	
	27	Lucius,	Pike, *r.*	4d. to 6d. *per* lb.
	28	Sturio,	Sturgeon, *r.*	6d. to 8d. *per* lb.
9. Leathermouthed Fifh.	29	Cyprinus,	Carp, *r.*	7d. to 10d.
	30	Tinca,	Tench, *r.*	8d. to 10d.
10. Cruftaceous Fifh.	31	Aftacus,	Lobfter, *r.*	4d. to 8d.
	32	Cancer,	Crab, *r.*	4d. to 8d.
	33	Squilla major,	Prawn, *r.*	6d. to 10d. *per* fcore.
	34	Squilla parva,	Shrimp, *c.*	2d. to 6d. *per* quart.
	35	Pagurus,	Crubbin, *r.*	12d. *per* doz.
	36	Aranea marina,	Sea Spider, *c.*	non efc.
11. Teftaceous Fifh.	37	Patella,	Limpits, *c.*	ditto.
	38	Cochlea,	Periwinkles, *c.*	2d. to 3d. *per* pint.
	39	Buccinum roftratum	Whelks. *r.*	6d. *per* doz.
	40	Oftrea major,	Oyfters, *c.*	18d. to 10s. *per* 100.
	41	Pectunculus,	Cockle. *c.*	¼ *per* quart.
	42	Mufculus,	Mufcle, *c.*	¼ *per* ditto.
	43	Echinus Marinus,	Sea Egg, *c.*	non efc.
	44	Acus,	Horn, or Garr Fifh, *c.*	3d. to 6d. *per* lb.

In the Middle Ages fishing was a very important component of the local economy. Even as late as 1773 it was still thought to be a significant industry, as this table from William Enfield's History *shows. Some of the species are difficult to identify today, but Linnaeus and Darwin would be pleased with the scientific classification.*

and Roby – names which still survive in the area and much further afield. It is reasonable to assume that John de Hull and Henry de Whitby came from the Yorkshire ports with these names. Stephen le Walsh (Welsh) was a Welshman and the origin of Patrick de Irland, one of Liverpool's first known cobblers, is very obvious.

Names like Somenour (Sumner), Heley (Healey), Walker, and Bushell still survive but they originate from many different parts of the country so that it would be very difficult to identify later families from the names of their descendants, but names like Travers (Travis) and Lynaker (Linaker) are local names and the poll tax shows that these families were established in Liverpool at a very early date. It is interesting to compare some of the names with the occupations. We find that Thomas le Fleshewer was indeed a hewer of flesh, for his occupation is a butcher (carnifax), but Richard le Mustardman is a brewer and Nicholas le Clerk is an agricultural worker. Robert le Shephird does not tend sheep but is listed as a servant. All this does not preclude the possibility that some were able to do more than one job, but it is of interest to see how quickly the generations could change their occupation when they moved from the countryside into the town.

Thus by the fourteenth century we begin to get an idea of the town and the people who populated the Lancashire bank of the River Mersey. They were a small and isolated community, many days' travel away from the capital. They suffered from rats, lack of sanitation, frequent outbreaks of plague and all the usual problems of the medieval village, but by comparison with some of the crowded cities of the middle ages they lived in a healthy situation with the advantage of a clean, south-westerly breeze from the open sea. The streets were narrow but paved, the countryside was always near and the open 'H' of the town street plan was such that there were no back alleys and every house had open land behind, where swine were tended and chickens ran in and out of the doorways. Village craftsmen plied their trade in the streets and the houses, but Liverpool still relied heavily on agriculture and fishing for its economy.

A small flotilla of fishing vessels lay at anchor in the waters of the Old Pool. On market days the farmers came from many miles around to sell their wares, some from the villages of Lancashire and others who crossed in the tiny boats which plied from the Cheshire shore. Early in the fourteenth century the monks at Birkenhead built a hostel for the use of the 'great numbers of persons' wishing to cross the estuary who were often delayed by reason of 'contrariety of weather and frequent storms'. Tolls were a farthing for a man on foot, a ha'penny on market days, a penny for travellers with excessive baggage and two pence for a man and a horse. The little town stood small and picturesque against the backcloth of the thick forest and woodland which clothed the hills behind. The castle stood high and impassive as it towered above the heavily thatched houses where wisps of dark smoke ascended from the peat fires which warmed the hearths of the burgesses.

As the sun set over the Irish Sea and bathed the high towers of the castle in shades of orange and red, the labourers in the town fields guided their ploughs behind the lumbering teams of oxen, and in the last dying rays of sunlight they still turned the heavy clay soil in deep furrows before they could wend their way homewards at the end of their long working day.

Liverpool New Town

VERY town was once new, of course, but the title of this section is quite deliberate. For, much like the post-war new towns of our own era, Liverpool was an 'artificial' creation. Although there may have been a peasant's hut or two on the peninsula of high ground next to the Pool, there was no established settlement until King John decided in 1207 to found a new borough. This was a common enough occurrence in the Middle Ages, with English kings establishing 'planted' or 'planned' settlements wherever they wanted to set up trading stations, strategic towns or military strongholds. Beginning with St. Albans in around 950AD, dozens of towns were thus created from nothing, including Leeds, Portsmouth, Caernarvon – and Liverpool.

There were several distinct components to a medieval new town – a regular street pattern, neatly divided-up burgage plots and townfield, often a castle and usually a church. Liverpool had all of these, except the church.

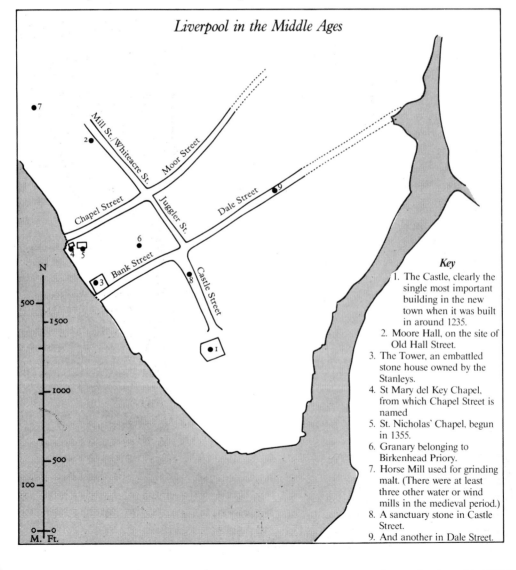

Liverpool in the Middle Ages

Key

1. The Castle, clearly the single most important building in the new town when it was built in around 1235.
2. Moore Hall, on the site of Old Hall Street.
3. The Tower, an embattled stone house owned by the Stanleys.
4. St Mary del Key Chapel, from which Chapel Street is named
5. St. Nicholas' Chapel, begun in 1355.
6. Granary belonging to Birkenhead Priory.
7. Horse Mill used for grinding malt. (There were at least three other water or wind mills in the medieval period.)
8. A sanctuary stone in Castle Street.
9. And another in Dale Street.

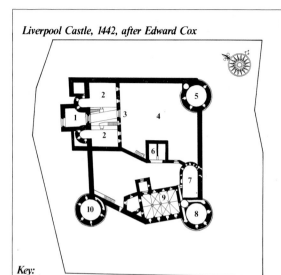

Liverpool Castle, 1442, after Edward Cox

Key:

1. Barbican and outer gate.
2. Gatehouse
3. Inner gate, with portcullis.
4. Outer ward.
5. South-east ('new') tower.
6. House covering the well.
7. Chapel.
8. South-west tower, called the prison tower.
9. The great hall.
10. Keep or 'great' tower.
11. Ditch or moat.

Left: Liverpool Castle, by Edward Cox. This plan was produced as late as 1892, but the author worked from original documents, descriptions of the castle and archaeological data – it may not be completely accurate, but it is a remarkable and painstaking reconstruction by a Victorian enthusiast.

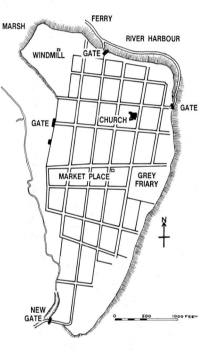

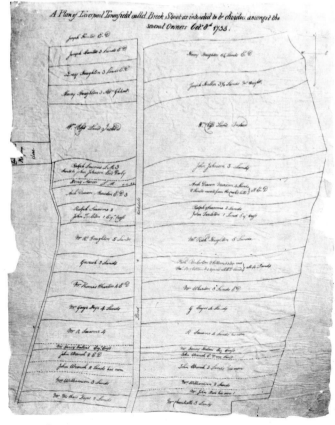

Above: An excellently preserved street grid pattern, from a typical medieval 'new town' – New Winchelsea in Sussex. Liverpool was never laid out on such a grand scale, of course, but there is evidence that the seven original streets of the town were laid out with similar forethought and care. See M. Beresford, New Towns of the Middle Ages *(1967).*

Left: The Townfield as it appeared in 1733, showing the names of the tenants on each strip. It is usually unwise to extrapolate evidence from the eighteenth century to the thirteenth, it seems fairly certain that the townfield looked pretty much like this when it was first laid out as part of the new town of Liverpool in 1207.

Chapter Two

Fishing village

HE FAMILIES of Molyneux and Stanley were the most powerful in Liverpool. Both families had a proud record of military achievement. Sir John Stanley served with the Black Prince in Poitiers and Richard Molyneux fought at Agincourt in 1415. At the beginning of the fifteenth century the Molyneux were constables of Liverpool Castle and their neighbours the Stanleys built a solid stone house on the north side of Water Street, situated right on the waterfront. The house was large and substantial with a courtyard flanked by outbuildings on each side and with gardens to the north and east. In 1406 Henry IV granted the Isle of Man to Sir John Stanley in return for his fidelity to the crown during the Percy Rebellion, and for the token rental of two falcons to be presented to the royal commisioners on the anniversary of the Coronation Day. John Stanley was authorised to embattle and strengthen his house in Liverpool and the Stanley town house thus became a fortified military base known as the Tower, making a second stronghold in Liverpool and challenging the Molyneux family who were established in the castle.

Stanley
'Argent on a bend azure three harts' heads cabossed or'.

The Stanleys were the most powerful and influential family in the area. In 1485 Thomas Stanley's support for the Earl of Richmond at Bosworth was decisive in founding the Tudor dynasty, and he was duly rewarded with the Earldom of Derby.

The Stanleys usually supported the Crown, and family fortunes reached a low ebb during the Civil War, when Lathom was the last royalist stronghold in Lancashire to fall to the parliamentarians.

There were times when Liverpool was simply not big enough to contain two such powerful dynasties without some kind of friction breaking out between them, and it was perhaps inevitable that the families of Stanley and Molyneux eventually came to blows. 'That great rumour and congregation of routes existing between Sir Richard Molineux Knt. on the one part and Thomas Stanley the younger of Lierpull Esq of the other part', wrote the historian Roger Dodsworth, 'Wheron the said conservators of the public peace by order of the Sherrif repaired to Lierpull early in July 1424 and there they found the said Thomas of Stanley in his father's house, and with a multitude of people in the town, to the number of 2000 men and more.' If we are to believe the figures quoted by Dodsworth, then Thomas Stanley raised two thousand men and Richard Molyneux one thousand. Considering that the whole population of Liverpool, including women and children, hardly exceeded a thousand, this was a huge number of followers, who must have been drawn from the whole of the extensive Stanley and Molyneux estates throughout Lancashire and Cheshire. It fell to the poor sheriff to try and avoid bloodshed; luckily he was a skilled negotiator and Roger Dodsworth described what happened next:

> We asket him the cause of that assemble of King's people and he informed us that the said Richard Molineux will come hither with great congregations, riots, and great multitude of people, to slea [slay], and beat the said Thomas, his men and his servants, the which he would withstand if he might. And he, the said Thomas, said that he would find sufficient surety of the peace for him and all his, so the said Richard would find the same; and hereon, the Friday next after the Sheriff arrested the said Thomas, and committed him to ward: and the said Sheriff made cry, that the people that there was should go with him to help him execute his office, after which he proceeded to West Derby Fen, and there, on a mow, within the said town, he saw the said Richard with great congregations route and multitude, to the number of 1000 men or more, arrayed in manner as to battle, and coming fast towards Lierpull town; and the said Sherriff arrested the said Richard, and committed him to ward.[1]

Molyneux

'Azure a cross moline or'.

The Molyneux family was second only to the Stanleys in terms of power and influence in south Lancashire. They became the Earls of Sefton and the family have many minor and interesting branches.

In 1972 the so-called moline cross was adopted as the emblem of the new Metropolitan Borough of Sefton.

With the exception of a few veterans and perhaps some hired men, the majority of the thousands who assembled on West Derby Fen were not professional soldiers – they were mostly servants, tenants and farm labourers from the Molyneux and Stanley estates. They didn't want a battle any more than did the sheriff whose job it was to keep the peace, and in the event common sense prevailed and no fighting took place. It seems that neither party had their headquarters in Liverpool, for in the attempt to keep the peace Thomas Stanley was ordered to withdraw from his stronghold at Clitheroe to the castle at Kenilworth and Richard Molyneux was similarly instructed to withdraw his private army from Lancaster Castle to Windsor.

At first there was little to choose between the power of the two rival houses and both found plenty of outlets for their military prowess in the interminable wars with the French and again in the great struggle for power between the houses of Lancaster and York which broke out just as the French wars ended. The fame of both families went far beyond Lancashire. When the House of York reached the lowest point of its popularity after the murder of the little princes in the Tower of London, and when Henry the Duke of Richmond faced the Yorkist army at Bosworth Field, the Stanleys were deeply involved in the conflict.

Richard III knew that Thomas Stanley, with his army of five thousand, held the balance of power at Bosworth. He expected Stanley to fight on his side, but Stanley was married to the widowed mother of Henry Tudor, and Richard had therefore taken the trouble to hold Stanley's son as hostage to ensure his loyalty. Thomas Stanley unwillingly found that the future of all England lay in his hands as he debated with himself over which side to support. The story of Bosworth is too well known to recount in a local history, and perhaps the tale that Stanley snatched the crown of England from a thorn bush and placed it on the head of Henry Tudor is apocryphal, but whatever happened when the battle was over the anecdote cannot be far removed from the truth, for history remembers Stanley as the king maker. In 1495 Henry VII and his queen visited the Stanley estates at Lathom and Knowsley and Thomas Stanley's part at Bosworth was rewarded with the Earldom of Derby.

There was another great battle, fought a generation later and many miles to the north when our greatly to be dreaded defender of the faith,

Henry VIII, was King of England. The House of Stanley again played a major part and won great renown. The battle was at Flodden, where Sir Edward Stanley, second son of the first Earl of Derby, was noted for his great gallantry on the field. Stanleys and Molyneuxs fought side by side at Flodden and witnessed together the fall of the Scottish nobility. Sir William Molyneux's efforts were equal to those of Edward Stanley; he captured two Scottish banners and received a personal letter of thanks from the king:

> Lancashire like Lyons, layden them aboute!
> All had bene lost by our Lorde! had not those leddes bene!
> But the care of the Scottes, increased full sore
> For their king was downe knocked, and killed in their sight,
> Under the banner of a bishop, that was the bold Stanley!
> Then they fetilde tham to fly, as fast as they might.[2]

For so many years the threat of Scottish incursions had been so real that England north of the Trent considered Flodden to be a more important victory than Bosworth. It was Flodden which enabled the Northerner to sleep more safely in his bed, as the fear of invasion from the Scots was effectively removed, whereas Bosworth was seen only as the sequel to a long struggle between rival factions for the Crown. It was not until long after Bosworth, with the advantage of hindsight, that the benefits of the strong and stable dynasty of the Tudors became apparent.

In Liverpool and the surrounding district many local men fought in the private armies of Stanley and Molyneux, but in the town itself the merchants were more interested in the new charters issued by successive kings. Early in the fifteenth century a royal charter was issued under Henry V which attempted to extract greater dues from the burgesses. They complained and wrote a humble petition in Norman French to 'the very wise Commons of this present Parliament', claiming that their liberties had been usurped and that they had been 'grievously molested, vexed and disturbed' by the king's officers.[3]

In the reign of Henry VIII the royal charter was again confirmed, but the Crown suspected that the merchants were using the tolls 'for their own singular use and advantage' and a royal commission was formed to investigate the issue. No evidence of fraud was found but the crown was still suspicious and in 1528 another commission was appointed to inquire into allegations that the local people were depriving the crown of the revenue from wreckage. There was no coastal community anywhere in England which did not consider a shipwreck to be a golden opportunity for plunder and the Crown was almost certainly right in this latter suspicion.

The permanent fabric of Liverpool changed very little throughout the fifteenth century. The castle acquired a new bakehouse in 1441 and the following year a new tower was built which replaced an older tower at the south-east corner. Windmills were beginning to appear alongside the water mills and the horse-driven mills. Eastham windmill was repaired in 1450 and Townsend Mill, a wooden post-mill, was replaced in the same year.

It is not until 1515 that there is any evidence of a town hall. A 'gilde house and court house' are both mentioned in 1511 and are probably references to the building which was given to the mayor and aldermen of the borough by John Crosse in 1515. From references in the town books the building is known to have had two storeys with a roof of stone slates and an outside flight of steps to the upper floor. The sixteenth century was not noted for its high standards of hygiene and, although Liverpool was not one of towns where it was customary to empty chamberpots out of the upstairs windows, problems of fouling the streets inevitably arose at frequent intervals. On one occasion, when the mayor and aldermen ascended the outside stairway regaled in their best robes for the council meeting, there was an acrid smell on the stone steps leading to the upper room. It was very obvious what the problem was. John Cross was most irate about it and demanded a heavy fine from the offenders if they could be found:

> Wheras divers unmanerlie persons have moost undecentlie made water upon the top of the steyres by this hall doore, wherebie groweth not onlie evyll sentes and sights but also is noyiouse, to the grief of mayster maior and his brethren, and to all persons havyng gownes, in theyre ascendyges and descendyges. In reformacion whereof wee agrie that every [person] or persons, whoe ever he or they be, that from henceforth is knowen or shalbe knowen to make water and pisse on that place, or anye other upon the same, shall forfiet and paye for everie tyme xiid wythowt delaye, and if he shall resist and wythstand the payment of that xiid he shall be distreynyd for the same, and have punishment of bodie at mayster maiors will and pleasure.[4]

In keeping with the general custom of the times, the building was used for many purposes. The upstairs was used as a court room and a meeting place for the guild, downstairs served several other purposes, being used as a town warehouse, a customs house and as a prison for both freemen and common criminals. The benefactor, John Cross, who gave the building, lived on the south side of Dale Street at no great distance from the Town Hall. His estates extended at the rear of his house as far as the Old Pool, and his descendants later built a stone wall at the bottom of his land to protect it from the tidal waters of the Pool. The tithes had belonged to Shrewsbury Abbey since the eleventh century, long before the foundation of Liverpool, but in the fifteenth century the Molyneux family was able to purchase them and a stone tithe barn was built by Sir William Molyneux of Flodden fame, a building which is still remembered by the streetname Tithebarn Street.

In 1515 John Cross also left money for the foundation of a grammar school, the first of its kind in Liverpool. The school was founded soon afterwards, but little is known about it until 1565 when an entry in the town books records that 'wee agre that it is nedefull to have a lernyd man to be oure Schole mayster for the preferment of youth in this towne'.[5] The mayor called a special meeting at which the question of his salary was discussed 'to take ordre for his wayges, over and above that the quynes majestie doyth allow us.' A salary of £5 13s 8d seems to have been agreed and was paid from the chantry rents at St Nicholas Chapel. Mr John Ore, a learned man from London, took up the post on the 16th of February and his salary was made up to £10 per annum.

There is no reason to suppose that the school differed much from the normal Tudor grammar school. Entry was for children aged seven or eight. The schools were called grammar schools because the high point of the curriculum was the teaching of Latin grammar. Science and literature were unheard of, mathematics consisted of elementary arithmetic, and history was that of the ancient world. The highest academic achievement was the study of Greek in the upper school, which some children aspired to at the age of ten or eleven. Once established, the grammar school managed to survive and the children of the burgesses became a little more literate, but academic standards varied greatly and in 1577 the schoolmaster John Riule was fined 'for neglectinge his dewtie towardes his schollers to the greate decaye of the youth of this towne w[hi]ch ought to be redressed'.

In Tudor Liverpool there was always plenty of activity in the way of games and pastimes. The archery practice, formerly a statute of the realm, was continued long after the Middle Ages. Cock fighting was certainly popular from very early times, particularly among the gentry, and it was even seen as a way of attracting custom to the town. In 1567 the town books record that 'for further and greater repair of gentlemen and others to this town we find it needful that there be a handsome cockfight pit made'. The popularity of the cockfight may be judged by the fact that in a later age the tenth Earl of Derby enjoyed the sport so much that he staged fights in his own bedroom and actually watched two cocks sparring with each other as he lay on his deathbed.

Bull baiting was another popular pastime, and all the traditional spectator sports of Elizabethan England seem to have been practised in Liverpool. The Elizabethan passion for drama was very much in evidence; entertainments were held in the castle and the tower, and performances were given at the Town Hall and later in the yard of the new cockpit. Travelling musicians, jugglers, ballad singers and companies of players were very popular, but when a group of travellers appeared with a monstrous and frightening animal (probably a bear) the authorities became concerned about things getting out of hand:

> We agree that no players of interludes, jugglers, jesters or wandering people bryngyng into this towne any monstrouse or straunge beasts, or other visions royde or rayre, to theyr lucre and distresse of the q[uee]ns subjects without licence of Mr Maior tyme beyng.[5]

Travelling players and other offenders who performed without a licence risked a spell in the stocks or the pillory. An example was 'the wandres and turners wythe the hobie horse', two wandering performers who did a turn with a hobby horse and were probably quite ignorant of the puritanical Liverpolitan bylaws. They were rewarded for their performance with a spell in the stocks at the High Cross.

Dancing became very popular, particularly on the occasion of a wedding or civic function. A hall known as the Comyn or Common Hall, standing centrally very near the Town Hall, was used for dancing but the stomping of great numbers of feet on the wooden floor caused great concern to the worried burgesses, who felt that the floor could not stand the strain. They did not attempt to stop the frivolities but decided that 'noe licence be or shall be grantyd and gyvyn to make any weddyng diners or pleyes of dawnsyng' in the Comyn Hall.

On one occasion Lord Strange, later to become the fifth Earl of Derby, was obliged to stay two weeks in the Tower of Liverpool whilst he awaited a fair wind to carry him to the Isle of Man. He was entertained by morris dancing, military displays, fireworks and banquets. Lord Strange became a great patron of the arts; it was his company of players that performed in Stratford-on-Avon in 1579, the very company which Shakespeare himself is reputed to have joined as a young man.

In the sixteenth century, for the first time, we begin to get accounts of Liverpool written by travellers and visitors to the town. These eyewitness accounts mention things out of the ordinary which local accounts do not always record. They thus offer a detached and unbiased viewpoint to complement the details in the town records. The earliest traveller to write such an account was John Leland, who arrived at the fishing village in 1530. His account is brief but full of interest. It was natural for him to comment on the tower and the castle, and the fact that there was no parish church, but his most interesting observation was the fact that the streets were paved – something which he found very unusual in his time. Local people took the fact for granted, for there is reliable evidence that they had been paved for two hundred years.

> Lyrpole, alias Lyverpoole, a pavid towne, hath but a chapel. Walton a iiii miles of, not far from the se[a] is a paroche chirch. The king hath a castelet there, and the Earl of Darbe hath a stone howse there. Irisch merchants cum much thither, as to a good haven. After that Mersey water cumming towards Runcorne in Cheshire, lisith [loseth] amonge the commune people the name, and is wllid [called] Runco[rn]e Water. At Lyrpole is smaule custome payed, that causith marchantes to resorte thither. Good marchandis at Lyrpole, and much Yrish [Irish] yarrn that Manchester men do b[u]y there.[6]

Later in the same century came Camden, who in 1586 published a longer account in his *Brittania*. Most of his description adds little to the details in the town books, but he confirms that the common pronunciation 'Lirpoole', with only two syllables, was widely used at the time. Camden also implies that in the sixteenth century Liverpool was already well known for its beauty:

> The Mersey spreading and presently contracting its stream from Warrington falls into the ocean with a wide channel very convenient for trade, where opens to view Litherpole, commonly called Lirpoole, from a water extending like a pool, according to the common opinion, where is the most convenient and most frequented passage to Ireland; a town more famous for its beauty and populousness than for its antiquity; its name occurs in no ancient writer except that Roger of Poictou who was lord, as then stated, of Lancaster, built a castle here, the custody of which has now for a long time belonged to the noble and knightly family of Molineux, whose chief seat is in the neighbourhood of Sefton, which Roger aforesaid in the early Norman times gave to Vivian de Molineaux. This Roger held, as appears by Domesday Book, all the lands between the rivers Ribble and Mersey.

It is unfortunate that Francis Bacon, who represented Liverpool in parliament from 1588 to 1592, mentions nothing of the town in his writings. There is a third account, however, which was written between those of Leland and Camden. It is an official report on the state of the castle from soon after the accession of Queen Elizabeth in 1559. The report was by three royal commissioners called Francis Samwell, Raffe Assheton and John Bradwell. The value of the report lies in the realistic detail which it gives. We see the rain falling through the broken roof of one of the towers and other minutae giving vivid life to the scene.

> Firste the said castell is scituate [situated] upon a rokk of stone and

joyneth harde to the towne of Litherpole, beinge a port towne, in so much that the castell yate [gate] is full into the face of our strete of the said towne. And also the said castell is scytuate neare upon the haven ther, in which haven, by reporte of honeste marchauntes of the said towne, ther may lye at harbour three hundreth sayle of shipps. The said castell is but a smale thinge, beinge in manner square, and the longeste waye within the same by estimacione not lx yardes, havinge three rounde towres of stone scytuate at thre severall corners therof. And the gatehowse, beyinge made tower fasshyone sware [square], serveth for the fourth corner. All which said towres, with the gatehowse, ar in utter rwyne [ruin] and decay, so that ther remayneth neither tymbre or lead, other then [than] such as hereafter is expressed, for that ther was no lead at any tyme in the rememberance of man remayninge upon any buyldynge within the said castell.[7]

The haven for three hundred sail of ships, by report of the 'honeste marchauntes of the said towne' refers to the Mersey estuary and not the Old Pool – the estuary was a safe enough anchorage, but far less convenient and more exposed than the Pool. The difficulty of getting in and out of the Mersey, because of many treacherous sandbanks and the strong offshore currents, was well known to the sailors. The commissioners go on to describe the delapidated state of the castle towers, but they conclude that the fortress was not decayed beyond all hope and would be worth repairing for use as a crown court for the hundred of West Derby (the wapentake):

Also ther is one tower of the three rounde towres which is the greatest of them all, which towre hath hadd a rooffe of tymbre and coverede with slate, as it appereth, nowe utterlie decayede. And within the said towre ther is too [two] flowres [floors] of tymbre much in decaye, for that the rayne doth contynuallie fall upon the said flowres to the great consummacion [consumption] and waste of them, which is great pytie. Nevertheless, if the said rouffe [roof] of the towre were newe made agayne, and well coverede with slate, and some lead to make the gutters, the said towre would be made for to contynewe a longe tyme, wherin the Quenes Majesties courtes for Her Graces Wappentacke of West Derbyshire, beinge a very greate soken, may be from tyme to tyme therin kept; and also a conveyent place may also be made for the salfe [safe] custodie of the Quenes Majesties courte rollees [court rolls] toiuching the said Wappentack, with others, beinge great in numbre.

The castle walls were found to be basically in good repair, even though stones had fallen in places and had since disappeared. They estimated that about thirty pounds would be required to repair the walls. They decided that the castle was of little use to safeguard the Mersey estuary from invasion by an enemy fleet, but that the entrance to the Mersey was so dangerous that it offered its own defence and no enemy fleet could hope to get safely in or out of the estuary without local knowledge. The castle, they concluded, was still of use as a safe place of refuge in times of war:

Furthermore, the said castell is of little effecte for the defence of the haven, for that the entre [entry] into the said havyn is so daungerous that ther is no navye that will gyve the attempte to entre therin endomage [and damage] the countrie theraboute, in asmuch as yf they shuld comme in, they cannot quyetlie [quietly] get owt agayne, for that both Worrall [Wirral], Lancashyre, and also Walles [Wales], do back and also adjoyne unto both sydes of the said havyne, by reason wherof hit is thought in the countrie ther the said haven is sure inough [secure enough] for any invasione therin to be made by the adverserie. Otherwyse if nede shuld so requyre that the inhabitauntes of the countrie theraboute shulde for salfgarde of themselves be enforcede to secke [seek] succour at the said castell, hit would for a tyme preserve them untill such tyme as they may be rescwede by the inhabitauntes of the hole countrie theraboute, which is verie populus.

The mayor and inhabitants 'doth humblie make request' that the castle be repaired, feeling that it was a defacement to the town in its state of ruin and decay. The total cost was estimated at about one hundred pounds, with a sum of forty shillings a year needed for maintenance.

Some people have visions of great fleets anchored in the Mersey in Tudor times, but in reality there was seldom more than twenty sail of small ships at anchor, and ships of over a hundred tons were rare. The total shipping registered at Liverpool in 1555 was 222 tons for twelve ships, averaging under twenty tons per ship. Two years later the records show only one ship of 100 tons, one of fifty tons, seven smaller vessels and four between ten and thirty tons. The total number of mariners in the town was given as two hundred.

Some of these vessels were employed in the Irish linen trade, as noted by John Leland, and Ireland was always one of the most important trading destinations for the Liverpool merchants. Thence and elsewhere mixed cargoes of coal, woollens, Sheffield knives, leather goods and small wares were exported. Return cargoes were invariably yarns, hides and sheep skins or fells. Other vessels were coastal traders engaged in carrying a variety of merchandise linking the west-coast ports, from Scotland to Cornwall, and sometimes further afield. Some merchants traded with Spain and Portugal for wine and spirits, mostly through foreign vessels but with a growing number of local ships. The trade was so small, however, that the Liverpool merchants were not required to submit to the regulations of the monopolist Spanish trading company which was formed in 1578.

There was a wooden jetty to serve the shipping in the Pool. It was destroyed by a storm in 1561 and the mayor gave a gold pistol towards a fund to get the jetty repaired and in working order again. The greatest storm of the century came soon afterwards, in 1565, when considerable damage was done both on the sea front and further inland. The burgesses were concerned for their houses and barns and the merchants were concerned about their ships and the cargoes that were ready loaded to sail for Ireland.

On Saturday, the 22nd of December, a fleet of ships awaited a fair wind, including the ship of the Queen's treasurer, Sir Henry Sydney, who was on his way to take up his new post of Lord High Deputy of Ireland. In his party were other 'worshippfuls and theyr ladies', a great many horses, soldiers and 'a great abundant tresoure of riches'. The storm which delayed them was so ferocious that it put the fear of God into the people. A windmill in the town was blown over, masonry fell from the chapel building and the sea wall was breached, with large stones carried six or seven yards inland:

And Sondaye mornyng than next after [23 Dec 1565], beyng wyndie cold froste and snowe myestie dercke and dyme [misty dark and dim] wythout ceassyng, the snowe dryvyng and wappyng [beating] to and froe, that all Christen people calld and cryed, praiyng and making theyr moost humble prayers unto all myghtie to ament the weyther soe fearefull and terrible, and to save the forsaydes [foresaid] shypps and barckes, wyth all the Christen people in theyme beying, and all Christen people upon the seas els wheare [elsewhere]. But it continewd al daye, and abowte sonne settyng it somethiyng calmed, and abowte x or xi of the clocke that Sondaye at nyght sodenlie spronge and roose [rose] the marvelioust and terribliest storm of wynd and wether that cont[i]nued abowt six howres or lytyll lesse, as well upon land as water, to the great hurte of the cominaltie, and theyr howsies and barnes, wyth many wynd mylne [wind mill] cleyne overthrowen [clean overthrown]. and all to broken, wyth great hurt upon churchies and chapells. In whiche stormes divers pinacles and borders of the chapell of this towne of Liverpole were blowen downe, and wyth fallyng brookyn [broken] all to p[i]eces, and other hurtes of glasse wyndowys, but, to sey the truth further, in this nyght storme was a part of our chapell wall of this towne next the full sea marke brostyn [burst, broken] and wasshyn owt, and some of the greatist stones moved cleyn, and wyth they extremenes of the seas car[r]i[e]d six or vii yardes owt of theyre places.[8]

Henry Woddes, John Bastwell and John Fynne, three masons from the parish of Aughton, were employed to repair the damage, which was estimated at upwards of thirty pounds.

Liverpool did not compare in ships and tonnage to the neighbouring port of Chester where in the same year as the great storm the merchants sent a request for details of imports and exports. Liverpool was technically still a creek of the port of Chester, and the fact that the Chester merchants requested this information may well be an indication that the amount of traffic through Liverpool was sufficient for them to bother about collecting their dues. The Chester merchants threatened to take their Liverpool counterparts to court when they refused to pay. In 1580 the matter came to a head when the Chester men demanded a duty of twenty-five per cent on the returns of every Liverpool ship which had traded with Spain and Portugal in the past four years. The Liverpool traders certainly could not afford to lose such a high percentage of their profits and again refused to pay, whereupon the Chester merchants took three of them to the High Court for illegal trading. The Master of the Rolls declared in favour of Liverpool, but the burgesses set up a tax or insurance on their own merchants to defend their trading rights against further lawsuits from Chester. The tax cost more than paying the dues but it proved to be a wise investment in the long term. The River Dee changed course often as it meandered out of its wide estuary and by the middle of the next century, Chester had lost its position to its better placed rival. This was a mixed blessing, however, as Liverpool's dependence on Irish trade was clearly demonstrated when the Irish economy collapsed in 1641, a set-back which was sufficient to halt the town's growth for some time.

Liverpool appears to have grown very little in population during the sixteenth century. Only one or two new streets appeared in Tudor times; old streets were renamed but retained their medieval courses. Housing development spread further along Tithebarn Street, and Pool Lane was formed to the south of the castle. Dale Street crossed the upper reaches of the Old Pool at the stone-built Townsend Bridge, first mentioned in 1564. The stocks and pillory were situated centrally near the Town Hall, and a ducking stool stood on the outskirts of the town where a suitable pond existed to cool off the unfortunate miscrents.

After the Reformation, when most of the leading local families remained with the Catholic faith, many religious differences were created but little open hostility broke out and the Catholic recusants and the Protestant families lived side by side in a reasonable state of harmony. In common with all towns of comparable size Liverpool was visited by plague at random intervals. The death toll was horrific in the great plague of 1558, when between 240 and 260 people died; this could have been as much as a third of the total population and was a local disaster as severe as the Black Death.

Tudor Liverpool was in many ways a very typical English town, with all the trappings of an Elizabethan community and with strong local customs, some of which have been recorded in the town books. The tradition of walking the bounds took place every seven years on Easter Monday when the walkers followed the boundaries with Everton, Kirkdale, West Derby and Toxteth. The burgesses were invited to join the mayor every midsummer eve, as well as on St Peter's Day and the two annual fair days, in a ceremonial procession through the streets dressed in their best attire and armed with their ceremonial swords and weapons 'as of old'. Every year on St. Luke's Day (18 October) the assembly of burgesses met to elect a mayor and a bailiff. The Great Portmoot met the following day to elect all the minor officers, including the serjeant at mace, two churchwardens, two leve-lookers, two moss-reeves, four mice-cessors and prysors, two stewards of the common-hall, a water bailiff, a hayward and two ale-testers.

The town was small enough for every person to know all their townsfolk. They worked side by side in the market place and they stood together every Sunday at worship in the chapel. Bachelors, apprentices, and servants were not allowed to walk out at night after 9 o'clock, but in true English fashion the people never lost an opportunity to celebrate. Ascension day was a happy and relaxed occasion when a race took place along the open shore and the winner was presented with the silver bell given by Mr Tarbuck of Tarbuck (Tuebrook). They lit bonfires to celebrate the Queen's birthday and when news of the Spanish Armada arrived in 1588 a single gun was stationed to guard the entrance to the Liver Pool.

Liverpool Exchange, from an eighteenth-century engraving. There are no contemporary illustrations of the first Liverpool Town Hall. This one dates from the late-seventeenth century. (L.R.O. DP 175).

'The crow's nest' — 17th-century Liverpool

BY THE time of the Civil War Liverpool was a fairly prosperous market town. The only truly authentic view of Liverpool at this time is a painting by an unknown artist of the Dutch school which was in the possession of the Peters family when John Eyes made this engraving from it, depicting the buildings with much greater clarity than on the original. The parish church, the Tower, the Castle, the old Customs House and the Town Hall are all easily identified. The entrance to the Old Pool was to the right, just outside the picture. It is interesting to compare this engraving with other near-contemporary views and plans, for example by Buck and Chadwick (pages 50-1 and 64-5).

Right: *The proposed fortifications to make Liverpool into a walled town at the time of the Civil War, showing the castle and the simple street pattern of the time. It was the light line, rather than the heavy fortification, which was actually built.*

Left: *The ancient Tower of the Stanleys, as it appeared shortly before it was demolished in 1821. After the Civil Wars, The Stanleys' lands were forfeit but by 1665 the Eighth Earl had recovered the Tower and let it to a Liverpool merchant.*

Below: *Liverpool 1680, by John Eyes (after an unknown 17th-century artist). See above for details.*

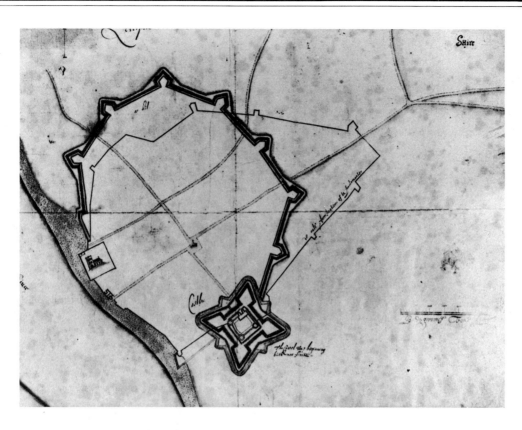

Chapter Three

'The Crow's Nest'

ASSING down Dale Street, with Crosse Hall standing back from the street on the right, the road left the confines of the little town and came to the Townsend Bridge, a small stone bridge which spanned the Moss Lake Brook flowing down the hill from Everton. The bridge gave access to the heathland on the far side of the Pool. Nobody lived over the bridge, but there was a crossroads with the Fall Well on the right where many of the townswomen went to gossip and draw their water. Straight ahead was the road to West Derby and Prescot; to the left was the muddy lane to Everton where on Saturday the farmers and countrymen came driving pigs and cattle before them to the market. To the south and across the heath was the mossland where peat was cut for use as fuel to warm the hearths of the burghers. Beyond the moss was the boundary with Toxteth Park.

It was at Toxteth that one of Liverpool's greatest sons, Jeremiah Horrox, was born in 1618. Little is known of his youth. He may have attended the grammar school in Liverpool or he may have been tutored privately by Richard Mather, the puritan minister of Toxteth who emigrated to the American colonies and became the author of some of the earliest works to be published in the New World. Young Horrox was an able pupil and in 1632, at the customary age of about fourteen, he gained a place as a sizar to read divinity at Emmanuel College, Cambridge.

In Horrox's time the great majority of university students prepared to enter the Church. Horrox was no exception and he admitted to being a deeply religious young man, but his first love had little to do with theology. He was interested in the secrets of the universe and the motions of the heavenly bodies. 'Astronomy is natural and true', he wrote, 'The sea is agitated with the winds; but the aether is clear and open, without wind or any other resistance.' The planets were not blown around like the fishing smacks in the Mersey estuary, their motions could be calculated with mathematical precision.

In the early decades of the seventeenth century the universities of Oxford and Cambridge were superbly equipped for the teaching of Latin, Greek, classics and theology, but science was little more than a vaguely defined word in their dictionaries. There were a few capable mathematicians and a few confident but less capable astrologers.

Some of the sages dabbled in alchemy in the hope of finding the philosopher's stone which would turn base metals into gold. It was the age when Galileo was called before the Inquisition in Rome for daring to assert that the earth moved around the sun and not the sun about the earth. When it came to the serious study of astronomy on which Jeremiah Horrox had set his heart, he was virtually on his own. He bemoaned his predicament in writing:

> There were many hindrances. The abtruse nature of the study, my inexperience, and want of means dispirited me. I was much pained not to have any one to whom I could look for guidance, or indeed for the sympathy of companionship in my endeavours, and I was assailed by the langour and weariness which are inseparable from every great undertaking. What then was to be done? I could not make the pursuit an easy one, much less increase my fortune, and least of all, imbue others with a love of astronomy; and yet to complain of philosphy on account of its difficulties would be foolish and unworthy. I determined therefore that the tediousness of study should be overcome by industry; my poverty (failing a better method) by patience; and that instead of a master I would use astronomical books.[1]

Horrox managed to obtain copies of Ptolemy's *Almagest*, Copernicus' book *de Revolutionibus*, which proposed the controversial system of the sun at the centre of the universe, and the *Progymnasnmata* of the great Danish nobleman Tycho Brahe who had spent virtually his whole lifetime measuring the positions of the stars and the planets in the sky. He graduated from Emmanuel College and returned home to Toxteth. Every night when conditions and circumstances allowed, Jeremiah Horrox was at his window measuring the positions of the moon and the planets against the stars. He found to his great consternation that they did not fit the positions given by the tables of Longomonitus from which he was working and which were in turn based on the *Almagest* – the 'Great Work' of Claudius Ptolemaus which had remained unchallenged as the bible of the astronomers for thirteen centuries. It was only when he was introduced to the work of Kepler that Horrox was able to fit his observations to an astronomical theory. His delight was beyond all bounds. He became an ardent admirer of the controversial and radical theories of Copernicus and Kepler and he expressed what he unfairly called 'the puerile fictions of the pagan Ptolemy' in verse:

> Why should'st thou try, O Ptolemy, to pass
> Thy narrow-bounded world for ought divine?
> Why should thy poor machine presume to claim
> A noble maker? Can a narrow space
> Call for eternal hands? Will thy mansion
> Suit great Jove? or can he from such a seat
> Prepare his lightnings for the trembling earth?

Horrox goes on to explain why it is not necessary to have the sun, the planets and all the stars moving daily around the earth. On the Copernican theory, the earth rotates and 'saves to all the distant stars the useless labor of unceasing motion'. Never before or since have the theories of Copernicus been put with such force and beauty as in the lines of Horrox:

> Thou God of truth whose certain laws direct
> The starry spheres, whilst all the powers above

Admire and tremble; the projected Earth
Rolling along its planetary path
Hath learned to hail thy triumph; and this age
Enables mortal eyes in thy great works
To view thee nearer, and with nobler thought
To trace the stars whose order proves them thine.
In vain the Sun his fiery steeds would urge
In vain restrain them, or attempt to guide
Their rapid course within the laws of fate.
The Earth performs their task, and by each day's
Revolving saves to all the distant stars
The useless labor of unceasing motion.
The clouds which once obscured our mental sight
Are gone for ever; great Copernicus.
Sent from above, lays open to our view
The arduous secrets of wide heaven's domain.

It was at Hoole, a coastal village about twenty miles north of Liverpool, that Horrox made his famous observation of the transit of Venus across the face of the sun. It was a triumph of his practical astronomy to be able to predict that the transit was going to take place at all, but his more startling advances were in the theoretical rather than the practical side of astronomy. He used his observation of the transit of Venus to correct the known orbit of the planet, and he used his measurements of the size of the Venus on the sun's disc to estimate the astronomical unit, the distance from earth to sun.

His practical skill appeared again when he discovered that the two planets Jupiter and Saturn were not in the places predicted for them by Kepler's laws of planetary motion. He correctly concluded that the two giant planets exerted some unseen influence on each other. His crowning mathematical achievement was his theory of lunar motion in which he recognised that the motion of the moon was influenced by the sun as well as the earth – he was on the verge of the discovery of universal gravitation. It was a theory so far ahead of its time that when Newton and Flamsteed came to study it fifty years afterwards Newton found it to be the best theory ever advanced and he based his own lunar theory on the ideas of Horrox.

Jeremiah Horrox' premature death at the age of twenty-three, and the loss of many of his papers, meant that he never achieved his full potential or recognition. His misfortunes did not end with his death. Many of his papers were lost when his house at Toxteth was plundered during the Civil War and at least one of his papers perished in the Great Fire of London.

His fellow astronomers, however, have always been fulsome in their praises and they acknowledge him to to be the father of English astronomy. Edmund Halley studied the various theories of the moon's motion and concluded 'that alone of our Horrox which attributes to the moon's orbit a libratory motion of the apsides, and a variable eccentricity, seems to approach the truth of nature; for it represents the diameters more agreeably to observation, and shews her motion more accurately than any other hypothesis which I have hitherto seen'. Lord Brougham claimed that 'nothing can be more clear than the great merit of Horrox, and the severe loss sustained by science from his early death.' Isaac Newton acknowledged his debt to Horrox when the *Principia* was first published in 1686, and Herschel referred to him as 'the pride and boast of British astronomy'.

Horrox died in 1641, and in the following year came the start of a great conflict which pushed the advances of pure science into the background. It was the civil war between the King and Parliament which drew the whole country into a long and bitter conflict.

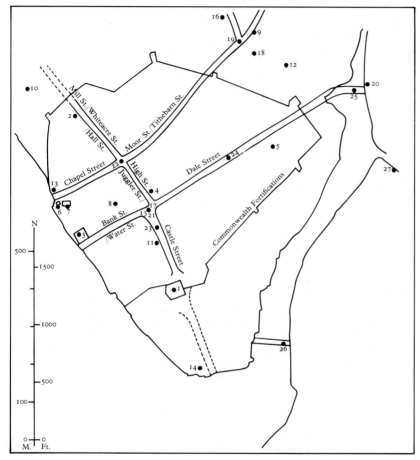

Tudor and Stuart Liverpool.

From the sixteenth century onwards the amount and quality of documentary sources increases dramatically and we are therefore able to re-construct much more clearly what the town actually looked like. It is interesting to compare this plan with the engraving on pages 34-5.

Key:
1. The Castle.
2. Old (Moore) Hall.
3. The Tower (see p. 34).
4. The Town Hall, first mentioned reliably at the beginning of the sixteenth century. For many centuries the Town Hall also housed the Exchange, a court house and, for a time, the customs house.
5. Crosse Hall.
6. St. Mary del Key Chapel.
7. St. Nicholas Chapel, not yet a parish church in its own right.
8. Granary, sold after the Dissolution of the Monasteries.
9. The tithe barn.
10. Horse mill, still in existence at the beginning of this period.
11. Horse mill.
12. Middle Mill, one of the few mills which we can reliably date and locate.
13. Salt House, which may have been used as part of the Civil War fortifications.
14. Pool House, used as a poor house.
15. Stocks.
16. Pinfold.
17. Pillory.
18. Ducking stool, many references to which are to be found in the town books!
19. St Patrick's Cross.
20. Townsend Cross, near the bridge of the same name.
21. High Cross, mentioned from around 1500.
22. White Cross.
23. Castle Street sanctuary stone.
24. Dale Street sanctuary stone.
25. Townsend Bridge, certainly in existence by 1564.
26. Pool Bridge, dating from the mid-17th century.
27. Fall Well.

The Liverpool burgesses, with their strong Puritan influence, for the most part supported Parliament, but the families of Stanley, Molyneux and Norris were active Royalists and the town was therefore divided. At the outbreak of the war Liverpool was considered to be a Royalist stronghold with the mayor, John Walker, supporting the King, as did Colonel Edward Norris of Speke, who was governor of the castle. As long as Lord Derby held south-west Lancashire for the Royalists, no attempt was made to fortify the town and the only defensive action taken by the Royalists seems to be the import of thirty barrels of gunpowder from Warrington.

Lord Derby was active in the Royalist cause and Preston and Lancaster changed hands more than once in the early phases of the fighting. By 1643 Parliament was gaining the upper hand and Colonel Tyldesley appeared with his Royalist troops to be quartered in Liverpool, which thus became a garrison town. In April came the first active hostilities when the Roundheads under Colonel Assheton came in pursuit of Tyldesley and attacked the Royalist stronghold. There was a bloody battle, with two days of hand-to-hand fighting in the streets. Thirty lives were lost, Liverpool was taken by Parliament and about 300 Royalists were taken prisoner in the castle and the tower.

The Roundheads decided to fortify the town and a wide ditch, twelve yards wide and about twelve feet deep, was excavated from the Townsend Bridge to a point on the Mersey just north of St Nicholas Chapel. The spoil from the ditch was used to build a high mud wall. Where the wall crossed over Dale Street, Tithbarn Street and Oldhall Street fortified gates were built and were guarded by cannon. The wall continued south-east to meet the castle, a short stretch was built from the castle to the Mersey and the street ends leading down to the river were blocked up against attack from that quarter, making Liverpool into a fortified town. There were plenty of cannon to defend the walls. The castle served its purpose of covering the shipping in the Pool and a covered way was built so that stores could be loaded and unloaded more easily under fire.

At about this time a clerk called Adam Martindale came to work for John Moore, the Colonel of the forces in the castle. Martindale had a poor opinion of his employer. He admitted that he was paid regularly but claimed that Moore and his family 'was such a hell upon earth, as was utterly intollerable. There was such a packe of arrant thieves, and so artificiall at there trade, that it was scarce possible to save anything out of their hands'. He left the employment of John Moore and accepted a lower salary as chief clerk to the foot regiment. Subsequent events meant that Martindale's opinion of his employer was soon to be shared by many others in Liverpool.

Roundhead soldiers continued to occupy the town for over a year. A strict military discipline was maintained and there was apparently some reluctance among the townspeople to buckle down to their new masters:

> Wheras divers of the Inhabitnts of this Towne have refused and contemptiously neglected contrarie to divers Orders to appeare wth their best Armes att ye beating of the drume, these are therefore to give publicke notice & warninge to all p[er]sons whatsoever inhabitting wthin this Garreson, hertofore appoynted for ye observing of ye watch wthin ye same; That if they or any of them shall hereafter refuse or neglect to appeare at the beatinge of ye Drume for ye settinge of ye watch wthin this Garrison, or for ye performinge of other duties wthin ye same or any p[er]son whatsoever sett upon his watch or Guard shall come of the same or neglect his duties therein, till he be hence called and releeved by an officer, shall for everie such offence pay to the use of his fellow soldiers ye some of xiid or lie in Prison in ye towne hall untill he have paid the same.[2]

All families known to be Catholics or 'papists' were suspected of having Royalist sympathies and were given fourteen days in which to collect together their belongings and leave town. There is evidence that women and children were moved out of the town for their own safety, and the townspeople were not allowed to receive any strangers in their houses. The military occupation was not welcomed by the burgesses, but most of them were Roundhead sympathisers and they could do very little about it. Adam Martindale liked their company, however, and 'enjoyed sweet communion with the religious officers of the company, which used to meet every night at one another's quarters, by turnes, to read scriptures, to confer of good things, and to pray together'. As a clerk he was not required to carry a musket, pike or halberd but for fashion's sake he wore a sword. 'I was not furnished with a charging-horse, warre-saddle, pistols, holsters, or carabine, but onely with a little hackney, and an ordinary saddle and bridle to ride along with the rest.'[3]

The garrison was used as a base from which to besiege Lathom House, where Charlotte de Tremiolle, the Earl of Derby's gallant French wife, was still holding out after four months of siege. In May Prince Rupert advanced northwards with the main Royalist army and in one of the most romantic episodes of the whole Civil War the Prince relieved the Countess at Lathom and prepared to advance and take Liverpool with his army. Lord Derby assured him that it would be an easy task, as there were no more than fifty soldiers in the garrison.

Rupert made his encampment on Beacon Hill at Everton, from where he had an excellent and panoramic view of Liverpool and its fortifications. 'A mere crow's nest which a parcel of boys might take', was Rupert's comment as he studied the town from the Low Hill and Copperas Hill. The hills around the little town were ideally placed for his batteries. It would be a simple matter to dig trenches and besiege the town which lay on the low ground below and which was designed as a seaport, not a fortified town to withstand a siege.

For several days Rupert tried to storm the town without success. The defences held, but in the castle John Moore concluded that Liverpool could not hold for much longer and without giving any notice to the burgesses he embarked his troops onto the ships lying in the Pool and made a cowardly escape by sea. Deserted by Moore's troops, Liverpool fell to the Royalists at three o'clock in the morning of the 13th of June after a night attack through the field to the north of Old Hall. The final attack was led by Caryl, the brother of Lord Molyneux, who was able to use his local knowledge to help with the advance. The people did not surrender easily. There was bitter hand fighting in the streets with much plunder and slaughter as the soldiers forced their way in as far as the cross by the town hall. It was the bloodiest and most terrifying night ever known in Liverpool. Nobody knew if they were facing friend or foe in the darkness, and when dawn came on the 14th, bodies were lying everywhere. The Royalists 'did slay almost all they met with', claimed Adam Martindale, 'to the number of three hundred and sixty, and, amongst others, diverse of their owne friends, and some artificiers that never bore arms in their lives, yea, one poore blind man'. Yet he added that the first soldier he met with offered him quarter without even asking. 'We finde that a great company of Inhabitants were Murthered and slaine by Prince Ruperts fforces', reads the town books, 'the names of the Murtherers we cannot as yet be c[er]tified of any of them or their names.'

After the fall of Liverpool about twenty thousand Royalist supporters flocked to Rupert's banner, and he departed for York where he hoped to repeat his success. The battle of Marston Moor was a turning point of the war and after the battle the Parliamentarians soon gained the upper hand again in Lancashire. The Royalists held Liverpool for only three months before the town was recaptured by Sir John Meldrum with apparent ease. Meldrum did not waste time on assaults; he simply dug a line of trenches and remained there for two months. In October fifty soldiers in the castle deserted and left to join Meldrum's forces, then the remainder of the garrison mutinied, imprisoned their officers and surrendered the town without a fight.

Thus Liverpool changed hands for a third time. It became a military garrison town again with Parliamentarian troops. The townspeople were heartily sick of the whole war, but there was little they could do about it. The bodies of their dead still lay in the fields awaiting a decent burial. The year 1644 marked the end of the bloodshed in Liverpool itself but troops were garrisoned in the town for several years afterwards and as late as 1647 the people were petitioning for a reduction in the number of troops from 600 to 200 so that they could all be garrisoned in the castle and the town could get on with its own business again.

Cromwell's victorious Protectorate recognised that Liverpool was the only port on the west coast which had remained loyal to their cause. Five hundred tons of timber were needed to rebuild the port which was described as 'in a greate p[ar]te destroyed and burnt downe by the Enemie'. The Government granted the timber to the town. The wood was to be taken from the grounds of James Earl of Derby, Richard Lord Molyneux, William Norris, Robert Blundell, Robert Molyneux, Charles Gerrard and Edward Scarisbrick – altogether an impressive list of Lancashire gentry who had chosen to support King Charles.

In 1645 the mayor, John Holcroft, was in London petitioning Parliament for compensation against the losses sustained in the Parliamentarian cause.

> That in ye Seidge very much of yr Peticoners Corne Cattel Beere and other p[ro]visions were taken and siezed on by the Governor Coll[onel] Moore for ye use of ye Garrison and yor Peticoners would not suffer onie of ye Inhabitants of the said Towne to Ship away the rest of their Goodes lest ye Soldiers sh[oul]d thereby have beene discourraged Whereupon when ye said Towne was at last taken without anie Condicon very many of ye Inhabitants of ye said Towne were killed all their Goods plundered and spoyled and many of their howses pulled down and burned whereby the said Inhabitants are utterly undonne unles they be releved by this hon[oura]ble howse.[4]

John Holcroft was joined by Thomas Bick(er)steth who remained in London for several months petitioning on behalf of his townsfolk. The negotiations were long and protracted, but Cromwell's government acknowledged the truth of the petition and eventually a grant of ten thousand pounds in compensation was agreed. This was a princely sum, but the Government did not actually pay the money. They decided to grant the burgesses the rental of land in Ireland instead. The burgesses had to abide by the decision but asked that the land be as near Dublin as possible – their request went unheeded and land in Galway was granted. The negotiations took so long that by the time the first rentals were due the monarchy had been restored and those who had supported Parliament were no longer seen in such great favour. In the 1650s the town books show occasional references to the Irish properties but there is no record that Liverpool ever received any rentals from them.

Liverpool's setbacks during the Civil War were certainly no worse than many other places, and as the effect of the war receded there appeared small but significant signs of an increase in prosperity. The town hall roof was repaired and 'tiered over with lime and hair, and made handsome'. A lantern was fixed at the High Cross and another at the White Cross to supply lighting on the nights when there was little moonlight – these two crosses were situated at the crossroads of the H plan which still represented the street pattern in the middle of the seventeenth century. A second bridge over the Pool was built some time before 1648. The Townsend Bridge at the end of Dale Street was repaired and in 1654 the hated mud walls were levelled and the fortified gates were taken down and removed. Tithebarn Street was given a new pavement, stepping stones were laid in the market footway, a second road to Everton was made by widening out an existing bridleway sufficiently to take a cart, and a new ducking stool was erected to help to cool off the ardours of the scolding fishwives.

In 1660 the unpopular Caryl Molyneux, who had led the Royalists into Liverpool, laid out a new street called Lord Street running eastwards from the castle through the remains of the orchard to the Pool. He petitioned to extend Lord Street and to build a third bridge across the pool. The bridge was actually built but the burgesses considered it illegal and in a heated confrontation between Lord Molyneux and the town council the bridge was pulled down again.

The steady increase in population was checked by regular outbreaks of plague. Serious outbreaks occurred in 1607 and 1651 and it was a miracle than none occurred during the Civil War sieges. Plague was a well known fact of town life. The great plague which struck London in 1665 was particularly violent and when in the following year London was decimated by the great fire, many of the merchants lost their houses and their fortune and were forced to start again from nothing. In 1668 Edward Moore negotiated with a Mr Smith of London, a sugar baker, to set up business in Liverpool and offered him a site forty feet square on which he could build a four-storey stone house. The bargain was not completed, but sugar refining did come to Liverpool soon afterwards when another London merchant called Daniel Danvers came and set up in business.

At this crucial stage in Liverpool's development Sir Edward Moore compiled a list of his tenants, describing their properties and mundane details such as the number of chickens they were obliged to give him as part of their rent, but he also described their personalities and even snatches of their family histories.

The people had long memories. They had not forgotten the time when Sir John Moore deserted Liverpool in the time of its greatest need and they refused to vote for Edward Moore either as mayor or as a member of parliament, partly because of his father's cowardice and partly because of his unpleasant personality. The rental was written as advice to Edward Moore's heirs. It tells us far more about the character of the people of Liverpool in this troubled century than any of the dry, official records of the borough.

Edward Moore warns his heirs not to let anybody take stones from the sea bank or it will cause the sea to waste the bank away. 'Here belong to this fish house fish yards and a free fishing', he writes, 'which our ancestors have had above four hundred years, as you may see by the original grant. If any wise body had these fish yards, might much advantage be made of them; they used to maintain your ancestors'

family with fish three days a week, when they were above thirty in a
family, and lived at the Old Hall'.

He points to a site in the town centre, explaining that it used to be
Moore property many generations ago. 'How the town came by the
little shops where the women now sell apples, and the cobbler works?',
he asks, 'Because in an exchange from Sir Richard Mullinex, I find
them granted to my great great great grandfather, John More.'

Some of the Moore tenants were honest and hardworking people.
Edward March was a poor but honest man, as was Edward Howroben
(Horobin) and his wife Margery. Widow Plome was a 'good honest
woman' living in a 'pretty new house', and Johnathan Hunter had been
his landlord's butler for fourteen years. William Whittle lived in
Chapel Street with his children Robert, Ellen and Elizabeth – 'He is a
very honest man; use him and his children well', said Edward Moore
and he repaired the gable end of their house for seven pounds. George
Glover the schoolmaster is also approved of as 'a very honest man,
with a good wife Margaret and with children Jane and Ellen, his
annual rent is five shillings plus two hens to be given at Christmas.'[5]

William Gardiner in Dale Street was another honest tenant, 'but his
wife is an odd kind of cunning woman; will never pay rent or hens, but
hath several times cozened me; therefore make her pay the rent on the
day, otherwise she will swear she hath paid you'. John Higginson in
Old Hall Street was a 'good honest man' but John Lorting was 'a sour
dog fellow, yet one who loves me and my family' – he had no children
of his own, so at his death the house became available for rental to
another family. Richard Livesey was long dead and left a fine house;
worth at least one hundred and twenty pounds and rented out at two
pounds per annum.

Henry Mason was an elderly and honest man who had been a
servant to the family for some fifty years, but Moore described his wife
as 'a most notorious whore, and a wicked woman', and he managed to
have her sent to the ducking stool. 'She hath cursed me and mine
without any cause[!], and much abused me, till I was glad to send her
to the house of correction; since which she has been much better. She
hath been once at Bridewell, twice carted, and once ducked . . . if she
outlive him, turn her out, for God can never bless anything she hath to
do withal'.

Edward Moore was well acquainted with all his tenants' scandals
and he explained that Henry Mason's son had no legal claim to the
rental after his father's death. 'If this old man's son (who many know is
a bastard gotten by one Topping, being great with child when she was
married) come to take it, you may tell him he is none of Mason's son;
yet, if he will give you one pound a year till he be able to fine for it, let
him have it'.

In Chapel Street lived Thomas Lancelot (remembered by Lancelot's
Hey) and his neighbour William Mosse; both are tagged with the
description of drunken, idle fellows. 'This Baly March is a most
notorious knave', said Edward Moore, 'one of those who openly
refused me in the election for parliament man'. In Juggler Street lived
Peter Lurting, who also refused to vote for his landlord. 'He is a very
knave and hath deceived me twice . . . he was the man who would
neither give me his vote when I stood for a parliament man, neither
would he give me his vote when I stood to be mayor of this town; but

treacherously, contrary to his promise and faith, having engaged at his going out of his mayoralty to name me, and so give his vote for me. It's true he named me amongst others, and then gave his vote for another . . .' Anne Young had died recently and her grandaughter was living in the house 'whose father by name Baly March is a most notorious knave, and her husband one Rob. Prenton as bad'.

By this time we begin to suspect that the reason why the Moore tenants were branded as knaves was connected with the way they voted and Edward's next words confirm the suspicion. 'Both of them hath been against me in all elections, and in this particular hath several times abused me by bad language behind my back, and said I was the worst landlord in England . . .'

Edward Moore then tells a long and amusing story about how he once arranged to meet Robert Prenton in London to transact some business. Moore turned up attired in his fine gentleman's clothes only to find that the rendezvous was a seedy public house in Billingsgate. 'I found his ship; and having a suit of apparel on my back worth forty pounds, and taking my man's cloak and throwing it over my clothes, I did so far condescend to go into a pitiful ale house, where I sat watching for him to come to his ship, in a room where there was at least five or six several companies of the meanest sort of people you can imagine.'

Moore was convinced that his failure to get into Parliament had cost him a fortune and all his life he harboured a grudge against those of his tenants who had not given him their vote. Alderman Formby in Water Street 'is one who, when to have chosen me a parliament man would have saved my whole estate, he would not give me his vote; but when I sent Mr Shaw the minister to him, he returned him the answer, I was too young to be a parliament man, therefore he would not give me his vote this parliament or the next, but the third he would'. Joan Holt was branded as 'One who hath much abused me. Her son James was one of those who promised me his vote, and when it came to the election, left me and went to the other party.'

He also had a grudge against Widow Blundell in Castle Street and her son in law, Scarisbrick, 'a very cunning woman; hath to her son-in-law a notorious knave, and one who, I charge you never trust . . . I will her tell you a pretty story of him', he continues and as he rambles on again in his niggardly and miserly fashion and we wonder at what scandal is about to be unveiled next:

I intending to build a stable at my horse mill door, to make it bigger I would take in a little gennell, in length some three yards and in breadth not one yard wide which lay at the south end of Will Riding the cooper's. But William Riding was extremely unreasonable, and demanded to have two shillings yearly abated out of his rent for it; when in truth nobody in England would give threepence a year for it; and I seeing him so base to me, desired he would refer it to anybody, to which he agreed. Then I named this fellow Scasbricke and Tho. Bridge, as indifferent betwixt us; and after two days they awarded me to abate two shillings yearly and the three rent hens, which was as good as four shillings per annum, and awarded me, besides, to make the said William Riding a back door in the wall to his back side in Phoenix Alley, with locks and key, in all which would have cost me at least fifteen shillings. Thus you see what it is to rely on such knaves; when I could have had it for two shillings, they would have made me pay fifteen shillings fine, and four shillings yearly; and these were both my own tenants and arbitrators. Thus you see what unreasonable souls these common people hath, and perfectly hates a gentleman.

Richard Williamson was described as a most notorious knave. 'You never trust any of that name in this town, for there is a great faction of them and their relations, and what is in them always lies underhand', he wrote. All of which leaves us with the conclusion that perhaps Edward Moore was indeed the worst landlord in all England, a view which would certainly be endorsed by some of his tenants. But there were many worse in his times and Edward Moore was not entirely without compassion. When Jane Tarleton's husband was drowned at Dublin, Edward Moore leased her house for thirty shillings when when he had been offered twice as much for the same house by another tenant.

By the seventeenth century the burgesses had gained the upper hand in Liverpool, and although landowners other than Edward Moore sometimes represented the borough in parliament and were sometimes elected as mayor, their influence was gradually dwindling. The population, which for centuries had barely crept above the thousand mark, only to be cut back again by war or plague, began to pick up in the seventeenth century and was certainly over two thousand by the time the Civil War broke out. By the middle of the century the numbers had reached about four thousand and very radical changes were afoot.

Liverpool was able to gain a much greater part of the Irish trade. London merchants found it more economical to bring their Irish goods overland from Liverpool rather than brave the long passage through the English channel which was attended by the increased danger of pirates, enemy action and shipwreck. A part of the Cheshire salt trade was being shipped through Liverpool and foreign trade was on the increase, particularly with France and Spain.

In 1666 came a significant event and a new venture. The *Antelope*, a tiny ship of only sixty-tons displacement, was prepared for a long voyage which would take her far beyond Ireland and across the Atlantic to Barbados. The *Antelope* carried a cargo worth about two hundred pounds, most of which consisted of three thousand yards of linen cloth valued at £130 15s 9d, and the rest made up of shoes, slippers, nails, spikes and coal. Nearly a year later, in August 1667, the gallant little vessel arrived back in the Mersey amid great rejoicing and laden with a cargo of sugar cane. When the profits of the voyage were counted the merchants got back twice the sum they had invested. Ten years later there were twelve ships trading regularly with Barbados while, at the same time, trade developed rapidly with Virginia, where tobacco proved even more profitable than sugar. Spain and Ireland no longer represented the farthest horizons of the Liverpool merchants. There was a new world of trade beyond the Irish Sea. It was a world for which the port on the Mersey was well situated.

Chapter Four

'The Wonder of Britain'

ELIA FIENNES travelled light for a gentlewoman of her times. She rode the muddy roads of England sidesaddle, with often only one servant to accompany her. In 1698 she crossed the Mersey from Cheshire into Lancashire. The boat was large for a ferry. It carried her horses easily and looked big enough to carry a hundred people, but the passage was rough, it took an hour and a half and the water was choppy – it seemed to her as dangerous as a sea passage:

> From Burton which was on the side of England the shore I went to the ferry 9 miles to the river Meresy, another great river, indeed much broader and a perfect sea for 20 mile or more; it comes out of Lancashire from Warrington and both this and the Dee empts themselves into the sea almost together a few leagues from Leverpoole, which poole is formed by a poynt of land that runs almost around the entrance from the sea, being narrow and hazardous to strangers to saile in in the winter, the mouth of the river by reason of the sands and rocks is a gate to the river; this I ferry'd over and was an hour and halfe in the passage, it's of great bredth and at low water is so deep and salt as the sea almost, tho' it does not cast so green a hew on the water as the sea, but else the waves toss and the rocks great all round it and is as dangerous as the sea; its in a sort of Hoy that I ferried over and my horses, the boate would have held 100 people. [1]

As they tacked nearer to the Lancashire shore the ferry threaded between the cosmopolitan selection of merchantmen standing in the Mersey. Anchored in the estuary were traders from all around the coast of Britain, from Scotland, Ireland and the Isle of Man. They shared the harbour with ships from Norway, Holland, Denmark, Flanders, Spain, France, Portugal, the Baltic and Hamburg and with the tall ocean-going three-masters trading with Virginia, Maryland, New England, Pennsylvania and other English colonies in the New World.

The view of the town from the river was impressive, with St Nicholas Church on the left, the square embattled Tower and the stone customs house standing at the waterside, the crumbling but still massive castle dominating the town to the south. In the centre the new town hall rose above the houses. It was topped with a small cupula which was dwarfed by the lookout tower with its railed platform and tall flagstaff,

Shipping in the Mersey. (by Frederick Calvert).

Small craft battle with a, choppy sea, with the Liverpool skyline behind. Probably about 1840; an early steamboat is depicted.

The Mersey, though a fairly sheltered estuary, could still be whipped up into a stormy and treacherous stretch of water by north-westerlies, as this painting shows.

from where the merchants trained their telescopes on the horizon to look for the first signs of their ships returning home from afar. Miss Fiennes was very impressed with her findings:

Leverpool which is in Lancashire is built just on the river Mersy, mostly new built houses of brick and stone after the London fashion; the first original was a few fishermens' houses and now is grown to a large fine town and but a parish and one church, tho' there be 24 streetes in it; there is indeed a little chappell and there are a great many Dessenters in the town; its a very rich trading town the houses of brick and stone built high and even, that a streete quite through lookes very handsome, the streetes well pitched; there are abundance of persons well dress'd and of good fashion; the streetes are faire and long, its London in miniature as much as ever I saw anything; there is a very pretty Exchange stands on 8 pillars besides the corners which are each treble pillars all of stone and its railed over which is very handsome town hall; over all is a tower and cuppilow thats so high that from thence one has the whole view of the town and the country round; in a clear day you may see the Isle of Man. . . [2]

The 'streete right through lookes very handsome' was Dale Street, with the Exchange which so much impressed Celia Fiennes standing at the west end near the High Cross and serving also as the town hall. It was built in 1674 when the old town hall was rebuilt and let out for business premises. The eight triple pillars supported the council chambers above, whilst the merchants conducted their business below. The 'little chapel' was that of St Mary del Key, a small but very ancient

A watercolour, by Herdman, of Celia Fiennes' 'very pretty Exchange'. The pillars supported the council chambers above, while the merchants conducted their business below.

Below: Isabella, Viscountess Molyneux, later Countess of Sefton, by Thomas Gainsborough. One of the finest portraits of the Molyneux family, a fine period piece and every inch a Gainsborough.

building next to the larger chapel of St Nicholas. Outside the west door was a statue of St Nicholas where the superstitious sailors, well aware of the dangers they had to face at sea, made offerings before leaving port on a long voyage. The many 'dessenters' in the town were Protestant Dissenters who had broken away from the Church of England and who, after the accession of William and Mary, were legally allowed to hold their own religious meetings provided that their meeting place was properly registered for the purpose. The Dissenters met in Key Street and the Quakers met at their meeting house in Hackin's Hey. Celia Fiennes arrived in the very year that Liverpool first acquired the status of a parish and she may have heard gossip from the locals about the application which was made in the previous year:

> It was formerly a small fishing town, but many people coming from London, in the time of the sickness and after the fire, several ingenious men settled in Leverpool, which caused them to trade to the plantations and other places, which occasioned sundry other tradesmen to come and settle there, which hath so enlarged their trade, that from scarce paying the salary of the officers of the customs it is now the third part of the trade of England, and pays upwards of £50,000 per annum to the king; and by reason of such increase many new streets are built, and still in building; and many gentleman's sons from the counties of Lancaster, Yorkshire,

Liverpool in 1725.

CHADWICK'S map of 1725 is full of interest and gives a very good impression of how the town looked at an important period of its development.

Chadwick's was the first reliable street plan of Liverpool and it complements very neatly the near contemporary view of the town drawn by S. and N. Buck in 1728 (see pages 64-5). Together these provide a fairly comprehensive guide to finding one's way around early-Georgian Liverpool.

The new wet dock was now completed and fully operational. It is clearly visible, together with the later addition of the octagonal basin and graving dock (number 49).

A few buildings are drawn – among them, the Customs House which can clearly be seen at the head of the dock; the churches of St Nicholas and St Peter and the Exchange.

Chadwick has given us a general street map, showing the various street, alleys and squares which were in existence in that time. In general, however, the frontages to the streets were not all solidly built up, as shown here.

It is also interesting to compare this plan with another, supposedly showing the town in 1720, which was included in the corner of Swire's map of Liverpool in 1824; the maps are similar but with some intriguing differences.

Derbyshire, Staffordshire, Cheshire, and North Wales, are put apprentices in the town. And there being but one chapel, which doth not contain one half of our inhabitants, in the summer (upon pretence of going to the parish church which is two long miles, and there being a village in the way) they drink at the said village by which, and otherwise, many youth and sundry families are ruined, therefore it is hoped the bill may pass, being to promote the service of God [3]

Celia Fiennes was not the only traveller to write about Liverpool at this crucial stage of its development. Daniel Defoe, better known as the author of *Robinson Crusoe,* visited Liverpool several times between 1680 and 1715 and was always impressed by the amount by which the town had grown between his visits. Defoe gives his own description of the ferry crossing from the Wirral, along with an amusing account of how the wealthy passengers were carried to the shore so that they did not spoil their fine clothes:

I entred Lancashire at the remotest western point of that county, having been at West-Chester upon a particular occasion, and from thence ferry'd over from the Cestrian Chersonesus, as I have already call'd it, to Liverpoole. This narrow slip of land, rich, fertile, and full of inhabitants, tho' formerly, as authors say, a meer waste and desolate forest, is called Wirall, or by some Wirehall. Here is a ferry over the Mersee, which, at full sea, is more than two miles over. We land on the flat shore on the other side, and are contented to ride through the water for some length, not on horseback but on the shoulders of some honest Lancashire clown, who comes knee deep to the boat side, to truss you up, and then runs away with you, as nimbly as you desire to ride, unless his trot were easier; for I was shaken by him that I had the luck to be carry'd by more than I car'd for, and much worse than a hard trotting horse would have shaken me.[4]

Nicholas Blundell, the squire of Little Crosby, described the means of summoning the ferry with a smoke signal for travellers who found themselves stranded on the Cheshire shore. 'We dined at Chester & thence went to the Rock hous', he writes, 'but the boat was gon, so we got a smoke made, but no boat coming to us, we went to the Wood Side, where Mr Darcy Chantrell came to us and got a Boat for us so we came home.'

Daniel Defoe was very interested in the spectacular growth of trade in Liverpool. It was no longer Chester which was used for comparison, but Bristol, the second port in England. Defoe could not help but compare the symmetrical placement of the two west-coast ports:

The people of Liverpoole seem to have a different scene of commerce to act on from the City of Bristol, which to me is a particular advantage to both, namely, that though they may rival one another in appearances, in their number of shipping, and in several particulars, yet they need not interfere with one another's business, but either of them seem to have room enough to extend their trade, even at home and abroad, without clashing with one another. One has all the north, and the other all the south of Britain to correspond in. As for Wales, 'tis, as it were, divided between them by nature it self. Bristol lies open to South Wales, and into the very heart of it, by the navigation of the rivers Wye and Lug, and by the many open harbours all the way to Milford and St David's, and the counties of Monmouth Hereford and Salop, by the Severn; Liverpoole has the same with North Wales, by the water of Dee, the Cluyd, the Conway, Canal of the Mona, and all the rivers in Carnarvon Bay. [5]

Shipping fees were 6d for vessels drawing up to ten feet of water and

Early Georgian Liverpool.

Key:

1. The Castle,
2. The Old Hall.
3. The Tower.
4. Town Hall (until c.1674.)
5. New Town Hall.
6. Crosse Hall.
7. St. Mary del Key Chapel.
8. St. Nicholas, at last designated a church in 1699.
9. St. Peter's Church, built 1704.
10. Castle Hey Presbyterian Chapel, probably late 17th-C.
11. Key Street Prebyterian Chapel, built in 1707.
12. Friends' Meeting House, in use from around the first years of the 18th century.
13. Baptist Meeting House, from around the same date.

12d or one shilling for every stranger's ship drawing more than ten feet of water. The locally registered ships paid only half of this sum. In 1672 the tonnage of shipping in West Derby hundred was 2,175, with sixty-five vessels and forty owners. The size of the ships was steadily increasing and larger vessels had to be held by three splayed-out anchors to prevent them from drifting with tide and current. A water bailiff was responsible for the moorings and he was given a coat with a silver oar as a badge of his office. The water bailiff was also responsible for the upkeep of the Rock Perch beacon on the Cheshire side of the Mersey, built in 1683 as a guide to the shipping. The beacon was originally a tall wooden structure with an iron basket at the top to hold coals and fuel. It served for 150 years as a primitive lighthouse to warn the ships of the dangerous rocks offshore. A boundary stone near the mouth of the Dee marked the end of the Liverpool liberties and the start of those of Chester.

'The town house is a fine modern building', wrote Defoe, 'standing all upon pillars of free-stone; the place under it is their Tolsey or Exchange, for the meeting of their merchants; but they begin to want room, and talk of enlarging it or removing the Exchange to the other part of the town, where the ships and merchants business is nearer

14. Granary.
15. Tithe barn, probably demolished before 1674.
16-17. Horse mills of various dates.
18. Middle Mill.
19. Middle Mill.
20. Paul's Mill.
21. Salt House.
22. Sugar refinery, established by Richard Cleveland and Daniel Danvers in a five-storey building.
23. Sugar refinery, owned by John Hughes.
24. Sugar refinery, also owned (until around 1708?) by Daniel Danvers.
25. The Custom House was situated for a time in Moor Street.
26. It was moved around 1680 (see engraving on page 34) to a new building on the shore.
27. Tannery.
28. The Old Dock, constructed on the site of the Pool in the 1710s. Traces of the original dock walls were found during excavations in 1980.
29. Pot works, evidently the earliest Liverpool pottery.
30. Pool House, now in use as a 'House of Correction'.
31. Poole's Almshouses, built in the late-17th century.
31. Richmond's Almshouses, built as an annexe to Poole's
32. Warbrick's, dating from around 1708 and built to benefit poor sailors' widows.
33. Charity School.
34. Stocks, still here until 1674.
35. The new site of the stocks.
36. Pinfold.
37. Pillory.
38. Pillory.
39. Ducking stool; a new one was ordered in 1712.
40. Cage or lock-up.
41. St Patrick's Cross.
42. High Cross.
43. White Cross.
44. Castle Street sanctuary stone.
45. Dale Street sanctuary stone.
46. Townsend Bridge, no longer needed, presumably, after the construction of the dock.
47. Pool Bridge, similarly, disappears from the records at around this time.
48. Dry Bridge.
49. Lord Street Bridge.
50. Fall Well.

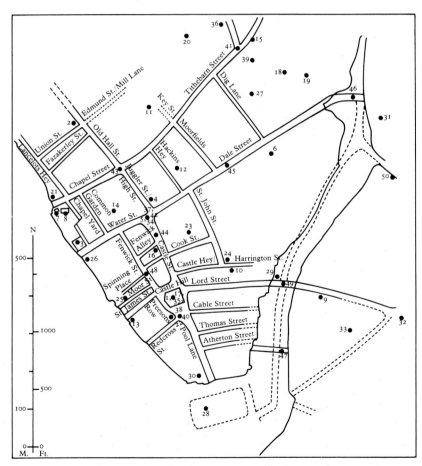

Old Customs House
   Built in 1720-21, a few years after the opening of the Old Dock, the customs house of red brick and stone was very much part of the eighteenth-century scene. The artist, W. G. Herdman, was born in 1805 – he would have known the customs house in his childhood but his painting is a reconstruction from earlier pictures.

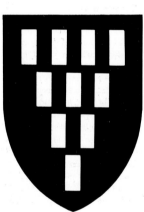

Blundell of Little Crosby
'Sable ten billets 4, 3, 2 and 1 argent'.
   There were several branches of the Blundells among the gentry of south Lancashire. The Little Crosby branch included Nicholas Blundell, whose diary records various minutiae of Liverpool life in the early-eighteenth century. He knew many people in the town and he witnessed the building and opening of the first wet dock.

[to] hand.' When the new town hall was built, the customs house was located in the newly cut Moor Street, but by 1680 it was relocated in a two-storey stone building near the waterfront – the landlord was Sylvester Moorecroft who was elected mayor in the year 1707. In the 1670s Daniel Danvers, a London merchant, with his partner Richard Cleveland, had built a five-storey sugar refinery near the corner of Red Cross Street. A second and a third sugar refinery followed early in the eighteenth century. By 1700 there was a dyeworks and the pottery industry was beginning to expand into a full-scale manufacturing industry – by 1760 there were no fewer than twenty potteries.

Apart from Lord Molyneux's Street, Edward Moore of Moore rental fame was the first to add new streets to the medieval pattern. Fenwick (Phenwyck) Street and Fenwick Alley, Bridge Alley and Moor Street were all his creations. Fenwick Street was spelt in several different ways, sometimes as Phoenix Street; it was named after Dorothy Fenwick from Northumberland who was the first wife of Edward Moore, and her family crest was a phoenix in flames. At the south end of Fenwick Street was a little bridge known as the 'dry bridge', which carried the street over the dry moat of the castle to a bank near the north wall. Bridge Alley, on the other hand, running at right angles from Fenwick Street to Castle Street, paradoxically contained no bridge at all and Edward Moore facetiously tells us that 'a drunken fellow' called Thomas Bridge lived at one end. Pool Street ran down from the castle to the quay past lodging houses, warehouses and yards, a sugar refinery and a salt works. By 1677 the municipal record shows that several other streets had appeared, including Lancelot's Hey named after Thomas Lancelet (a 'drunken, idle fellow'), Hackin's Hey named after that 'very honest man', John Hackin, in Edward Moore's rental, also Castle Hill, Preeson's Row, Red Cross Street and St James' Street, giving a total of eighteen streets.

By 1697 ten more streets had been added, making a total of 28, very close to the figure of 24 quoted by Celia Fiennes. By 1708 the number had increased to 36. Henry Peet, in his excellent article on 'Liverpool in the Reign of Queen Anne', compiled a list of these streets with the numbers of inhabited houses in each. For convenience the town was divided into north and south, with Dale Street, the most populous street in Liverpool, as the boundary. The total number of rateable houses in 1708 was 1,287, from which Henry Peet was able to estimate a population of about seven thousand.

Among those who knew Queen Anne's Liverpool intimately was Nicholas Blundell, the squire of Little Crosby. Nicholas was essentially a countryman and the diary he kept shows a love of the countryside and rural sports. 'I heard cookow and saw one swallow', he wrote on a journey back from Aigburth in April 1704. 'I went to a hors Rase on Leverpoole Sands where a Grey Mair gave a Dunn Hors half a Mile at the Start' – the dunn horse won.

He went into town two or three times every week and kept a diary of local events for over twenty years. He knew many people in the town and would visit them in their homes or dine with them at the Woolpack in Dale Street. Nicholas Blundell's horse had to pick its way over the mooring ropes as he arrived at the town along the coastal track from the north. He was on his way to visit his friends the Tarletons who lived in Castle Street. Nicholas wanted to arrange for the passage of a young kinsman called John Blundell on one of Tarleton's ships to America. When young John arrived in America he was to take up an apprenticeship with Richard Blundell, brother of Nicholas, who was a trader in Virginia. The formalities were completed and John Blundell sailed with Captain Edward Tarleton on the *Laurel,* a vessel of two hundred tons, with a cargo of clogs and other manufactured items.

Near the Tarletons, also in Castle Street, lived John Gildus, a barber surgeon. A man of many parts, John Gildus not only shaved his customers' beards but for a suitable fee he would cut and bleed them and explain how he was drawing the poisonous fluids from their bodies. He was also a dentist, and extracted two of Mrs Blundell's teeth for the handsome fee of five shillings.

Nicholas sometimes called on his old friend Robert Broadnax in John Street. Colonel Broadnax was a veteran of the Civil War who had been a captain of horse and a gentleman of the bedchamber to Oliver Cromwell and subsequently a Lieutenant Colonel under William III. In 1701, at the advanced age of eighty-three, the Colonel was taken by a sickness which he was convinced would finish him off. He took a philosophical view of his illness and ordered a local carpenter to make a coffin in preparation for his decease. Colonel Broadnax slept in the coffin expecting to find himself transported to higher (or lower) realms, but when he awoke in the morning he was still in Liverpool. Robert Broadnax repeated the performance the next night – the carpenter had done a fine job and the coffin was very comfortable. 'I went to Leverpoole and made Major Broadnax a viset', wrote Nicholas Blundell in 1727, 'He told me that in March next he will be 108 years of aige; he has his memory perfectly well, and talks extreamly strongly and heartally without any seeming decay of spirits'. The next week Robert Broadnax died. He had slept in his coffin every night for twenty-six years.[7]

In Red Cross Street lived the wealthy sugar dealer Daniel Danvers, the largest ratepayer in town and one of the men who sponsored the

Inhabited houses,
Liverpool 1708
(vide Henry Peet) [6]

South

Castle Street	80
Phenwyck Street	31
Phenwyck Alley	8
Bridge Alley	10
Castle Hill	18
Moor Street	30
St James' Street	19
Preeson's Row	26
Red Cross Street	35
Back of the Castle	18
Pool Lane	38
Waterside	18
Over the Pool	10
Cook Street	35
Saint John Street	39
Harrington Street	38
Lord Street	62
Cable Street	43
Atherton Street	24
Thomas Street	34
About the new church	20

North

Water Street	98
Juggler Street	54
Chapel Street	61
Chapel Yard	19
Common Garden	25
Lancelot's Hey	45
Rosemary Lane	35
Union Street	18
Old Hall Street	28
Tythebarne Street	42
Hackin's Hey	27
Moorfields	38
Dale Street	161

Liverpool's first wet dock

BY the beginning of the eighteenth century, it was becoming clear that better facilities would have to be provided for the increasing number of ships using the port. In 1708, with considerable foresight, the Corporation consulted Thomas Steers, one of the country's foremost engineers, who suggested the bold solution of draining the Old Pool and building a large, stone dock in its place, about two hundred yards in length and nearly one hundred yards wide, with gates to hold back the tide. It was only the second of its kind in the country and provided shipping with much-needed protection and a still-water berth at which to load and unload. The Corporation was clearly pleased with the project, for it continued to sponsor dock projects for many years to come, so that eventually nearly eight miles of the Liverpool seashore was fronted by docks and basins. Steers' original dock was eventually drained in 1827 to make way for a new Customs House.

Right: *An 18th-century plan of the estuary, showing some of the landmarks and shipping lanes into the Mersey. (L.R.O. DDX 99/5)*

Below: *A reconstructed plan showing the town centre and its dock system in around 1824. The extent of the later dock developments to seaward is immediately evident when one compares it to the original shoreline – the shaded portion shows where the Pool had once been, and the extent of the reclaimed land. The map is based on a reconstruction of the Pool by Charles O'Kill and the later street plan is a simplified version of a detailed town map by William Swire in 1824.*

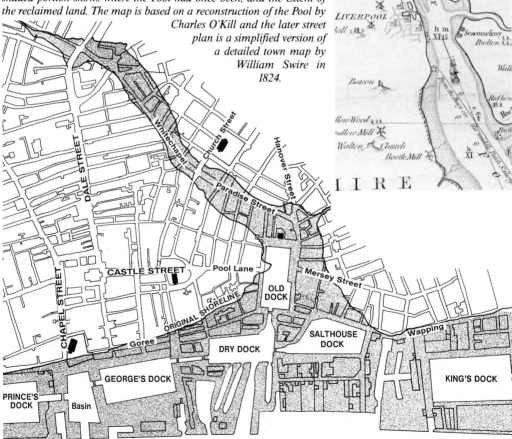

Above: A detail of Bucks' view of Liverpool, 1727, showing Steers' wet dock not long after it was opened.
Below: A detail of Eyes' plan of 1760, showing how by this date the Old Dock had become almost landlocked by the later dock developments to seaward. (L.R.O. DDX 99/6)

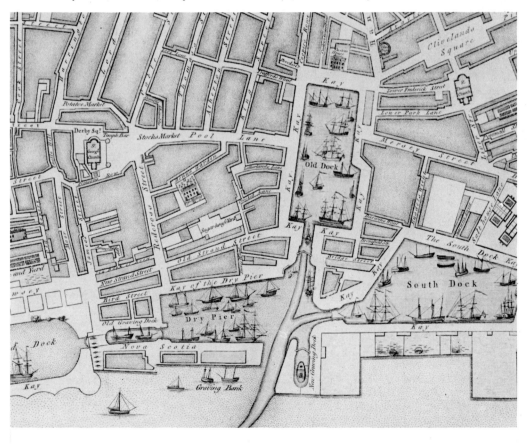

pioneering voyage of the *Antelope*. He could tell tales of the great fire of London which caused him to leave the capital soon after 1666. He was married to Sarah Pemberton the daughter of the late John Pemberton, an apothecary in Moor Street.

Also in Red Cross Street were the Aspinalls, the Newtons, the Formbys and the Brownbills. In Castle Street lived branches of the ancient families of Scarisbrick, Molyneux and Standish, a branch of the Robinsons, and John Ainsdale living next door to Mrs Litherland. In Harrington Street lived the Battersbys, the Penningtons and another branch of the Aspinalls. In Water Street lived William Denton and Henry Mercer the brewers, Thomas Dugdale the carver, Edward Nicholson the shoemaker, Robert Sher the silversmith and Prescott Ranicars who married Elizabeth Tarleton. In Tythe Barn Street were branches of the Halsalls, Tyrers and Rigbys. Dale Street was the longest street in town; here lived the artisans like John and Thomas Bulman the clockmakers – Thomas Bulman was another emigrant from London and the man of the same name listed as a clockmaker at Swan Alley near London Bridge in the 1690s. Over the Pool the new church of St Peter was commenced in the early 1700s and consecrated in 1704. Daniel Defoe described St Peter's as 'a noble large building all of stone, well finish'd; has in it a fine font of marble placed in the body of the church, surrounded with a beautiful iron pallisado'. He liked the beautiful tower and the peal of eight good bells.

With the rapid expansion of Liverpool came the pressing problem of how best to load and unload the cargoes in the difficult tidal waters of the Mersey. The Old Pool was quite inadequate for the numbers and size of the vessels and it was never a particularly safe harbour. In 1708 the engineer Thomas Steers was appointed as adviser, and he recommended a bold and drastic solution which involved draining the Old Pool and building there a great stone dock with floodgates to hold back the tide. It was an ambitious project. Nothing quite like it had ever been undertaken before and, along with a similar but smaller dock at Rotherhithe on the Thames, it set the pattern for future docks all over the world, but it needed all the resources of the merchants to finance and it took five years to build. On Daniel Defoe's final visit to Liverpool the dock was completed, he was very impressed with the work:

> . . . the situation [of the port] being on the north bank of the river, and with the particular disadvantage of a flat shore. This exposed the merchants to great difficulties in their business; for though the harbour was good, and the ships rode well in the offing, yet they were obliged to ride there as in a road rather than a harbour. Here was no mole or haven to bring in their ships and lay them up, (as the seamen call it) for the winter; nor any key for the delivering of goods, as at Bristol, Biddiford, Newcastle, Hull and other sea ports; Upon this the inhabitants and merchants have, of late years, and since the visible encrease of their trade, made a large basin or wet dock, at the east end of the town, where, at an immense charge, the place considered, they have brought the tide from the Mersee to flow up by an opening that looks to the south, and the ships go in north; so that the town entirely shelters it from the westerly and northerly winds, the hills from the easterly, and the ships lye, as in a mill-pond, with the utmost safety and convenience. As this is so great a benefit to the town, and that the like is not to be seen anywhere in England but here, I mean London excepted, it is well worth the observation and

imitation of many other trading places in Britain who want such a convenience, and, for want of it, lose their trade.[8]

The dock was rectangular, about 200 yards long and nearly 100 yards wide, with the line of the south side stepped near the middle, it was constructed of brick and imported yellow sandstone. Many ships could anchor safely within the lock gates and a short time later an octagonal basin was built at the entrance with a dry dock on one side of the octagon and at right angles to the entrance passage.

There were plenty of poor and underprivileged in Queen Anne's Liverpool; the filthy and insanitary living conditions of the poor were barely above the basic level of subsistence. There were casual unemployed dockers, there were the sick and the infirm, there were penniless sailors discharged from foreign vessels. But the local council was wealthy and very progressive. They levied a poor rate which raised hundreds of pounds every year, local people had somewhere to appeal to and the poor in Liverpool were no more numerous than anywhere else of comparable size. Nobody had seen more of England than Daniel Defoe, and nobody was better placed to make a fair judgement:

> Liverpool is one of the wonders of Britain, and that more, in my opinion, than any of the wonders of the Peak; the town was, at my first visiting it, about the year 1680, a large, handsome, well built and encreasing or thriving town; at my second visit, anno 1690, it was much bigger than at my first seeing it, and, by the reports of the inhabitants, more than twice as big as it was twenty years before that; but, I think, I may safely say that at this my third seeing it, for I was surpriz'd at the view, it was more than double what it was at the second; and, I am told, that it still visibly encreased both in wealth, people, business, and buildings. What it may grow to in time, I know not.
>
> In a word, there is no town in England, London excepted, that can equal Liverpool for the fineness of its streets and the beauty of the buildings; many of the houses are of free stone, and compleatly finished; and all the rest (of the new part I mean) of brick, and handsomely built as London itself.

The Liver Pool was no more. The town had left its origins far behind, though it still retained the atmosphere of a country market town where farmers came to trade their produce every Saturday from the smaller towns and villages of rural Lancashire and Cheshire. Dale Street still led to the dale at the Townsend Bridge where the Moss Lake Brook flowed down from Everton. Cattle grazed in the meadow near the new church of St Peter. To the north was a firm beach of golden sand where horses raced on high days and holidays. New developments beyond Chapel Street were eating into the sandhills, but when the wind was from the north the scent of sand dunes and star grass still pervaded the northern limits of the town. Windmills put their sails to the breeze on Brownlow Hill and ground the corn to make the flour for the people's daily bread. Below in the Mersey other sails billowed to carry the wooden ships across the wide Atlantic. The village of Everton with its ancient beacon stood on the green hills behind and overlooked the rippling corn which in high summer stood tall and golden in the town fields of old Leverpoole.

Chapter Five

Georgian sea port

ICHOLAS BLUNDELL loved horse racing, cock fighting and bull baiting. In 1713 one of his servants, William Ainsworth, returned from Blackburn Fair with a fighting cock, and three weeks later Ainsworth brought back another cock from the market at Ditton. Nicholas acquired two more cocks and put them all on a special diet for the great cockfight which took place on Easter Monday. As early as March he was taking bets on his 'Ditton Cock Clumsey' against an inferior-looking bird owned by his neighbour, John Rose. Nicholas was pleased with the success of his fighting cocks, but in his enthusiasm it is difficult to know exactly what happened, except that feathers were flying everywhere and Nicholas got a good scolding from his wife for neglecting his duty as host for the evening:

> We had a great Cocking at Mrs Ann Rothwells, they played Battle Victory, I had two Cocks in the Battle and one of them got two Battles, there were nine battles played this after-noone. Captaine Robert Fazakerley and Wiliam Atherton etc. Lodged here. Mrs. Blundell and Mr Turvill made a Viset here, but I came not to them from the Cocking.[1]

When Nicholas had finished building his new marl pit he decided it would be an excellent place for bull baiting. The poor beast was tethered to a stake in the marl pit whilst a pack of yelping dogs was set snarling at his heels, but the bull proved to be so good at defending himself with his horns that nearly all the dogs suffered injuries of one sort or another:

> I baited a Large Bull in the Bottom of my New Marlepit in the Great Morehey, he was never baited before as I know off, yet played to admiration, there was I think 8 or 9 Doggs played the first Bait & only two the 3rd Bait, I think there was not above two Doggs but what were Lamed or very ill Brused, I gave a Coller to be played for but no Dogg could get it fairly so I gave it to Richard Spencer of Leverpoole being his Dogg best deserved it.[1]

Nicholas Blundell was not a follower of fox hunting or deer hunting and not all his entertainments were as bloody as the bull bait. A week later, when the marling of the fields was over, there followed a country celebration for the neighbours and the farm workers, with maypole dancing, sword dancing and other entertainments. All the neighbours were invited over to join the celebrations, and they arrived with presents of country produce to give to Nicholas' wife, Francis. The Blundell household was always well supplied with ale and little luxuries such as tobacco and French brandy, because Nicholas was a leading light in the highly organised smuggling racket run by the country gentry of the Lancashire coast, and against which the Liverpool customs officers fought a continuous, losing battle:[2]

> I had on my Finishing day for my Marling and abundance of Neighbours & Tenants eat and drinke with me in the after none. Severall of them had made presents to my Wife of Sugar, Chickens, Butter &c. All my Marlers, Spreaders, Water-Baylis, & Carters din'd here except one or two Carters as I think were absent, I payed of my Marlers & Spreaders and some of my Carters. We fetched home the May Powl from the Pit and had sword dansing & a Merry Night in the Hall & in the barne, Richard Tatlock played to them, I drunk in the Paintry with Mr Aldred, Mr Burton, Thomas Syer, William Tarleton, Walter Thelwell, Mr Shephard of Ince &c: There was also here John Rose, Thomas Tyrer, John Tarleton &c.

In the February of 1714 he met Patrick Norris and a Mr Branagen at the Woolpack in Liverpool. They rode back together to Little Crosby, where Nicholas provided accommodation for the night. Mr Branagen brought a new horse with him which was to race along the sands on the morrow. 'I went part of the Way towards Formby with Mr Branagen & Patrick Norris to look at the Road as Walter Thelwell has set out over Ince Mosses', wrote Nicholas. The horse was to run from Formby to Liverpool Sands, back to Formby, then back again to Liverpool, covering the same stretch of sand three times. The betting was that the course could be covered in under four hours. 'He performed and finished his course in less time by above a quarter of an Hour', wrote Nicholas with pleasure and characteristic confusion.

Racing at Hoylake, by J. Dalby.

In 1716 we find Nicholas Blundell undertaking a long journey to the continent. He could have sailed from Liverpool to Ostend but he chose instead to travel via London, where he could see old friends and do some sightseeing. He left London in March 1716 and returned in August 1717, having visited his aunt in the meantime and his three sisters at a convent in Flanders. In common with many of the Lancashire gentry, Nicholas Blundell was a Roman Catholic, and the reason for his journey was not simply a sightseeing tour. It was a flight from the authorities because of his active involvement with the Jacobite rebellion during the rising of the Old Pretender in 1715.

Most people in Liverpool supported the Protestant succession of 1688 and the port became actively involved with the transport of troops to Ireland. In supporting the succession of William and Mary, however, Liverpool was at variance with much of the surrounding countryside. Lord Derby, after dithering a little before making up his mind, took the side of William of Orange, but Lord Molyneux supported the Jacobites. Discontent simmered for a very long time and it was not surprising to find that when both the Old and Young Pretenders came south from Scotland they chose the route through Lancashire in the hope that the Catholic sympathisers there would rise to join them.

The Whigs were fiercely against the Jacobites and at the time of the 1715 rising Liverpool was the only Whig stronghold in Lancashire. As the rebel numbers swelled and they advanced further south, the townspeople regretted that they had built no fortifications with which to defend themselves – the Jacobites well knew that in Liverpool there were plenty of ships, supplies and ammunition for a rebel army. A trench was hurriedly dug out and the lower parts of the town were deliberately flooded. Seventy pieces of artillery were mounted around the outskirts of the town and all the ships in the river were stationed in a position to give the maximum defence. Daniel Defoe described the panic as the rebel advance came nearer:

> There are no fortifications either to landward or seaward, the inhabitants resting secure under the protection of the general peace; though when the late northern insurrection spread down their way, and came to Preston, they could have been glad of walls and gates; and indeed; had the rebel party had time to have advanced to Warrington, seized the pass there, and taken Manchester, as they would certainly would have done in three days more, it would have fared but very ill with Liverpoole; who could have made but little resistance against an arm'd and desperate body of men, such as they appeared to be, and by that time would have been: Besides the invaders would here have found not the sweets of plunder only, but arms, ammunition, powder and lead, all which they extreamly wanted; they would have had ships also to have facilitated a communication with their fellows in Ireland, who would have throng'd over upon the least view of their success, if it had been only in hopes of plunder.[3]

The castle still existed but it was no longer Crown property and no longer an impregnable fortress. It had been bought by the town and the council had no intention of retaining it as a military stronghold. The castle had not been repaired for years and was of little use in the defence of the town. Luckily for Liverpool the Jacobites were defeated before they got anywhere near. Four of them were hanged on the Prescot Road at a place which became known as Gallows Hill and the people heaved a great sigh of relief. 'Heaven had Liverpoole in its particular protection', said Daniel Defoe, 'as well as the whole kingdom.'

The castle was crumbling into a great state of decay but until about 1720 people still lived in the ruins of the round corner towers. Parts of the castle wall still stood in 1725, but in the following year the council ordered the last remaining stretch of wall, at the end of Lord Street, to

Above: *The Customs House from Trafford's Wient.*

A superb plate from Enfield, designed by Edward Rooker and engraved by P. Burdett. The picture has many later imitations, but the original dates from 1770, showing the carved prows and figureheads of the merchant vessels in the Old Dock. The fourth Customs House is on the left, with the tall spire of St Thomas in the background. There is plenty of lively and authentic eighteenth-century dockside activity.

Left: *St Nicholas Church and Quay.*

The picture claims to be prior to 1711, but it is clearly a much later fabrication, as the spire was not added to the tower until 1746. In many respects, however, such as the decorated stern of the ship on the right and the dockside buildings, the view has some authenticity.

be pulled down to make room for the new church of St George.

By 1745, when Bonnie Prince Charlie led his supporters through Lancashire, the castle was a thing of the past. In Liverpool batteries were erected against the Young Pretender and the town was again put in a state of panic, but, as with the earlier rising, the precautions proved to be unnecessary. At the time of the 'forty-five' a regiment called the Liverpool Blues was raised by public subscription to help put down the rebellion, and during Bonnie Prince Charlie's flight back to Scotland they played a part in the siege of Carlisle. When the rising was over, anti-Jacobite feeling rose high in Liverpool. There was an outbreak of violence and the only Catholic chapel in town was

Bucks' view of Liverpool, 1728

THE South West Prospect of Liverpool by S. & N. Buck was one of several that these engravers executed at around this date in the north of England. It is a fine representation of the town as it probably appeared at that date. Wherever it is possible to check, the view seems to be extremely accurate, but in order to be really up-to-date, the artists depicted St. George's Church as standing proudly in the centre of the picture, whereas it was only just on the drawing board at this date, and was not completed for a further seven years. Here, Bucks' original key to the view is preserved and short additional notes given where appropriate. The buildings in the background have been deliberately faded, apparently to give a greater feeling of perspective. See page 57 for an enlarged detail of part of the engraving around the area of the dock.

4. 'The Beacon'. Further north than Everton, perhaps at Kirkdale.

5. 'The Exchange'. Dating from around 1679, it was 'a famous town house, placed on pillars and arches of hewn stone', doubling as a town hall. It was just in front of the present Town Hall, which replaced it in 1754. See page 33.

THE SOUTH WEST PROSPECT OF LIVERPOOL

1. 'St. Nicholas's Church'. Dating originally from the middle of the fourteenth century, St. Nicholas' became the town's only place of worship at the Reformation when the Chapel of St. Mary del Key was closed. It was extended on the north side in 1697 and, two years later, it was at last made into a parish church. In 1746 a spire was added to the tower, both of which tragically collapsed in 1810 (see page 99). The present tower was built shortly afterwards. but the church was again badly damaged during the last war.

2. 'Water Street', one of the original seven streets of Liverpool.

3. 'The Tower'. By this date the Tower was often in use as a prison, although the upper parts were used for public meetings and assemblies while the new Town Hall was being built. The new prison opened in 1811 and the Tower was pulled down in 1819.

6. 'The Tobacco Pipe', about which little is known, though seemingly the chimney to a tobacco factory.

7. 'The New Church' depicted here is St. George's. It was built more or less on the site of the Castle which had disappeared finally in 1726, the same year in which the plans were passed for the new church. Presumably the artists did not want to depict an empty building site.

8. 'Yerton' is the name that the Bucks gave to the little village on the hill behind Liverpool. It is shown here as a fairly large village, but Yates' map of 1769 (page 82) only depicts around thirty houses clustered around the Everton village square, so one must presume some degree of artistic licence here.

12. 'The Charity School'. The town's first Charity School appears to have been opened in a small house on the south side of School Lane in 1708. By 1726, just before this view was completed, Blundell's Blue Coat School had been built and the school was transferred there. This appears to be the building shown both here and on Chadwick's plan of 1725 (see page 51).

15. 'Law Hill', where Prince Rupert viewed the town before setting up his cannon there. By the middle of the 18th century, Low Hill had several houses and was a distinct community outside both Liverpool and Everton.

17 'The Bowling Green House'. This bowling green is shown on Eyes' plan but, being situated on Wapping, it was soon overlooked by a huge tobacco warehouse, among other things, and was built over shortly afterwards.

11. 'The Custom House' at the head of the dock. Unfortunately it is barely visible here, hidden behind a forest of masts. See, however, the illustrations on pages 54 and 63. The first idea of building a Customs House near the new dock seems to have been in 1717; built in stone and brick over the next four years, it was demolished soon after the dock was filled in.

13. 'The Copperas House'. The Copperas Works produced copper parts for the shipping industry until it was closed in 1756, apparently because of the noxious smells that the factory produced.

16. 'The Sugar House'. The location of this particular refinery is unknown since it does not seem to appear on any of the contemporary maps. At least three others existed in the town at this time.

THE COUNTY PALATINE OF LANCASTER.

9. 'St. Peter's Church'. Soon after Liverpool gained parish status, but before the more central castle site became available, it was decided to build a church 'across the Pool'. Consecrated in 1704, St. Peter's housed the town's first library which was given by one John Fells in 1715. The church was sadly demolished in 1922.

14. 'The Glass House'. A glassworks opened by Josiah Poole in 1715. On Eyes plan of 1760 it is shown as a substantial building built around a courtyard and with a circular structure, perhaps a furnace, in the centre. Shortly afterwards it appears to have disappeared, like the nearby bowling green, under warehouses and new streets.

19. 'Rock House Ferry Boat', a small, exposed sailing smack making its way across the river and threading its way between larger vessels.

10. The New Dock – see pages 56-7 for a more detailed illustration and commentary.

20. 'The River Mersey', here depicted as full of sailing vessels.

18. 'Eastham Ferry Boat'.

attacked and set on fire.

The boundaries of the port were formally defined in 1723:

> From the Redstones, in Hoylake, on the point of the Wirral southerly, to the foot of the river called Ribble-water, in a direct line northerly, and so upon the south side of the said river to Hesketh Bank easterly, and to the river Douglas (or Astland) there, and so all along the seacoasts of Meols and Formby, into the river Mersey, and all over the rivers Mersey, Irwell and Weaver. [4]

The excellent street plan by Chadwick (1725) and the beautifully detailed South-West Prospect drawn by the brothers, S. and N. Buck, (1728) are complementary and invaluable guides to the Liverpool as it appeared in the 1720s. Chadwick's plan labels all the streets and the notable buildings of the time. He shows the Old Dock crammed full of sailing ships, with many others vessels outside in the Mersey. Buck's prospect depicts the view from the river in a realistic scene which shows a forest of masts jostling together in the dock and, like Chadwick, with ships in the Mersey flying the flags of many different nations. On Buck's prospect the Rock House Ferry with square sail billowing is shown sailing smartly out from the shore.

A long jetty runs out from the dock entrance into the river with steps at the end leading down to the water where two small boats are moored. The waterside is a hive of activity, with shipwrights and carpenters building new ships on the beach where wooden hulls stand propped up with sterns to the river.

Houses are gabled with two storeys, tall chimneys and many windows. Most of them are detached, but with an occasional terrace. The tallest spire is that of the recently built St George's Church, with St Peter's to the south and the squat tower of St Nicholas's on the waterfront to the north – a fourth tower with a large flag flying turns out to be the merchant's lookout tower on the Exchange. The new customs house, already the fourth house to serve this purpose in Liverpool, is just visible behind the forest of masts in the wet dock. To the south stands the tall conical tower of the glassworks with a wisp of smoke emitting from the top, and nearby is a smaller chimney known as the tobacco pipe, its function to burn off damaged tobacco. The castle is no more, but the turreted tower of the Stanleys still stands at the end of Water Street. The Copperas Works on Copperas Hill stands outside the town, and the surrounding hills are dotted with many windmills, some of which rise between the houses on the outskirts of the town. A bowling green stands to the south, with a house for the benefit of the bowlers.[5]

The rise in prosperity and population continued unabated. It was decided that the customs house was too small. Another dock was needed. The pillars of the Exchange were sinking and Liverpool needed a new and grander town hall.

Many reasons have been given for the rapid expansion of the Liverpool trade in the first half of the eighteenth century. One reason is that, unlike other ports, the Liverpool apprentices received next to no wages until they reached the age of 21. Samuel Derrick thought one reason for the competitive advantage was the security of the passage through the Irish Sea, which meant the Liverpool merchants could dispense with part of their insurance premiums. Another important factor was certainly the quality of the Manchester linen and woollen

goods that were held in great demand on the West Indian markets, but Bristol too was expanding very rapidly and was almost as well supplied with textiles by the Cotswold woollen industry.

One advantage enjoyed by Liverpool was the choice of the passage to and from North America via the north or the south of Ireland and, as the colonisation of America progressed, the centres of population tended to grow further northwards. As ships became larger the Bristol vessels lost precious time in the tortuous six-mile passage down the River Avon where they had to be towed by hand and oar. Yet another factor may have been the state of the art of navigation, which was not very advanced in the first half of the century, with very few navigators being capable of following a great circle route. Vessels tended to run down the longitude to make a landfall in America and this again made the southerly route longer.

Growth was fuelled primarily by overseas trade, especially with the New World. Tobacco and sugar began to be imported in large quantities, whilst cotton later became a principal raw material import of great value to the town. Liverpool's export growth reflected the growth of trade generally and especially of its Lancashire hinterland. In particular, Manchester, Bolton, Wigan, Preston and a host of other towns were developing large manufacturing trades, and the great majority of it was exported from Liverpool. Import processing industries such as metalworking and sugar refining were also crucial for the town, employing increasing numbers. There was a great 're-exporting' trade and Liverpool became by far the most important

North Shore, Liverpool. (by Samuel Wilkinson).

Fishing boats on the North Shore in the early-nineteenth century. The tower of St Nicholas', in the centre of the picture, is the only surviving landmark in this view.

entrepôt after London and Bristol.

The first dock was such an immense commercial success that a second dock, called the South Dock or the Salthouse Dock, was commenced in 1734. It was another ambitious scheme and took nineteen years to complete. The docks provided far greater security for the shipping and convenience for loading and unloading, but there were still occasions when even they did not guarantee perfect security.

The great inundation of December 1720, recorded in Nicholas Blundell's diary, was probably the highest sea on the Lancashire coast in the eighteenth century. Liverpool did not suffer as much as the parishes to the north, but at one point the tide rose so high that a Norwegian ship called the *Tabitha Priscilla* was carried right over the jetty and deposited into the dock where she was brought to a standstill by her anchor.

In 1757 a severe hurricane hit the port and five ships were sunk in the Mersey, several windmills were blown down and the spire of the new St Thomas's fell. 'The upper part of the high spire of the church was blown down in the late storm', observed John Wesley. 'The stones, being bound together by strong iron cramps, hung waving in the air for some time. Then they broke through roof, gallery, pews, and pavement, and made a deep dent in the ground.' Five years later what was described as a tornado hit Liverpool and in two hours did considerable damage to the town and the docks. In 1768 houses near the river were flooded by exceptionally high tides and the bowsprit of a vessel called the *Wheel of Fortune* was driven right through the middle window of a house in James Street.

John Wesley's observations of Liverpool are full of interest. His first visit was in April 1755 and his findings echo the views of earlier travellers. There is little doubt that eighteenth-century Liverpool was considered to be a very attractive town:

> I rode by Manchester (where I preached about twelve) to Warrington. At six in the morning, Tuesday the 15th, I preached to a large and serious congregation, and then went on to Liverpool, one of the neatest, best-built towns I have seen in England. I think it full twice as large as Chester; most of the streets are quite straight. Two thirds of the town, we are informed, have been added within these forty years. If it continue to increase in the same proportion, in forty years more it will nearly equal Bristol. The People in general are the most mild and courteous I ever saw in a seaport town; as inded appears by their friendly behaviour, not only to the Jews and Papists who live among them, but even to the Methodists (so called). [6]

Wesley became a regular visitor, returning three more times in the 1760s. In 1766 he expressed his disapproval of the deed drawn up for the new Methodist chapel, which was 'verbose beyond all sense of reason', and which had been written on such good-quality parchment that it must have cost six guineas when the frugal Wesley claimed he could have produced a copy for as many shillings. Liverpool clearly didn't understand what the new Methodism was all about, and in 1768 the sober and austere preacher disapproved of 'some pretty, gay, fluttering, things' who interrupted his sermon. Such frivolities had no part in the world of John Wesley.

It was unfortunate but necessary that the second town hall, Celia Fiennes' 'pretty exchange', had to be pulled down to make way for a larger and grander building, but the pillars were sinking and the

Exchange was no longer large enough or fashionable enough for the expanding town. In 1748 a foundation stone for a new exchange was laid and inscribed with the names of the mayor Joseph Clegg, James Crosbie and Richard Cribb the bailiffs, Owen Brereton recorder and the architect John Wood of Bath, who designed the new town hall in the grandest Georgian traditions. It took six years to build and the opening ceremony was a great and pompous occasion attended by 340 ladies and presumably by an equal number of gentlemen, who between them managed to prolong the festivities for a week:

> . . . this magnificient building was opened in the mayoralty of James Crosbie, Esq., with a splendid ball, graced by the presence of three hundred and forty ladies. The whole week was a scene of festivity; concerts followed balls in great succession; a public breakfast was given at the rooms, and the inhabitants, as well as the strangers, were entertained with boat races on the river, and other popular amusements. The stately edifice, which gave rise to all this rejoicing, was built under the direction of the Woods, of Bath, according to the Corinthian order of architecture, in the form of a square, round which there were piazzas, to shelter the merchants in unfavourable weather. [7]

Samuel Derrick, Master of Ceremonies at Bath, visited Liverpool in 1760. He noted that the new town hall was crowded in on two sides with older houses which blocked out much of the light on the ground-floor rooms. He commented on the elegance of the ladies and the lavish scale of the entertainment, even though his visit did not coincide with any particular celebration. 'The assembly room of the town hall is grand, spacious and finely illuminated', he wrote, 'here is a meeting once a fortnight to dance and play cards; where you will find some women elegantly accomplished and perfectly well dressed. The proceedings are regulated by a lady styled 'the Queen'; and she rules with very absolute power.'

Derrick was a great lover of good food and drink – he found the merchants to be very hospitable, 'friendly to strangers, even to those of whom they have the least knowledge, their tables are plenteously furnished and their viandes well served up, their rum is excellent, of which they consume huge quantities . . . but they pique themselves greatly on their ale'. Derrick also sampled the fare at Liverpool's leading inns, the Golden Lion and the Fleece in Dale Street, at the Millstone in Castle Street and the Talbot in Water Street. If we are to believe his account, Samuel Derrick was a gourmet capable of consuming twelve dishes at one sitting. 'For tenpence a man dines elegantly at an ordinary, consisting of ten or a dozen dishes. Indeed it must be said that both in Lancashire and in Cheshire, they have plenty of the best and most luxurious food at a very cheap rate.'

'The docks are flanked with broad commodious quays', he continued. 'Surrounded by handsome brick houses, inhabited for the most part by seafaring people, and communicating with the town by drawbridges and floodgates, which a man must be wary in crossing over, as they are pretty narrow.'

Between the gluttonous bouts of feasting and drinking the merchants occasionally found time for a little culture and in the middle of the century the first permanent theatres began to appear. The cockpit yard, the market place, and the castle were typical of the earlier informal venues for drama. In 1712 Nicholas Blundell saw *The*

Yeoman of Kent performed in the castle and in 1714 he went to the New Market where he saw 'a Play acted called *Mackbeth'.*

The first regular theatre was known by the downbeat name of the Old Ropery. It was soon followed by the Drury Lane Theatre which was able to charge the handsome sum of two shillings for admission to the pit. The Drury Lane Theatre was renovated and reopened in 1759. Among the first productions were *Bold Strike for a Wig,* Shakespeare's *Henry IV,* and *The Conscious Lovers.* 'It is a most beautyful and regular structure: the scenes and clothes are entirely new and very elegant', reported the *Liverpool Chronicle.* Samuel Derrick was hardly likely to miss the Drury Lane Theatre on his visit to Liverpool, but his compliments may well be coloured by the quantity of food provided at the interval. 'The scenes are perfectly painted . . . They play three times a week; and behind the boxes there is a table spread, in all the manner of a coffee house, with tea, coffee, wine, cakes, fruit and punch.'[8]

The Theatre Royal opened in 1772 in Williamson Square, at a cost of six thousand pounds – the opening number was the tragedy *Mahomet.* The theatre was very selective in its taste and was able to survive for several years by employing only the best London performers. In 1777 Sarah Siddons was paid nearly a hundred pounds for her part as the Queen in *Hamlet,* with her husband playing opposite her as the King. The audience was delighted and became very discerning in their appreciation of good drama, but the following year the theatre made the drastic mistake of employing a provincial company. Audience participation in the eighteenth century was very real, and according to the memoirs of Mrs Inchbald they 'threw up their hats, hissed, kicked, stamped, bawled'. The poor provincial thespians were greeted with a volley of potatoes and empty bottles. On one occasion the theatre itself was the scene of a tragedy when a nearby house caught fire. The alarm was raised and in the stampede to get out one man was trampled to death and many others were injured.

Liverpool continued to grow in wealth and population, with the size of the town doubling with every generation. But the increase in wealth brought with it a corresponding increase in poverty. The number of homeless immigrants was always on the increase. Under an Act of Parliament in 1748 a commission was established, independent of the town council, for the watching, lighting and cleansing of the town. A force of sixty night watchmen was appointed. They were keepers of law and order, but they soon proved inadequate to police the whole of the town and it was another forty years before their numbers were increased. The wealthier inhabitants built new houses on the rising ground to the south of Hanover Street and around St Paul's Square and Mount Pleasant, while the poorer inhabitants crowded into the narrow alleyways of the centre near their work on the docks and the waterfront.

The medieval townfield survived the eighteenth century, retaining its original function as a place for agriculture. It was enclosed in 1733 and was later surveyed by John Eyes who produced a very accurate plan naming all the tenants at that time. The field was remarkably unchanged since the Middle Ages, in that the holdings were arranged in strips, running at right angles to the Walton road which ran right through the centre of the field for a distance of about half a mile.

The Theatre Royal, painted by H. Christian in 1884.

There existed other medieval customs which died hard, including the obligation of the inhabitants to repair the roads, and they were required to do three days' statutory work to maintain them. For most of the eighteenth century the approach roads to Liverpool were atrocious. The Prescot road, consisted of a cobbled track which had been designed for packhorses and it was badly damaged by the wheeled vehicles that were being used to carry coals from the inland coalfields. As late as 1741 some sources claimed that there were only two closed carriages kept in Liverpool, one by Mrs Isabel James and the other by Madame Clayton, and their use was limited to the confines of the town because of the state of the approach roads.

The situation was improved slightly when the Douglas Navigation Canal was opened and coal could be brought from the Wigan coalfield by sailing barge, partly by canal and partly by sea from the Douglas estuary. The road to Prescot was eventually made into a turnpike, which meant that a toll could be charged for its upkeep, but it was only comparatively late, after the completion of the turnpike as far as Warrington, that stage coaches were able to enter Liverpool. The first through service to London was inaugurated in 1761 by Horn and Company. It was a thrilling sight for the people of the town when the first stage, splattered in mud from a dozen counties but smartly painted and drawn by four fine horses, rattled down the hill and into Hanover Street, having left the capital only four days previously.

Five years later two stagecoaches were plying to London and the journey time was reduced to three days in the winter and only two days of hard jolting in the summer when there was better weather and more daylight. Stagecoaches also ran regularly to Manchester and to more northerly parts of the kingdom. Gore's *Directory* gave information for travellers and mentions the main coaching inns of the period:

STAGE COACHES

There are two Stage Coaches which go constantly to LONDON, viz. in three days during the winter season, and in two days during the summer season; one from the Golden Talbot, in Water-street, Thomas Sutton, book-keeper; and the other from the Millstone, in Castle-street, Samuel Adams, book-keeper.

The KENDALL Stage Coach comes to the Black Horse and Rainbow; Mr Cuthbert Cottom's in High-street, every Saturday, and goes out every Sunday, and takes passengers for Lancaster, Kendall, &c.

The MANCHESTER Stage Coach comes to the Golden Lion, in Dale-street, every Monday Wednesday and Friday; and goes out every Tuesday, Thursday and Saturday, during the summer season; comes in every Monday and Thursday, and goes out every Tuesday and Friday, during the winter season, and takes passengers for Warrington and Manchester, &c.[9]

The Liverpolitan John Eyes was famous for his survey of the Sankey Navigation, and in the 1760s he came to survey his home town, which had doubled in size since the time of Chadwick's plan in the 1720s. Eyes dedicated his plan to the merchants and traders of Liverpool and to John Tarleton, the mayor; he used Thomas Kitchen as his engraver.[10] His scale of 300 yards to an inch enabled him to show not only the detail of every street and alleyway, but also the plan view of some of the buildings. Paradise Street followed the line of the Old Pool, Castle Street retained its original name but the site of the castle had become Derby Square. Eyes shows the South Dock (Salthouse Dock) and the 'Dry Pier' with the new 'intended dock' to the north – planned in 1761, this dock, which became George's Dock, did not open until 1771.

George Perry's plan, three years later than Eyes, was also engraved by Thomas Kitchen and shows even more valuable detail.[11] Perry showed the Red Cross market, the library in John Street, the playhouse in Drury Lane and the baths which had been built on the river side near St Nicholas' Church. George Perry also named many of the industrial sites and showed the local industries of Liverpool in the 1760s. He shows the sites of the sugar houses, saltworks, glass houses, a tan yard, brick yards, lime kilns, breweries, pot houses, and a stocking manufactury. An iron foundry and a copper works provided the metal parts for shipping and local industry, and the windmills provided for a more traditional and basic need. Roperies, timber yards, a pitch house and 'Mr Dutton's boat yard' are depicted, all serving the shipping industry. William Roscoe, born at Mount Pleasant in 1753, remembered the sights and sounds of the Liverpool of his childhood:

Where rise yon masts her crowded navies ride,
And the broad rampire checks the beating tide;
Along the beach her spacious streets extend,
Her areas open, and her spires ascend;
In loud confusion mingled sounds arise,
The Docks re-echoing with the seaman's cries,
The massy hammer sounding from afar
The bell slow-tolling, and the rattling car
And thundering oft the cannon's horrid roar,
In lessening echoes dies along the shore.

William Roscoe

Chapter Six

'The Wrongs of Africa'

 SHIP is worse than a gaol. There is, in a gaol, better air, better company, better conveniency of every kind; and a ship has the additional disadvantage of being in danger', opined the sagacious Doctor Johnson. 'When men come to like a sea-life, they are not fit to live on land. Men go to sea before they know the unhappiness of that way of life; and when they have come to know it, they cannot escape from it, because it is then too late to choose another profession; as indeed is generally the case with men, when they have once engaged in any particular way of life.'

If the corpulent doctor had visited Liverpool his opinions would certainly have remained unchanged. Shipboard conditions were so bad that naval officers sent their sons to sea in their early teens knowing that the youngsters would rebel against the life if they were left another few years before being packed off to the navy, and it was not unknown for prisoners to be taken from the jails to man the ships in times of war. Neither the Merchant Navy nor the Royal Navy were able to recruit all the men they needed and ships' complements were raised to the required quotas by the dreaded press gang whose strong-arm tactics were actually sanctioned by the law of the land. At the outbreak of the Seven Years War with France, Liverpool Council offered a handsome bounty of two guineas to every man who volunteered for service on board a ship of war. This brought an inadequate response and the bribe was raised to three guineas. It was still not enough and the press gang, working with the authority of the mayor, was given a warrant to go through the town and impress any men they could find to man the King's ships.

In 1758 and 1759 Though Thurot, a brilliant French privateer, sailed into the Irish Sea and caused so much alarm that fortifications were built on the Mersey in anticipation of an attack. Privateers like Thurot were commanders of privately owned vessels which had a government licence to attack enemy ships in time of war. Liverpool, too, had many privateers, of which the most successful and best known were Fortunatus Wright, with his Mediterranean exploits, and his pupil William Hutchinson who later became Dock Master at Liverpool.

Privateers occasionally appear on samples of Liverpool pottery, one example being the *Golden Lion* which had previously been a French man-of-war and which was converted to a Greenland whaler. The more fortunate privateers could become rich overnight on their prize money. The classic case was Peter Baker who risked his whole fortune on a leaky vessel called the *Mentor,* but somehow managed to capture the *Carnatic,* a French East Indiaman loaded with spices and diamonds, which turned out to be worth the staggering sum of £135,000. Baker became so wealthy that he was able to purchase the manor of Garston out of his prize money.[1]

At the time of the Seven Years War the great profits made from privateering meant that the expansion of trade was hardly checked at all, and towards the end of the eighteenth century Liverpool was dominating the Atlantic trade and also profiting from the improvements in transport and manufacturing which were being brought about by the industrial revolution.

By 1800 Liverpool was bigger than Bristol and its registered tonnage of shipping was third after London and Newcastle. It had become the main supply port for all the rapidly expanding industries of Lancashire.

At the lower end of the social scale, however, there was no security of employment for the sailors or the casual dock workers and Liverpool suffered from all the problems of violence, drunkenness and poverty that accompanied a large sea port. When times were bad, the sailors had to fall back on charity to subsist and it seems that some of them preferred this existence to that of signing on for a new voyage.

In the 1770s the American War of Independence brought about the only slump in the steadily increasing volume of trade into the port of Liverpool; during the war the figures quoted for the volume of shipping showed a decrease from 84,792 to 79,450 tons. This decrease of under seven per cent generated several thousand unemployed sailors, all trying to exist with no income, and things became so desperate that the sailors rioted and held the town to ransom for several days before the military could be brought in to restore order. Cannon were brought into the streets and according to some sources they were used against the rioters and lives were lost in the cause.[2] The unemployment problem was short-lived, however, and only a few years later bounties of two guineas were being offered to able seamen and one guinea to ordinary seamen who volunteered for active service against the Americans. The bounties were increased to the considerable sums of ten guineas and five guineas, but the ships could still not be fully manned without the efforts of the press gang.[3]

There was one particular trade in which the sufferings of the seamen were as nothing compared to the sufferings of the cargo. It was of course the African slave trade, which has always been traditionally assumed to be the most profitable trade of all. William Roscoe wondered at the morality of the wealth which had been accumulated at the expense of so much human suffering:

Ah! why, ye Sons of Wealth, with ceaseless toil,
Add gold to gold, and swell the shining pile?
Your general course to happiness ye bend,
Why then to gain the means neglect the end? [4]

In the seventeenth century Liverpool played virtually no part in the slave trade, which at that time was the monopoly of the Royal African Company and was operated exclusively from London. The monopoly

Slaves in Africa.
An African dealer, with weapons, arrives at the trading post with slaves already manacled. The slaves were traded for manufactured goods before sailing the middle passage across the Atlantic.

ended in 1698 and the first port seriously to challenge London for a share of the market was Bristol, where the merchants were so successful that within twenty years they had usurped London as the leading exponents. For two decades from the 1720s to the early 1740s Bristol dominated the African trade and at one time more than half of the slavers sailing from England were Bristol vessels. By the latter half of the eighteenth century, however, the Liverpool traffic had increased so rapidly that the northern port was unchallenged as the leading exponent of the slave trade.

The earliest record of a slaving vessel trading from Liverpool appears in the Norris papers of 1700, when the captain of the good ship *Blessing* received his orders from the Norris family:

We order you with the first fair wind and weather that presents to make the best of the way to King-sail [Kinsale] in the kingdom of Ireland where apply yourself to Mr. Arthur Izeik merchant there, who will ship on board you such necessary provisions and other necessaries you shall want for your intended voyage and . . . with the first fair wind and weather make

A LIST of AFRICAN SHIPS for the Year 1771.

When clear'd	Ships	Where bound	No. of Slaves
January 17.	Agnes,	Windward Coast,	200.
19.	Nancy,	Gold Coast,	300.
22.	Corsican Hero,	Do.	300.
24.	John,	Windward Coast,	200.
25.	Violet,	Do.	300.
February 6.	Lord Caffills,	Old Callabar,	400.
9.	Industry,	Windward Coast,	200.
15.	Friendship,	Gambia,	200.
---	Lively,	Do.	200.
---	Jelliwar,	Do.	100.
28.	Lark,	Windward Coast,	100.
March 6.	Providence,	Bonny,	350.
---	Two Brothers,	Gambia,	300.
7.	Juno,	Senegal,	100.
---	Dove,	Windward Coast,	100.
9.	Warren,	Do.	150.
20.	Hare,	Benin,	400.
21.	Sam,	Senegal,	100.
26.	Peggy,	Windward Coast,	250.
---	Benin,	Benin,	450.
28.	Hector,	Old Callabar,	400.
April 6.	Hawk,	Windward Coast,	300.
9.	Ferret,	Do.	250.
15.	May,	Old Callabar,	200.
18.	Tom,	Bonny,	450.
20.	Mary,	Sirralone,	300.
26.	Polly,	New Callabar,	350.
29.	Gregson,	Bonny,	500.
May 3.	Edgar,	Do.	400.
---	Elizabeth,	New Callabar,	350.
7.	King of Prussia,	Cammeroons,	250.
13.	St. John,	Gambia,	300.
15.	Betty,	Bonny,	450.
16.	Whim,	Cammeroons,	200.
---	John,	Windward Coast,	250.
22.	Effex,	Do.	200.
24.	Mercury,	Gold Coast,	200.
---	Jenny,	Windward Coast,	100.
June 1.	Dalrymple,	Old Callabar,	400.
6.	Rumbold,	Bonny,	450.
8.	Tom,	Windward Coast,	250.
13.	Lancashire Witch,	Do.	300.
15.	Prince George,	Do.	200.
17.	Little Will,	Do.	300.
---	Andromache,	Old Callabar,	200.
18.	Hazard,	Windward Coast,	200.
---	Nancy,	Bonny,	350.
19.	Molly,	Windward Coast,	200.
20.	Sportsman,	Old Callabar,	400.
21.	Afton,	Gambia,	300.
25.	Apollo,	Windward Coast,	200.
29.	Jenny,	New Callabar,	350.
July 2.	Nanny,	Bonny,	450.
July 4.	Ellis,	Bonny,	500.
---	Charlotte,	Gold Coast,	100.
---	Juba,	Old Callabar,	400.
6.	Plumper,	Bonny,	450.
8.	Harriett,	Windward Coast,	200.
9.	Corker,	Do.	300.
12.	Carrick,	Do.	100.
---	Ann,	Bonny,	350.
13.	Little Ben,	Windward Coast,	100.
19.	Rofe,	Do.	250.
23.	Jack,	Gold Coast,	250.
24.	Nancy,	Bonny,	400.
31.	Hannah,	Gold Coast,	300.
August 3.	Peggy,	Do.	100.
7.	Sisters,	Do.	100.
13.	Society,	Do.	300.
---	Unity,	Do.	300.
14.	Liberty,	Bonny,	400.
15.	Lord North,	Do.	400.
---	Barbadoes Packet,	Windward Coast,	200.
16.	Mentor,	Gold Coast,	500.
---	Townside,	Windward Coast,	200.
22.	Union,	Gold Coast,	300.
23.	Captain,	Windward Coast,	300.
26.	Bess,	Gold Coast,	250.
27.	Pearle,	Windward Coast,	200.
28.	Swift,	Old Callabar,	200.
30.	President,	Do.	200.
September 4.	Fox,	Cammeroons,	200.
5.	Prince of Wales,	Bonny,	600.
---	Patty,	Windward Coast,	250.
13.	Renown,	Do.	200.
17.	Nancy,	Do.	200.
18.	Myrtle,	Do.	300.
23.	Molly,	Gambia,	300.
27.	Merideth,	Sirralone,	250.
---	Portland,	Windward Coast,	250.
28.	Marcia,	Old Callabar,	200.
---	John,	Gold Coast,	300.
October 1.	William,	Windward Coast,	150.
17.	Matty,	Do.	250.
---	Hannah,	Angola, (wood)	----
20.	Integrity,	Old Callabar,	250.
November 2.	Austin,	Bonny,	350.
8.	Saville,	Windward Coast,	250.
---	Camaranca,	Do.	200.
20.	Dispatch,	Gold Coast,	300.
21.	Ferrett,	Windward Coast,	150.
23.	Sally,	Do.	300.
25.	Lilly,	Do.	200.
December 9.	Mars,	Do.	250.
19.	Bella,	Cameroons,	250.
		Total	**28200**

The Slave Trade 1771.

A page from Enfield's History, *showing all the ships which sailed from Liverpool to Africa in 1771, with their names and the number of slaves transported – over 28,000 in all. The table also gives a good indication of the places in Africa where the slaves were bought.*

the best of your way to the Coast of Guinea . . . where dispose of what of the cargo is most proper and purchase what slaves you can . . . I hope you will slave your ship easy and what shall remain over as above slaving your ship lay out in teeth which are there reasonable – when you have disposed of your cargo and slaved your ship make the best of your way to the West Indies . . . if you find the markets reasonable good sell there, if dull go down Leeward to such Island as you shall see convenient where dispose of your negroes to our best advantage and with the produce load your ship with sugar, cottons, ginger if to be had . . . and make the best of your way home . . . but call at King-sail for orders . . . read over your invoice frequently that you may be better acquainted with your goods, we have not limited you to any place, only if you can't do your business on the Gold Coast and Wida go to Angola your ship we think not proper to go into Byte. We leave the whole management of the concern to you and hope the Lord will direct you for the best. Be very cautious of speaking with any ship at sea for the seas are dangerous. Endeavour to keep all your men sober for intemperance in the hot country may destroy your men and so ruin your voyage. Let everything be managed to our best advantage, let nothing be embezzled. We commit you to the care and the protection of the Almighty, who we hope will preserve you from all danger and crown all of our endeavours with success to bring you home with safety which shall be the constant prayer of . . . Write from all places where you have convenience of sending.[5]

The slave route was a triangular operation, with ships sailing first for Africa with a cargo of pots and pans and other manufactured items such as alcohol, tobacco, cloth, firearms, gunpowder and metal bars. These items were seldom new wares, but usually second-hand goods picked up at the market stalls. The African dealers inspected the pans for holes before exchanging them for slaves. The slaves were captured by dealers in Africa who brought them down to the slaving ships already in chains, sometimes walking in a long procession down the road to the coast, sometimes shackled in a large canoe which brought them down river from the interior. Occasionally a ship would carry only a handful of slaves, but the larger vessels packed hundreds of negros into the hold, manacled together in appalling squalor and with hardly space to move and breathe. There followed the horrific 'middle passage', across the Atlantic:

> Deep freighted now with human merchandize,
> The vessel quits the shore; prepar'd to meet
> The storms, and dangers, of th' Atlantick main;
> Her motion scarce observ'd, save when the flood
> In frequent mumurs beats against her prow,
>
> Whilst groans and loud laments, and scalding tears,
> Mark'd the keen pangs of others. – Female shrieks,
> At intervals, in dreadful concert heard,
> To wild distraction manly sorrow turn'd;
> And ineffectual, o'er their heedless limbs,
> Was wav'd the wiry whip, that dropp'd with blood.[6]

The conditions of the slaves are described by John Newton, the captain of a slaving vessel:

> The cargo of a vessel of a hundred tons, or little more, is calculated to purchase from two hundred and twenty to two hundred and fifty Slaves . . . the Slaves lie in two rows, one above the other, on each side of the ship, close to each other, like books on a shelf. I have known them so close, that the shelf would not easily contain one more . . . the poor creatures, thus cramped for want of room, are likewise in irons, for the most part both hands and feet, and two together, which makes it difficult for them to turn or move, to attempt either to rise or to lie down, without hurting themselves or each other . . . The heat and smell of these rooms, when the weather will not admit of the slaves being brought upon deck, and of having their rooms cleaned every day, would be almost unsupportable to a person not accustomed to them . . . They are kept down by the weather to breathe a hot and corrupted air, sometimes for a week; this, added to the galling of their irons, and the despondency which seizes their spirits when thus continued, soon becomes fatal. And every morning perhaps, more instances than one are found, of the living and the dead, like the Captives of Mezentius, fastened together,[7]

The time taken to complete the middle passage varied greatly with wind and weather, but the average time spent in these atrocious conditions of human suffering was betwen fifty and sixty days. Lack of exercise, poor diet and the squalid, insanitary conditions meant that many negroes died on the passage. Figures available for the later decades show a mean mortality rate of 5.65 percent, but some voyages were far worse than this and it may be assumed that earlier in the century, before the ships were obliged to carry a surgeon, the death rate was far higher and commonly reached ten to twenty per cent.

The negroes were bound for the sugar plantations of the West Indies or to the southern colonies of America, where they were sold as slaves to the plantation owners. The ship was then loaded with sugar, rum, and mahogany in the West Indies, or with tobacco if the voyage was to Virginia, and the new cargo was transported back to England on the third and final leg of the voyage.

There were profits to be made on each of the three legs and it has therefore always been generally assumed that the slave trade was a highly profitable concern. It is certainly difficult to justify why such high risks would be taken for a low return on investment, and the accounts of William Davenport of Liverpool survive to show that he made a staggering gross profit of £28,332 on two voyages of the slaver *Hawke* in the years 1779 and 1780. This figure reduces to £14,803 after allowing for insurance, repair bills and other expenses, still leaving a net profit of over one hundred per cent on the original investment of £13,502. We now discover, however, that the profits from the *Hawke* were quite exceptional and that these two voyages were the most successful ever financed by William Davenport in his twenty-five years as a slaver. We also know that many slavers, unlike the *Hawke*, did not carry cargo on all three legs of the 'traingle'.

Davenport traded with two towns in the Gulf of Guinea: Old Calabar near the mouth of the River Niger and Cameroon about fifty miles to the east. His mean profits over a quarter of a century of human suffering were 7 per cent on 37 voyages to Old Calabar and 21.9 per cent on 26 voyages to the coast of Cameroon. Davenport was an experienced and committed trader and it seems, therefore, that the profits of the trade in general were no better than other more traditional forms of trading. At its height around a hundred slavers a year would make the triangular passage to Africa and the West Indies, representing only about five per cent of the tonnage leaving Liverpool.[8]

Only the hardened sea captains and their crews witnessed the atrocities of the middle passage. The majority of merchants and local people saw only the handful of slaves who were brought back to England as curiosities, perhaps to be dressed as pages or footmen in a wealthy aristocratic household. But the irons and shackles were displayed for sale in the shops and market places and the people were well aware of the inhumanities of the trade. Some took the attitude that whilst shipboard conditions were atrocious and inhuman, the slavery was little different to the appalling conditions experienced in England in the coal mines, where women and children still laboured underground, or the squalid cellars and alleyways of the inner cities where the poor died of dysentry and cholera every day of the week. The poor, however, were free to leave and beg for a living, but the slaves were taken by force and chained together in the hold of the ship. The trade was inhuman and immoral, and the social conscience of

England was troubled by it.

The Bill for the abolition of the slave trade is rightly connected with the names of men like Wilberforce, Pitt and Fox. Opposition to the Bill came mainly from the Liverpool merchants, with 64 petitions from there, compared to 14 from London and 12 from Bristol. In Liverpool it was generally thought that the loss of the African trade would create massive unemployment and loss of revenue for the merchants, and it needed a brave man to speak up for abolition when the debate became a public issue.

There was, however, a small but influential circle of Liverpool abolitionists who formed a branch of the Society for Abolition:

Liverpool Subscribers to the Society for Abolition, 1788 [9]

Anonymous (thought to be Dr James Currie)	£2 2s 0d
Dr Jonathan Binns	£1 1s 0d
Mr Daniel Daulby	£1 1s 0d
Mr William Rathbone	£2 12s 6d
Mr William Rathbone Jr	£2 2s 0d
Mr William Roscoe	£1 1s 0d
Mr William Wallace	£2 2s 0d
Rev John Yates	£2 2s 0d

William Roscoe was the best known of these abolitionists, but all these men fought for their humane principles against the opposition of their neighbours and they all deserve their place in the history of Liverpool.

James Currie was a Scottish doctor who did much good work in trying to improve the housing conditions of the poor. William Wallace was his father-in-law. Jonathan Binns was another doctor, whose practice suffered when his views on abolition became generally known. The Rathbones were a well-established Quaker family of timber merchants and Daniel Daulby was another well-known Quaker connected with them in the timber trade. John Yates was a preacher at the Kaye Street Chapel and he courageously denounced the slave trade from the pulpit. There were many other leading Liverpool abolitionists, such as Edward Rushton and John Newton. The latter was one of the few who had direct experience of the trade as a sea captain. He no longer lived in Liverpool but had become a completely reformed character and wrote some of the best-loved hymns in the English hymn book.

When the Bill for abolition was in preparation, two committee members, Thomas Clarkson and Alexander Falconbridge, visited the centres of the slave trade and spent some time in Liverpool collecting information. They lodged in the King's Arms tavern, where they had direct contact with the seamen and captains of the slaving vessels. When their mission became known they were harassed and forced to change their lodgings and Clarkson described what he thought was a definite attempt on his life:

> I was one day on the pier-head with many others looking at some little boats at the time of a heavy gale . . . I had seen all I intended to see, and was departing, when I noticed eight or nine persons making towards me. I was then only about eight or nine yards from the precipice of the pier, but going from it. I expected that they would have divided to let me through them; instead of which they closed upon me and bore me back. I was borne within a yard of the precipice, when I discovered my danger and

perceiving among them the murderer of Peter Green, and two others who had insulted me at the King's Arms, it instantly struck me that they had a design to throw me over the pier head . . . There was not a moment to lose. Vigorous on account of danger, I darted forward. One of them, against whom I pushed myself, fell down. Their ranks were broken. And I escaped, not without blows, amidst their imprecations and abuse.[10]

In 1806 William Roscoe was elected to represent Liverpool as a member of parliament and after thirty years of campaigning he had the satisfaction of voting in favour of the Abolition Bill. His two-part epic peom on *The Wrongs of Africa* was written and published in the 1780s. When Roscoe returned to his native Liverpool after the Bill had been passed he marched through the streets in procession with a large band of freemen, but he was waylaid by a gang of unemployed seamen who felt he was responsible for the loss of their jobs. A violent scene followed in Castle Street. Nobody was seriously hurt, but the procession was thrown into disarray and Roscoe was badly shaken by the episode.

He declined to stand again for parliament, but his friends insisted on putting his name forward as a candidate in the election of 1807 for the Whigs and Reformers. He was defeated by two generals, Banastre Gascoyne and Isaac Tarleton. Roscoe was not unduly dismayed by his defeat. He was a sensitive and high principled man who liked botany and poetry. He did not mix easily with the seasoned politicians and the over-confident riff-raff in the House of Commons.

Roscoe was of the people and knew the people. His father kept a public house in Mount Pleasant and is reputed to have served as a butler at Allerton Hall. Young Roscoe's first job was for six months with the bookseller John Gore, the man who published Liverpool's first directory, in 1766. He left to work for John Eyes, the surveyor, who produced the excellent street plan of 1768. Roscoe was already writing poetry when still in his teens. He became articled as an attorney and was admitted to the bench at the age of 21. He practised law with great success for over twenty years but then turned his talents to land speculation and property development. He dabbled in the coal trade and became involved with a project to drain Chat Moss near Manchester. His poetry never enjoyed the popularity of Wordsworth and Coleridge but it was well known in literary circles. He turned to biography and wrote an internationally acclaimed history of Lorenzo de Medici and his son, Pope Leo X. He became a collector of fine art and was able to purchase early Renaissance paintings of the Italian and Dutch schools and some valuable early manuscripts, though he had to sell his art collection when he lost money in a banking venture. In America he was known for his work on botany as well as his literary efforts and it was in this capacity that he helped to found

Edward Rushton (1746-1814), painted by Spiridione Gambardella.

At the age of sixteen Edward Rushton served as a second mate to Africa, where a negro saved him from drowning in a river. During the passage to the West Indies there was an outbreak of ophthalmia among the slaves. Rushton went among them to treat the sick and he caught the disease himself. He remained blinded for the rest of his life, became an active abolitionist and wrote poetry decrying the slave trade.

the Liverpool Botanical Gardens where he gave the opening address in 1802.[11]

The pompous and aristocratic Thomas Creevey reminds us that Roscoe worked his way up from a humble background. Creevy could not understand how Roscoe could achieve such distinction as an author. He described him as 'a man whose dialect was that of a barbarian and from whom in years of familiar intercourse I have never heard above an average observation, whose parents were servants (whom I well remember keeping a public house), whose profession was that of an attorney, who has never been out of England and scarcely out of Liverpool.'

But Roscoe is remembered as one of Liverpool's greatest sons, a judgement which surprises outsiders who know him only as the author of *The Butterfly's Ball and the Grasshopper's Feast*. Where Gladstone was a national figure, Roscoe was a local man and it is in his love and devotion to his native town that Roscoe's greatness becomes apparent. He belonged to the select number of great philanthropists who could turn their hands to all branches of knowledge and who saw no barriers between science and the arts. William Roscoe was a lawyer and a successful businessman and lived for a time in the classical splendour of Allerton Hall. When Washington Irving met him at the Athenaeum Club he was 'advanced in life, tall, and of a form that might once have been commanding, but it was a little bowed by time – perhaps by care. He had a noble Roman style of countenance; a head that would have pleased a painter; and though some slight furrows on his brow showed that wasting thought had been busy there, yet his eye still beamed with the fire of a poetic soul'.

As the battle over the abolition of the slave trade was being fought, many local manufacturing industries were growing rapidly. The clockmaking industry thrived and towards the end of the century ships' chronometers were being manufactured. The Liverpool potteries were well established at sites all over town. The famous Herculaneum Pottery opened in 1794 and collectors' pieces of fine porcelain were being produced. On the outskirts of the town the original Everton Toffee Shop established by Molly Bushell in 1753 had become a flourishing concern; her jealously guarded toffee recipe 'of which not even a single copy has been taken' was claimed to be the secret of success. A silk industry was established in the same year as Molly Bushell's toffee in what became known as Silkhouse Lane. A mill was built which took oil-bearing seeds and crushed them to produce oil for lamps and heating.

The rapid expansion of trade and industry, the privateering, the slave trade and population explosion brought many social problems. Wallace, writing in 1795, noted the great influx of Welsh and Irish;

William Roscoe (1753-1831), painted by John Williamson.

Roscoe was a humane man of many talents. He was an MP for a short time, and he voted in favour of the Bill for the abolition of slavery. He was a successful lawyer, banker, botanist, poet, writer, agricultural pioneer and a collector of Italian manuscripts and paintings. Outside Liverpool he is best remembered for his children's poem, The Butterfly's Ball and the Grasshopper's Feast.

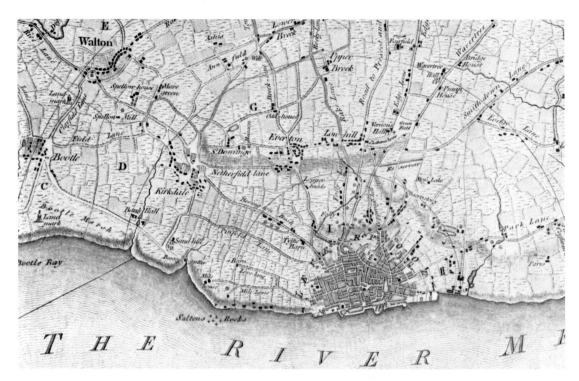

A detail of a map of the Liverpool area by George Perry, which was probably surveyed by William Yates, in 1769. William Yates was one of the most important eighteenth-century cartographers, whose map of Lancashire in 1786 is an invaluable source. This map of the 'environs of Liverpool', dating from some seventeen years earlier, is therefore of great significance.

It shows the town, with its expanding dock system, in relation to the surrounding villages and townships. It is tempting to ascribe the regular field boundaries to the north west of the town to being evidence of the original medieval townfield. This area was dug up just three years later when the navvies began the cut for the first section of the Leeds and Liverpool Canal here.

(L.R.O. DDX 99/8).

also the Scots who were heavily involved with the trade and the shipping. Building could not keep up with the rapid expansion of a population which was approaching eighty thousand by the year 1800. The poor and the immigrants were crowded into the older parts of the town, and an estimated one ninth of the population was living in damp cellars with an average of four people to a room. New housing was provided but in the absence of any building regulations the houses were shoddily constructed, back-to-back, with inadequate provision for light, air or sewage. Water was sold from a cart. So many public houses existed that in 1795 it was calculated that one house in every seven was licensed to sell strong drink. The town council urged the magistrates to reduce the number.

A curious feature of the political system was that Liverpool at this time was very solidly Tory, with the town council remaining firmly in control of local affairs. In the years following the French Revolution an attempt was made by the assembly of burgesses, who were predominantly Whigs, to challenge the authority of the council. Three times the burgesses brought the council to court and each time the verdict was given in their favour. However, the council was each time able to claim a new trial on the grounds of some legal technicality and the financial resources of the burgesses eventually became too depleted to continue the challenge. The Liverpool council remained steadily Tory right up to the eve of the Great Reform Act of 1832.[12]

Roscoe claimed that the trade of his native town would not suffer with the loss of the slave trade. He had the satisfaction of seeing this prediction come true, for when the tonnage and dues for 1806 and 1807 were calculated and compared the volume of trade through the ever-expanding port had increased yet again.

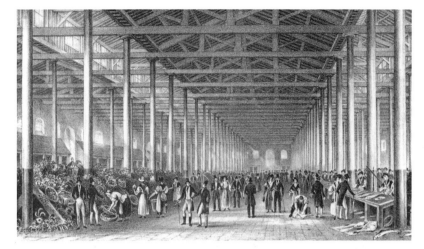

St John's Market, interior by W. Craus.

An excellent view of the interior of the market showing the roof structure in great detail. Essentially a food market, the picture shows some of the goods for sale and a very respectable, middle-class clientele.

Old Fish Market, James Street 1856, by W. G. Herdman.

One of the many Liverpool markets, this one specialised in fish and sea food. Herdman produced a whole series of valuable market scenes.

Gill Street Pig Market 1867. W. G. Herdman.

A good example of Herdman's work, a typical nineteenth-century market, showing Pembroke Street on the extreme right.

The great age of sail

STEAMBOATS were well established for tug and ferry services by the middle of the nineteenth century but sailing ships were still plying the long-distance trade routes. The diagram below shows graphically the transition that eventually did take place from sail to steam. Steamships overtook sailing vessels in tonnage in around the mid-1880s but, because of the larger average size of the steamships, sailing vessels remained more numerous until around the turn of the century. This means that sail, not steam, predominated almost throughout the period of Liverpool's greatest growth. Most of the docks were built to cater for them and much of the town's prosperity was based on them. The grandeur of the later steamships and liners should not allow us to forget the immense importance of windpower in what truly was Liverpool's great age of sail.

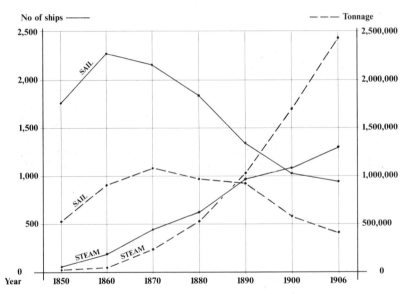

Below: A dramatic scene in the 1830s showing the sailing ship Maria Brand *in difficulties in the Mersey. St. Nicholas', the baths and the Town Hall can be seen in the background.*

Opposite, top: Samuel Walters' painting of the early Holt ship, Emma, *in full sail. The Customs House can be seen with dome just beneath the bowsprit.*

Opposite, bottom: Robert Salomon's painting of the Liverpool ship, Arctic, *is also a fine period piece, capturing all the romance and elegance of the era of the sailing ship.*

Top: *Liverpool from Toxteth Park 1834, by G. Pickering.*
An excellent view of housing, church sprires, and a forest of masts in the Mersey. Obviously a popular spot for drying the washing!

Centre: *Black Rock Fort and Lighthouse. by Samuel Austin.*
A welcome and familiar sight for mariners returning to Liverpool from all parts of the world.

Bottom: *The Port of Liverpool by Samuel Walters. The waterfront in the latter half of the nineteenth century with a mixture of steam and sail. The spire of St Nicholas is prominent in the centre of the picture, with three domes – St Paul's, the Town Hall and the Customs House – visible on the horizon.*

Chapter Seven

Venice of the North

S A YOUNG MAN John Gladstone was able to save up five hundred pounds working for his father in Leith. He arrived at Liverpool in 1785 and managed to buy himself into partnership with two corn merchants. The partnership prospered. He soon diversified into shipping and was running his own affairs. Gladstone's interests extended to the West Indies and after the abolition of the slave trade he became the owner of sugar and coffee plantations in Jamaica. When the monopoly of the East India Company ended in 1814, his ship, the *Kingsmill,* was the first to open up trade between Liverpool and the East Indies. John Gladstone claimed that the slaves on his plantations were well treated and he defended the West Indian planters against what he called 'the intemperate, credulous, designing or interested individuals who followed the lead of that well-meaning but mistaken man Mr Wilberforce'. His investment in the sugar planations was substantial and when emancipation came in 1833 he owned 1,609 slaves, for which he received compensation of a little over £75,000.

Gladstone used his wealth to build churches and to found charitable societies. He built St Thomas's at Seaforth in 1814-15, St Andrew's in Liverpool in 1816, another church at his birthplace in Leith, and an episcopal chapel at Fasque in 1847. He married his second wife, Anne Robertson of Dingwall, in 1800, and she bore him several children, including a boy child born at their home at 62 Rodney Street on December the 29th 1809. The boy was called William Ewart after his father's friend, a fellow Scottish merchant who was also a member of parliament for Liverpool. John Gladstone himself represented Liverpool for ten years in the House of Commons, but it was not he, it was his fourth son who became Prime Minister and one of the greatest statesmen of the age. The child was baptised at St Peter's, with his seven-year-old sister as godmother.

In his early years young William Ewart was not particularly precocious or academically brilliant, but he remembered his childhood with nostalgia. One of his first memories was a short speech of three words made as he stood on a chair at a family gathering in Rodney Street:

My next recollection belongs to the period of Mr. Canning's first election

for Liverpool, in the month of October of the year 1812. Much entertaining went on in my father's house, where Mr Canning himself was a guest; and on a day of a great dinner I was taken down to the dining room. I was set upon one of the chairs, standing, and directed to say to the company 'Ladies and gentlemen'.[1]

William Gladstone also recollected part of his early religious education. His pious upbringing did not make a very deep impression on him:

I was not a devotional child. I have no recollection of early love for the House of God and for divine service: though after my father built the church at Seaforth in 1815, I remember cherishing a hope that he would bequeath it to me, and that I might live in it. I have a very early recollection of hearing preaching in St. George's Liverpool, but it is this: that I turned quickly to my mother and said, 'When will he have done?' *The Pilgrims Progress* undoubtedly took a great and fascinating hold on me, so that anything I wrote was insensibly moulded in its style; but it was by the force of allegory addressing itself to the fancy, and was like a strong impression received from the *Arabian Knights,* and from another work called *Tales of the Genii.* I think it was about the same time that Miss Porter's *Scottish Chiefs,* and especially the life and death of Wallace, used to make me weep profusely. This would be when I was about ten years old. At a much earlier period, say six or seven, I remember praying earnestly, but it was for no higher object than to be spared from the loss of a tooth . . . And now I remember that I used to teach pretty regularly on Sundays in the Sunday-school, built by my father near the Primrose Bridge. It was, I think, a duty done not under constraint, but I can recollect nothing which associates it with a seriously religious life in myself.

The school attended by young William Gladstone was by no means typical of the majority of schools at that time, but his impressions still make interesting reading. Gladstone attended a small school of only twelve boys run by the Reverend Rawson, a Cambridge graduate whom he described as 'a good man of high no-popery opinions'.

His school afterwards rose to considerable repute, and it had Dean Stanley and the sons of one or more other Cheshire families for pupils. But I think this was not so much due

to its intellectual stamina as to the extreme salubrity of the situation on the pure dry sands of the Mersey's mouth, with all the advantages of the strong tidal action and fresh and frequent north-west winds. At five miles from Liverpool Exchange, the sands, delicious for riding, were one absolute solitude, and only one house looked down on them between us and the town. To return to Mr. Rawson. Everything was unobjectionable. I suppose I learnt something there. But I have no recollection of being under any moral or personal influence whatsoever, and I doubt whether the preaching had any adaption whatever to children. As to intellectual training, I believe that, like the other boys, I shirked my work as much as I could.

Although Gladstone was born into a privileged class, one of his natural traits was an ability to mix and communicate with ordinary workmen and local people. It was an ability which was later to take him far in life:

I had a great affinity with the trades of joiners and bricklayers. Physically I must have been rather tough, for my brother John took me down at about ten years old to wrestle in the stable with an older lad of that region, whom I threw. Among our greatest enjoyments were undoubtedly the annual Guy Fawkes bonfires, for which we always had liberal allowances of wreck timber and a tar-barrel. I remember seeing, when about eight or nine, my first case of a dead body. It was the child of the head gardener Derbyshire, and was laid in the cottage bed by tender hands, with nice and clean accompaniments. It seemed to me pleasing, and in no way

Above: W. E. Gladstone, by Percy Bigland. Born in Rodney Street in 1809, William Ewart Gladstone is Liverpool's most famous son. He became the most enigmatic Prime Minister of his times; he held office four times between 1868 and 1894, and he was eighty-five when he retired from politics.

Opposite, top: John Gladstone, by William Bradley. From Leith, in Scotland, he became a wealthy shipping merchant in Liverpool. He was the father of William Ewart Gladstone.

Opposite, bottom: William Ewart, by Alexander Moses. A Scotsman and close friend of John Gladstone and MP for Liverpool. William Ewart Gladstone was named after him.

repelled me; but it made no deep impression.

At the time Gladstone started his schooling, literary and scientific societies were flourishing in Liverpool, thanks mainly to the efforts of the Roscoe circle. The famed Athenaeum Club in Church Street was an exclusive gentleman's club founded in 1798 and the Lycaeum in Bold Street was established a few years later. Both clubs had regular meetings on scientific and literary affairs; they had libraries and news rooms for their members. The Liverpool Botanic Gardens dated from 1802. It was an exclusive establishment where admission was by ticket only, but the botanical collection soon attained a high national reputation. In 1812 a Philosophical and Literary Society was established, which held its meetings on the first Friday of every month. Five years later the Royal Institution was opened for 'the promotion of literature, science, and the arts, by academic schools; public lectures; the encouragement of societies who may associate for similar objects; collections of books, specimens of art, natural history, &c. by promoting a laboratory, and philosophical apparatus' – ambitious objectives which seemed to cover all possible aspects of human knowledge.

Medical knowledge was advanced by the flourishing school of hygiene and tropical medicine which was founded in the time of the slave trade when the ships were obliged to carry a surgeon to attend to the welfare of the negroes. Hospital care started in the eighteenth century, with the first general infirmary dating from 1749. The Seaman's Hospital was almost as old and was founded in 1752; the Lunatic Asylum was situated in the infirmary gardens and was founded in 1792. A local dispensary to supply medicines for the poor was formed in 1778. The House of Recovery convalescent hospital dated from 1806, there was a hospital for diseases of the eye, also a Military Hospital and in 1820 an American Seaman's Hospital to cater for the many American sailors who found themselves sick and stranded in Liverpool. The Infirmary was free to the poor of the town, but William Enfield, Liverpool's first historian, explains that entry was very restricted. Patients who were dying or incurable were not admitted:

> No woman big with child, no child under seven years of age, excepting in extraordinary cases, as fractures, or where cutting for the stone or any other operation is required; no persons disordered in their senses, suspected to have the smallpox, itch, or other infections, distemper; nor any that are apprehended to be in a dying condition or incurable, can be admitted as in-patients, or if inadvertantly admitted be suffered to continue.[2]

At one time Liverpool had aspirations towards becoming a spa town, a suggestion which is not as outrageous as it might seem at first sight. In theory all that was needed to become a spa was an assembly room, a place to promenade, spa water and a medical practitioner to pronounce the health-giving properties of the waters. Liverpool had a town hall which, as Samuel Derrick of Bath discovered, could entertain as well as anywhere in the country. It also had several fine streets for promenading, especially after the widening of Castle Street in 1786, and there was an abundance of people of fashion living in the town, or at least on the immediate outskirts. There were natural springs in the hills round about and plenty of eccentric medical practitioners prepared to testify that the water was the cure for all kinds of ailments. Considering the large percentage of hypochondriacs among their patients, it would not be difficult to produce some remarkable cures of patients with psychological ailments. William Enfield described St James' Walk in the 1770s, with its elevated view of the town where a chalybeate spring issued forth with mineral waters:

> Among the public places, the Terrace, at the south end of the town, called *St. James's Walk*, deserves to be particularly mentioned. It is upon an agreeable elevation, which commands an extensive and noble prospect, including the town, the river, the Cheshire land, the Welch mountains, and the sea. It is of a considerable length, and much improved by art. Behind this eminence is a stone quarry, which plentifuly supplies the town for every purpose of building. Here labour has exposed to view one continuous face of stone, 380 yards long, and in many parts 16 yards deep. The entrance to this quarry is by a subterraneous passage, supported by arches; and the whole has a pleasing and romantic effect. There is found here a good chalybeate water, which appears upon trial to be little inferior to many of the Spaws [i.e. Spas].[3]

The spa waters of Liverpool did not become famous, but there was one annual event which came to attract the members of the aristocracy. Horse racing on the sands had been practised certainly since Tudor times and probably even earlier. In the eighteenth century Nicholas Blundell used to organise races on the sands at Crosby. The Derby, with sponsorship from Lord Derby, was first run in 1780. In 1827 John Formby arranged a race meeting at Maghull, on land which belonged to the Molyneux family. His enterprise was copied in July 1829 by William Lynn, landlord of the nearby Waterloo Hotel, who opened a second race track and organised a rival meeting near his hostelry at Aintree. 'Maghull is as far superior to any land in Aintree for racing purposes as the light of the meridian sun is superior to that of a farthing rushlight', claimed John Formby. But the Maghull racetrack went out of business, the Aintree course survived, and in 1836 William Lynn opened a new grandstand and staged a four-mile steeplechase which was won by the famous Captain Becher riding the 'Duke'. The next thing to happen was that aristocracy took an interest in the events at Aintree and in 1839 they planned to stage a large national meeting with the powerful backing of the Earls of Derby, of Eglington, of Wilton and of Sefton, and with Lord George Bentinck among the chief organisers.

High society flooded in for the event and, overnight, Aintree found that it had became the national centre for steeplechasing. For a week beforehand the stately homes of south Lancashire were alive with feasting and merrymaking on a lavish scale. When the great day arrived the crowd was estimated at a staggering fifty thousand, with seats in the stand selling at seven shillings each. The local papers reported 'Piemen, chimney sweeps, cigar sellers, thimble riggers and all the small fry of gambling-table keepers', all joining the swarm of humanity which descended on Aintree in their crazy assortment of conveyances.

The favourite for the big race was 'The Nun' at 6 to 1, but as soon as they were off Captain Becher, known as 'the last of the leather breeches', set off at a spanking pace and took the lead on 'Conrad'. He thundered up to a jagged six-foot hedge where 'Conrad' stumbled and fell, depositing his rider unceremoniously into the water on the other side. Undeterred, the gallant Captain Becher remounted his steed and careered off at a great pace in an effort to catch up with the leaders who were already disappearing over the horizon. 'Conrad' however, had other ideas and at the next water jump he threw his disgruntled rider a second time and ended Captain Becher's hopes for the race. Becher need not have worried. His consolation prize was better than the prize money, for his fall had etched the name Becher's Brook on the racecourse for posterity. With 'Conrad' out of the race, 'Lottery' took up challenge from 'The Nun' and 'Paulina'. It was an exhausting race, with horses falling thick and fast. 'Dictator' appeared from behind and took the lead for a while. He stumbled, his jockey remounted and drove him to the next fence where he fell with a broken back and had to be put down. The favourite did not have the finishing power and fell away towards the end. In the final stages 'Lottery' took the lead again and thundered past the winning post in fine style, ahead of 'Seventy-four' and 'Paulina'.

'Lottery' became an immediate success with the race-going public. He was a horse with great spirit and personality. He hated his jockey, Jem Mason, so much that the rider had to mount furtively from the rear and on one occasion, hearing Mason's voice from outside his stable, 'Lottery' is reputed to have kicked down the stable door in anger. A journalist unofficially called the race the 'Grand National', though the name did not become official until 1847. The following year the horse 'Valentine' fell at another of the water jumps and added another piece of history to the Aintree course.

When it came to proving the salubriousness of the atmosphere, Liverpool was as good as any other seaside town or inland spa at exaggerating its claims to longevity. As 'proof' of the healthy atmosphere of Georgian and Regency Liverpool, it is possible to compile an impressive list of centegenarians who lived much of their lives in eighteenth-century Merseyside. As a set of statistics it is about as reliable as the predictions in *Old Moore's Almanac,* but in some cases anecdotes are given which show that even if the claimants could not substantiate their longevity, they were probably well into their nineties before reaching the end of their lifespan.

Liverpool Centegenarians, 1727-1838[4]

Robert Broadnax, d.1727, æt. 109.	Mrs Owen, d.1799, æt. 107.
Elizabeth Hilton, d.1760, æt. 121.	Mary Ralphson, d.1808, æt.110.
Mrs Bostock, d.1765, æt. 106.	David Salmon, d.1809, æt. 106.
James Birchall, d.1772, æt. 102.	Edward Simon, d.1821, æt. 104.
William Ellis, d.1780, æt. 136.	Ellen Tate, d. 1823, æt. 110.
Sarah Holmes, d.1783, æt. 114.	Margaret McKenzie, d.1823, æt. 104.
Mrs Bailey, d.1787, æt. 105.	Frances Dixon, d.1823, æt. 105.
Mrs Hunter, d.1796, æt. 115.	Charles Rigby, d.1829, æt. 100 +
Roger Pye, d.1796, æt. 103.	Hannah Waln, d.1838, æt. 112.
Mr Ingleby, d.1798, æt. 117.	

Of this doddering band of ancient Liverpudlians, Sarah Holmes lived in Frederick Street and Mrs Hunter in Cable Street. The eccentric exploits of Colonel Broadnax have already been described. Roger Pye was a young man on board the *Tabitha Priscilla* when it sailed over the pier and into the Old Dock in 1721, but the old salt who could tell the best sailor's yarns was David Salmon who had sailed with Commodore George Anson in 1740 during his epic voyage around the world. Anson returned with his scurvy-ridden crew in 1744, carrying the spoils from a Manila treasure ship which he captured in the Pacific.

Towards the end of the eighteenth century, the fashion of taking the waters changed to include the new fashion of actually bathing in the sea, and it was not until this time that anybody cared to notice the fact that Liverpool had exceptionally fine beaches to the north. When the data

Left: *Baths, Cornwallis Street 1864.*

The Cornwallis Street public baths opened in 1851, and were a good example of the architectural style of the 1860s. The size of the building is exaggerated by making the figures smaller.

Below: *North Shore, Liverpool. (British School 19th-C.)*

Showing the North Shore late in its career as a beach for bathing. Seaside souvenir shops still remain, with sea food and sweetmeats for sale. One of the windmills has been converted into a house.

comes under scrutiny there is plenty of evidence of sea bathing at Liverpool from very early in the eighteenth century right through to the first decades of the nineteenth. The rates assessment book of 1708 mentions Mr James Gibbons as living at 'ye bagniall', or the 'bathing place' in Water Street. 'I went part of the way towards the Sea with my children', wrote Nicholas Blundell in 1709, 'but turned back. My wife and Dorothy Blundell went with them, they were put into the sea for some out breaks.' It appears that Molly and little Fanny, aged five and three, were forced to bathe in the sea because of an outbreak of spots or rash, but we can hardly imagine that the little girls did not enjoy the novel experience of the seaside.

Public baths for sea bathing existed in Liverpool before 1765 and are shown on Eyes plan of that year situated at the southern end of the North Shore beach, at a part of the front which became known as Bath Street. The process of taking the waters was by no means simple. In 1774 Robert Thyer, a visitor from Manchester, described how a lady of his acquaintance had first of all to be cut and bled to draw the poisonous fluids from her body, the next day she had to take physic, and it was not until the following weekend that she was judged to be ready for sea bathing.[5]

The North Shore was a beautiful beach of golden sand backed by sand-dunes which disappeared around the northern horizon at Formby Point and lined the Lancashire coast for over twenty miles. The firm sands of the beach were used as a public highway to communicate with the coastal communities to the north. Situated near the beach was Ladies Walk, entered by the wishing gate and lined on both sides by an avenue of trees. Lover's Lane and Maiden's Green were nearby.

A windmill stood very close to the beach at this point, a tall brick mill called the Wishing Gate Mill with a railed gallery built around it at about twelve feet above the ground. The place was a beauty spot where wives and sweethearts traditionally came to say their fond farewells to sailors departing for the remotest ends of the earth. At some distance to the north was a second windmill called the North Townsend Mill. Near the beach were a number of traditional fishermen's cottages, and the old and new North Shore Houses, also known as the Half Mile Houses. There were two taverns much frequented by the bathers. One stood next to the nearer windmill and was called the Wishing Gate, the other was an inn called Vandries' House and was another popular bathing establishment.

Bathing machines were introduced some time before 1794 and the popularity of sea bathing grew steadily until by 1830 there was a full mile of bathing machines lining the shore at the height of the bathing season. Picton gives a general description with interesting detail, particularly regarding the lack of attire among the males:

> Long lines of bathing 'machines' stood in readiness to accommodate the visitors, while stalwart bathing men and women – amphibious creatures whose days were spent up to their knees in water – the terror of the juveniles, were in attendance, like Tritons and mermaids waiting the behests of Neptune. The shore at high water, during the months of July and August, presented a very animated appearance, being crowded with visitors from the manufacturing districts 'coom fur t' ha a dip i' th' saut weytur'. The bathing was conducted in a very primitive fashion. There was a sort of conventional separation between the sexes but the male bathers entered the water and disported there 'in puris naturalibus', the spectators promenading and looking

on with the sentiment of 'Honi soit qui mal y pense'.[6]

Local residents recollected the country 'dowkers' or 'dippers' whose job was to attend the bathing machines and help the bathers with the elaborate procedure of taking the waters. The dippers sold sweets and a cake they called 'parliament cake' which was covered all over with coloured sugar plums. In the first decades of the nineteenth century Liverpool was easily the most popular seaside town on the Lancashire coast and although many bathers were local people the clientele was by no means entirely local; some travelled from Manchester and the inland towns to take the water:

> Liverpool has become a town of considerable resort as a sea-bathing place; and the inhabitants from the interior of Lancashire resort hither in great numbers during the summer months to enjoy this salubrious and gratifying exercise. The floating bath, which is moored during the season off George's Pier Head, affords excellent accommodation to those who prefer this novel mode of immersion, and on the shore machines are provided as at Scarborough, Brighton and Ramsgate, for conveying the visitors into the briny waves and returning them in safety to the shore. Since the removal of the old baths to make way for the quays at the Prince's Dock, the bath accommodation is somewhat dimished, but a complete suite of new baths is now erecting on the west side of George's dock, which will, when completed, be an ornament to the town, and contribute to the health and comfort both of the inhabitants and those that repair hither for the benefit of sea-bathing.[7]

A little to the north was the beach at Kirkdale. Ellen Weeton lodged at Mile End House with a room which looked straight out onto the beach. She bathed at what she described as 'a very retired situation, pleasant and clean', offering good bathing where 'you might undress in the house and walk into the water'. She disliked the baths at Liverpool as being too noisy and crowded for her taste.

Liverpool's golden beaches had a few decades dedicated to the happy pursuit of pleasure, but the merchants on the council would only tolerate such idle pastimes provided that they did not interfere with commerce. The development of the docks pushed inexorably northwards so that by the middle of the nineteenth century the glorious mile of bathing machines was a thing of the past and even the isolated beach at Kirkdale was being developed as the Wellington, Huskisson and Sandon Docks.

As early as 1808 Ellen Weeton was expressing a preference for bathing at Southport, which was becoming frequented by 'many people of some consequence and fashion', and by 1825 Southport had become so popular that she was thrown into great trepidation by the mixed bathing which involved gentlemen's and ladies' machines standing promiscuously side by side in the water.

The later development at Liverpool makes it hard to believe that the seabathing interlude really happened. As a seaside resort Liverpool never approached the Victorian elegance of Southport or the total dedication to the seaside holiday which later characterised Blackpool. Sea bathing and spa waters were always secondary to trade and commerce. Even so, it was not until the 1820s that Southport took pride of place as Lancashire's leading seaside resort and not until the later decades of the century, when the working classes could at last afford to travel to the seaside, that Blackpool increased in popularity.

The bathing is referred to in a music hall song of the 1830s which mentions among other things the loss of the Old Dock, the closing of the

Rooker's painting shows the Liverpool waterfront in the 1790s, with the Goree Piazzas in the centre of the picture and the spire of St George's behind. On the right can be seen the spire of St. Thomas's, with the kilns of the Herculaneum Pottery near the waterfront. The dome on the left is St. Paul's.

old ropewalk and the introduction of newfangled ideas like policemen, gaslighting and even railway stations.

Liverpool's An Altered Town[8]

Once on a time this good old town was nothing but a village
Of fishermen and smugglers, that ne'er attempted tillage;
But things have altered very much, such buildings and Naccapolis,
It rivals far and soon will leave behind the Metropolis.
(Chorus) — Oh dear oh, for Liverpool's an altered town, oh dear oh.

Once on a time, were you inclined your weary limbs to lave sir,
In summer's scorching heat, in Mersey's cooling wave sir,
You'd only just to go behind the old Church for the shore sir,
But now its past Jack Langan's half a mile or more sir.
(Chorus)

When things do change you scarce do know what next is sure to follow,
For mark the change in Derby Road that late was Plumpton's fellow;
Now Atkins found it out so smug and changed its etymology,
He clapped it in his wild beast show, now its 'Gardens of Zoology'.
(Chorus)

A market was on Shaw's Brow, and it remains there still sir,
The Infirmary they have taken away and clapped on Brownlow Hill sir,
There's Gloucester Street and Nelson Street have had an alteration,
They've pulled the most part of them down and built a railway station.
(Chorus)

There's St Luke's in Bold Street, St George's in the Crescent,
St Peter's in Church Street, I'll name no more at present.
They tell the time to every one their hour that they may hop right
By day they go by clockwork but at night they go by gas light.
(Chorus)

The spire of famed St Thomas's, that long had stood the weather,
Although it was so very high they've downed it altogether,
And the Old Dock, the poor Old Dock, the theme of many a sonnet,
They've pulled it up and now have built a Custom House upon it.
(Chorus)

In former times our good old town was guarded from the prigs sir,
By day by constables, by night by watchmen with Welsh wigs sir,
But things are altered very much, for all those who are scholars
Can tell the new policemen by the numbers on their collars.
(Chorus)

In former times if you had taken a walk through Queen's Square sir,
You might have seen, if you had looked, a slashing ropewalk their sir,
Yet all those things the public thought were getting very stale sir,
On the ropewalk they've built a market and on the square a whale sir.
(Chorus)

Not long ago our sailor swells, they were so mighty grown sir,
They could not spent their evening elsewhere than the saloon sir,
But things are altered very much, the saloon is gone fair sir,
At every step the ladies go, policemen cry 'move on there'.
(Chorus)

The 'Naccapolis' (first verse) refers to the new cemetery called the Necropolis or the city of the dead. In 1832 Thomas Atkins took a lease on nine acres of land from James Plumpton, where he opened the Liverpool Zoological Gardens (verse 3). When the initial attraction of the animals died away, he gave firework displays, performances and exhibitions. 'By degrees it fell lower and lower in the [social] scale, until the gardens became notorious for the low, dissolute company which resorted thither'.[9] The market (verse 8) was St. John's Market, the railway tunnel from Edge Hill to Lime Street was excavated in the early 'thirties and references to the Old Dock etc. will be found elsewhere.

In the late-eighteenth and early-nineteenth century Liverpool was often styled 'the Venice of the North'. It was not a facetious title. Both places were great trading centres. The Liverpool dock system, with its footbridges and drawbridges, was open for visitors to wander round and explore at their leisure. They could watch the cargoes of the world being unloaded on the dockside and they could see the shipwrights at work on the wooden vessels in the graving docks. The dock system was a wonder that was

*Sailing vessel and Customs
House.*
   *A clipper-ship in Canning
Dock, with the Customs House
in the background.*

considered the equal of the canals of Venice and which, with its great
forest of masts and spars, embodied far more exciting activity. The
magnificent Goree Piazzas at George's Dock were designed as a covered
arched walkway like those bordering on an Italian square, and in the
nineteenth century they were as famous on the Liverpool waterfront as the
Liver Building is in the twentieth century. There were baths to seaward of
George's Dock, sea bathing on the North Shore and a chalybeate spring
on the outskirts of the town. Parades such as the one on George's Dock
and Prince's Parade on Prince's Dock were built on the waterside,
precursors of the promenades of the seaside towns.

It is fitting to end the chapter with a well-known quote from Lord
Erskine, who described his astonishment at the vista of Georgian
Liverpool spread out before him as he viewed the town from one of the
surrounding hills:

> If I were capable of painting in words the impression Liverpool made on my
> imagination, it would form a beautiful picture indeed! I had before and often
> been at the principal sea-ports of this island, and believing that having seen
> Bristol, and those other towns that justly pass for great ones, I had seen every
> thing in this great nation of navigators on which a subject should pride
> himself; I own I was astonished and astounded, when, after passing a distant
> ferry and ascending a hill, I was told by my guide – 'All you see spread out
> beneath you – that immense place, which stands like another Venice, upon the
> waters – which is intersected by those numerous docks – which glitters with
> those chearful habitations of well-protected men – which is the busy seat of
> trade and the gay scene of elegant amusements, growing out of its prosperity –
> where there is the most chearful face of industry – where there are riches
> overflowing, and every thing that can delight a man who wishes to see the
> prosperity of a great community, and a great empire – all this had been created
> by the industry, and well-disciplined management of a handful of men since
> you were a boy' – I must have been a stick or a stone not to have been affected
> by such a picture.[10]

Chapter Eight

Signs of change

 N 1810 the old parish church of St Nicholas was the scene of one of the most terrible and tragic accidents in the whole history of Liverpool. A spire had been added to the tower in the middle of the previous century and it was known that the tower was unsafe and needed repairs. The foundations at the north-west corner of the tower were being strengthened but the structure was judged safe enough to stand the ring of the bells to call the faithful to service.

One winter morning, on the 11th of February, a procession of children from the Moorfields Charity School was entering the aisle for the morning service. The time was 10.23 and the bell ringers had just entered on their second peal when, without any warning, and unseen by those inside the church, the whole tower fell into the centre aisle. The horror of the scene which followed is beyond description. The girls at the head of the procession had just entered the church and

St Nicholas' Church 1812, Thomas Rickman.

The view is dated two years after the spire fell into the nave, killing the children of the Moorfield's Charity School. The artist shows faithfully the remains of the tower after the tragedy.

twenty-three were killed outright; another died in hospital and three adults inside the church were also killed. At the parish church of St Nicholas the tragic circumstances and the memory of the children of Moorfields School who died on that Sunday morning is something which has never been forgotten.

An earlier tragedy, which fortunately involved the loss of only one life, involved Liverpool's third town hall, designed by the Bath architect John Wood. On the morning of January 18th 1795 the west side of the town hall caught fire. It might have been possible to save the building had it not been for a severe frost which had frozen the water pipes. The fire caught hold of the interior of the building and very quickly destroyed much of it.

Burning of Liverpool Exchange. (British School 18th-C.)

Sunday January 18th 1795. The night was so cold that the water pipes were frozen; the firefighters could not contain the flames and the interior of the building was gutted by the fire. The Town Hall has a remarkable history. It was attacked by cannon in 1775; in 1881 there was an abortive attempt to blow it up by a group called the Fenians, and it suffered damage from an air raid in 1941.

It was fortunate that a great part of Wood's original fabric did survive the fire and the architect James Wyatt was given the job of rebuilding. Wyatt produced a design which was both impressive and at the same time respectful to the earlier work of John Wood. He added a two-storey Corinthian portico and rebuilt the gutted roof by adding a large dome supported by a large cylindrical tower. A statue of Minerva in a seated posture with helmet and spear looked down from the top of the dome. The interior was not fully completed until 1820, but when it was finished the whole inside was an exceptionally fine example of late-Georgian decor, with two ballrooms and a lavish banqueting hall. It gave Liverpool one of the most impressive suites of civic rooms in the country. The building also housed the new exchange. It was traditional in Liverpool for town hall and exchange to share the same building, and Liverpolitans were fond of pointing out that the new exchange had more than twice the floor area of the Royal Exchange in London.

There were few places in Liverpool where the entertainment and decor matched that of the town hall, but one exception was at Knowsley, where in 1822 the diarist Thomas Creevey described the new dining room which did not meet with his approval:

> . . . We all dined at Knowsley last night. The new dining-room is opened: it is 53 feet by 37, and such a height that it destroys the effect of all the other apartments. You enter it from a passage by two great Gothic church-like doors the whole height of the room. This entrance is in itself fatal to the effect. L[ad]y. Derby (like herself), when I objected to the immensity of the doors, said: 'You've heard Genl. Grosvenor's remark upon them, have you not? He asked in his grave, pompous manner – "Pray are those great doors to be opened for every pat of butter that comes into the room?" ' At the opposite end of the room is an immense gothic window, and the rest of the light is given by a skylight mountains high. There are two fireplaces; and the day we dined there, there were 26 wax candles over the table, 14 on it, and ten great lamps on tall pedestals about the room; and yet those at the bottom of the table said it was quite petrifying in that neighbourhood, and the report here is that they have been obliged to abandon it entirely from the cold . . . My lord and lady were all kindness to me, but only think of their neither knowing nor caring about Spain or France, nor whether war or peace between these two nations was at all in agitation! [1]

Thomas Creevey claimed to be the son of a sea captain and a local girl called Phoebe Prescott. When Thomas was only one year old his father died, but his widowed mother was still able to afford a public school education for her son, who went on to become a leading politician and an active member of the highest circles of Regency society. One theory put forward to explain his expensive education was that Thomas Creevey was in fact an illegitimate son of the first Earl of Sefton; the marriage of Pheobe Prescott to William Creevey was one of convenience and Lord Sefton paid for the education and upbringing of his illegitimate son. The scandal is supported by the fact that Thomas Creevey was certainly a great friend of the Earls of Sefton and on his visits from London to Liverpool he regularly resided at Croxteth with the Molyneux family.

Creevey's diaries give an interesting account of parliamentary matters in Regency times and some amusing glimpses into London society, which is where their main value lies. As a Whig member of parliament for Liverpool and a regular visitor, his writings sometimes throw light on Liverpool society but usually at the higher social levels, beyond the reach of ordinary mortals.

A contemporary journal keeper who was more in touch with the common people was Ellen Weeton, a bright and active young woman just over thirty years of age. For twelve years she had been a schoolteacher in the village of Upholland, near Wigan. It was not until ten years after her mother's death that she inherited a private income which was just sufficient to maintain her independence and to make her the free agent which she always wanted to be. She decided to move from Upholland to Liverpool and lodged originally with the Chorley family in Dale Street before moving out to Kirkdale when she had found a more suitable place to stay. Ellen was prudish and prim, but she had a keen sense of humour and frequently let her hair down. She was a lively letter writer and journal keeper, and she had a mind which was sharp and critical. Her writings are full of detailed observations which make them always full of human interest. The excitement of the urban life after the quiet of the countryside did not always meet up to her expectations:

> When I came to Liverpool I expected to have found it filled with intelligent beings, imagining knowledge to be so generally diffused. I begin to discover that it contains as much proportionate ignorance as any little village in England, where perhaps the curate is the only intelligent man in it. How astonished am I daily to find so many more ignorant than myself, so few more knowing . . . Here, not one in ten can speak their native language tolerably; not more than one in twenty correctly; and of these last, scarce one tenth can boast any greater literary acquirement than that of their grammar. I thought myself very ignorant when I came here, expecting to find so many wise, so many learned – I find them not . . . The people here do not seize the opportunities of improvement that so frequently occur – Their ignorance is astonishing! It would almost appear as if ignorance was taught, as if it were something to boast of . . .[2]

Ellen, or Miss Weeton as she might perhaps prefer to be called until we know her better, lodged with Edward and Betty Smith 'Near Mile-end house, call'd Beacon's Gutter, A fine romantic name to utter' – she quipped in one of her letters to her correspondent, Miss Chorley. The gutter was a drainage ditch on the outskirts of town which served as the boundary of the ancient borough of Liverpool. Ellen might well have witnessed the ceremonial beating of the bounds which was still kept up by the mayor and corporation at that time.

Her lodgings were very close to the beach at Kirkdale but still only two miles from the town hall. Here she could watch the shipping from her window, walk along the fine open beach which was deserted for most of the year, and take the waters in the summer months when visitors came to bathe.

In her first fortnight at Kirkdale she witnessed a shipwreck just opposite the house where she lived. She described the heavy breaking sea as it washed over the deck and the attempts by the rescuers to save the ship's crew:

> On Friday, several vessels were wrecked: one of them in our view. Mrs H. and I went into a bathing machine just opposite the vessel in distress, and whilst we stood sheltered from the violence of the wind, we saw it beat against the rocks repeatedly. A crowd began to collect upon the shore within a few hundred yards of the ship. A reward was offered to any six or eight who would venture out in a boat to fetch the crew – for then the vessel lay quite down on one side, the waves dashing over the offside like drifting snow, and on the nearer side, washing over the decks and carrying away anything moveable. The men for a long time were busied in hacking at the masts, which at length fell overboard with a loud crash. A boat at length set off, but could not reach the ship. A second time the force of the waves drove them back in spite of all their exertions. A man then boldly waded into the water till he was within hearing of the poor crew, and said something to them by means of a speaking trumpet. The boat then set off the third time, and fortunately reached the ship and took out the men, all except the mate and two black sailors, who bravely, or fool-hardily, staid in the vessel by themselves from ten in the morning than four in the afternoon. In a few minutes the crew were safely landed, and gave a shout which was heard as far as our cottage. The vessel was too high upon the rocks to sink, so that every day since, she has been unloading, and yesterday was sold by auction on the shore for the benefit of the Insurers; and to-day two fields adjoining this house are almost covered with Irish linen, which was part of her cargo, and which they have been washing in the gutter that runs close by, to get out the salt water. She was just setting

sail for the Brasils.

In spite of her sharp criticisms, Ellen enjoyed Liverpool. She occasionally attended service at Christ Church, where she made some amusing comments on the vicar and the congregation. 'Mr Chorley is quite a buck, and dashes away in his silk stockings, his Dickey, and his quizzing glass', she noted. 'Mr. Martland, nick-named the Beauty of Holiness, is grown so attentive to his book, that he has quite forgot to admire the young ladies during Divine Service – alias the Beauties of Christ Church. And the Organ in that Church intends to cease roaring, as it is in danger of frightening away those who go to doze there.'

When her cousin, Henry Lathom, came to visit her they walked into town to see Sarah Siddons play Lady Macbeth at the Theatre Royal. The production came up to Ellen's exacting expectations. She enjoyed it thoroughly, but she and her escort were a great embarassment, tittering and chuckling in all the wrong places when the rest of the audience was sitting spellbound. She gave an account of the play in a letter to her brother:

> I wish you could have been here this week to have seen Mrs Siddons. It will be too late now, for she finishes her career in Liverpool for this summer on Friday next. Henry Lathom has been with me a fortnight, and on one day that week he and I went to see her as Lady MacBeth. We got a very comfortable front seat in the gallery, and I was highly gratified. I have seen her before at Lancaster as Belvidera, but had almost forgot her, it is so long ago. Much as I expected, my expectations were exceeded; particularly in that scene where Lady Macbeth is represented as walking in her sleep. The whole audience seemed wonder struck. I assure you I was. [In the next sentence she changes rapidly from praise to derision]

Everton Village. (British School, 19th-C.)

The village of Everton retained its rural aspect until the 1830s. It enjoyed a few decades as a prosperous suburb before the great influx of Irish immigrants into Liverpool changed the social aspect of the area. In 1879 the St Domingo Football Club changed their name to Everton, a move which was to make Everton into the best-known suburb of Liverpool.

The witches, the thunder and lightning, the ghosts – had not even the semblance of anything terrible. Henry laughed at them as well as me. The witches seemed such a merry set; the ghosts so substantial – the theatre and the stage too light to give a sufficiently awful effect to the lightning or the thunder (and that was not loud enough), that they must be weak indeed who are for one moment affected by them.

Ellen's abode at Kirkdale was in a very respectable area, but the most prestigious suburb to the north of the town was nearby Everton. The wealthy had abandoned the confines of the docks and the inner

Walton-on-the-Hill. (by John Pennington).
　An early-nineteenth century view of Walton, which retained its rural aspect until the end of the nineteenth century.
Liverpool was in Walton parish until 1698, and the suburb therefore has a very special significance in the ecclesiastical history of the town.

Old Plough Inn, Walton. (British School, 19th-C.)
　Haycarts and thatch add to the rural tranquility of Walton-on-the-Hill.

city and had built their large detached villas on the outskirts of the town. Everton, Kirkdale and Bootle to the north competed with Toxteth Park, Wavertree and Allerton to the south. 'I have seen wild roses growing upon the very ground that is now the centre of Bootle', wrote Gladstone in later life, 'All that land is now partly covered with residences and partly with places of business and industry; but in my time but one single house stood upon the space between Primrose Brook and the town of Liverpool.'

All the villages had their attractions. In 1800 Everton was described as 'a pretty village with a view which embraces town, village, plain, pasture, river and ocean. At sunset the windows of Everton Brow flash back the glowing radiance, showing that nothing impedes the wide prospect westwards.' Twenty years later the view from Great Mersey Street was one of handsome terraces with long gardens sloping down towards Kirkdale and Herdman's picture shows the village centre as it was in 1828 with a stone cross at the centre and surrounded by old stone houses with traditional mullioned windows. 'Everton now abounds with handsomely walled pleasure grounds and well-enclosed fields, and is conveniently intersected with admirable roads, most of them well paved, and many of the parapets are flagged for two thirds of their breadth with admirable, well-laid strong flags', reads a description written in 1830.[3]

During the Napoleonic wars, a semaphore signal station was established on the site of the beacon on Everton Hill. There was a proposal to build an army barracks at St Domingo, something which the Everton middle classes objected to as lowering the tone of their village. Opinion was divided, however; apparently the ladies of Everton liked the idea of having a few soldiers around as competition to their boring, beer-drinking husbands and some thought a barracks would actually add a bit of spice to the social life of the area. Sylvestor Richmond, a customs officer and a local wit, wrote a piece of doggerel which purported to state the case of the ladies. As an example of early nineteenth-century wit, it is a fair sample.

The Ladies of Everton Hill to William Ewart Esq.[4]

Come forth all ye females of Everton Hill
Ne'er shall woman be wronged and her clappers lie still,
Let us tell, one and all, these proud lords of creation
That we cannot submit to unjust domination.
And unless they will straightway express their contrition
Maids, widows, and wives, all will counter petition.
A barrack, my girls, which these men think so frightful,
Is just what we want – Oh a barrack's delightful!
We shall never stir out, be it good or bad weather,
But quite certain to meet a cockade or a feather:
And these terrible men, to our husband's alarming,
So far from a bugbear, to us are quite charming,
I'd give all I'm worth in the world, girls, by jingo,
For a summer night's ramble about St Domingo.
All the bands will be playing, the captain saluting,
Oh such drumming and fifing, such fiddling and fluting,
And instead of a fusty old brown coated varlet,
We shall have, at command, a smart fellow in scarlet.
What a difference ye gods! from an ale drinking clown;
Who quart after quart every night guzzles down;

A view of the conical kilns of the Herculaneum pottery works in the early-nineteenth century. Two distinctive windmills provided mechanical power for the works. The pottery works was established in 1796. It became the property of Josiah Wedgwood, and the works were moved to the Potteries in about 1833. The picture is a share certificate.

But the Captain's all life, full of fire and politeness,
With a beautiful hand of exquisite whiteness.
Mr Silvester Richmond

The elderly still remembered the time when the pack horse was the principal means of carrying goods from the inland towns to the docks, and when there was a toll between Liverpool and West Derby – a ha'penny for sheep and cattle, one penny for horses, sixpence for waggons with coals and a shilling for a coach. The pikemen at the toll gates wore tall black glazed hats, stockings and knee breeches, and short aprons with large pockets to collect the money. They were lowly paid but they had the toll house to live in, provided free of rent.

Herculaneum Pottery, 1808 (sketch by Edmundson).

A view only two years earlier than the share certificate and from almost the same angle. This is where Liverpool porcelain was made; a piece of Herculaneum pottery in good condition is now a valuable collectors' item.

Soon after the first stagecoaches were running between Liverpool and London the Sankey Canal was surveyed by John Eyes, the man who produced the town plan of 1765. It was built under the supervision of Henry Berry, the second of Liverpool's dock engineers. At much the same time, Leigh's cut was excavated to make the river Douglas navigable so that coal from the Wigan coalfield could be brought to Liverpool by canal and sea.

When the Duke of Bridgwater built his canal at Worsley he did not envisage that it would carry goods as far as Liverpool, but his scheme proved to be such a great success that the Bridgwater Canal was extended to reach the Mersey at Runcorn in 1773. Thus these three early canals, although none of them actually came into Liverpool as such, all served the needs of the town in different ways. When the success of the pioneer cuts became evident, a mania for canal building followed. Longer and more ambitious canals were projected with a national network serving all the industrialised areas.

In the Potteries the great entrepreneur Josiah Wedgwood was a promoter of a scheme to link the River Trent with the River Mersey. Wedgwood's wares were very delicate and he knew that transport by water would save his company a fortune in breakages. In 1777 his scheme became a reality and the fragile pottery of the famous

Brickfield, Liverpool. (British School 19th-C).
Many eighteenth- and nineteenth-century houses in Liverpool were built from locally made bricks. The medieval town field itself provided the bricks to build the houses which finally over-whelmed it as an outpost of agriculture.

When the Leeds and Liverpool Canal was first mooted, the Liverpool merchants were determined to gain a ready supply of coal from the Wigan area and, when they were over-ruled by the Yorkshire interests in the canal company, they initially withdrew all support for the canal and, largely because of this, no direct connection to the docks was built until a flight of locks was constructed down into Stanley Dock in the 1850s. This picture shows a detail from a remarkable aerial view drawn from the imagination (and perhaps based on the first Ordnance Survey) by Ackerman in 1847. It shows the original terminus of the Leeds and Liverpool Canal near Leeds Street.

Wedgwood factory could be transported to Liverpool for export with the perfect smoothness offered by the new canal.

At Leeds an even more ambitious scheme was mooted which involved building a canal across the Pennines to link Leeds with Liverpool and to give the Yorkshire manfacturing towns a cheaper means of getting their wares to the west coast for export. The Leeds and Liverpool Canal, unlike its predecessors, actually came right into the town and terminated at the docks. The first sod was cut at Halsall on the 5th of November 1770 and the canal carried its first boat in February 1774. The completion of the Leeds and Liverpool, however, took many years and it was well into the nineteenth century before the whole canal was finally opened and goods could be carried across the Pennines between Lancashire and Yorkshire. The original terminus was at Old Hall Street, very close to the town centre, where the canal had sidings very like a railway terminus, and as the dock system developed branches were built such as the branch to Collingwood Dock which opened in 1846.

The Leeds and Liverpool Canal became a well-established waterway through the northern suburbs. The canal was designed for commerce but it also carried a considerable passenger traffic. Travel was very slow, with the horses lumbering along at a pedestrian pace and by the time the canal had meandered around the contours and climbed through a few lock gates it was quicker to walk, but the ride was cheap and smooth and it was very convenient for people with heavy baggage to be carried. Ellen Weeton described some of her experiences on the packet boat:

> . . . most people who go in the tail end of the packet seem to think that
> eating and drinking is the most delightful amusement of travelling. The
> generality of those who sail in the upper end seem to have very different
> ideas. They appear as if ashamed of such a piece of vulgarity as the
> indulging of a propensity to eat . . . Some very odd faces are to be seen at
> times. Two old ladies got in a few miles from Liverpool. The very moment
> they could squat themselves on a cushion, they began to knit. One had a
> good hardy look, as if she had been stewed to make her keep. She looked
> more like a coddled gooseberry than anything else . . . A very nice old
> lady got in much about the same time, accompanied by almost as nice a
> young one; both of respectable appearance. The old one had rather an ill
> tempered look, but fortunately she was very deaf, so she could not often be
> put out of her way by what she heard. A clergyman sailed with us five or
> six miles; he had that wolf-like keenness in his eyes, as if he knew which
> was the best method of taking the tithe.

Ellen's private income was about sixty pounds a year after paying
the unpopular new income tax which had been introduced to finance
the Napoleonic wars. Some idea of the value of this money may be
judged by the fact that her lodgings cost only seven guineas per
annum. After about a year she tired of being a lady of leisure and
began to look for a paid post where she could use her education and
experience. In December 1809 she obtained a position as 'Governess to
superintend the Education of a Young Lady'. Her task was to educate
the new wife of a Preston banker called Edward Pedder. In a rush of
blood he had married a seventeen-year-old dairy maid and he wanted
his new wife to hold her own with the ladies' circle in Preston. Some
idea of Ellen's perspicacity may be judged from the fact that she
successfully obtained a salary of thirty pounds a year for her new job at
a time when the salary of a schoolteacher rarely exceeded twenty-four.

The Leeds and Liverpool Canal was a major contributory factor to
the final disappearance of the Liverpool Town Field. In the early
nineteenth century the canal cut a large gash right through the centre
of the field. The medieval strips had become allotments and the
cornfields had given way to pigsties and hen coops with an occasional
market garden, but the field still retained some of its rural appearance.
Some of the allotments had been used to dig clay to make bricks, so
that the field was littered with unsightly pits where clay had been
extracted and the occasional derelict brick kiln added to the general
lack of beauty. Houses soon began to appear on the southern part of
the Oldfield in the east and on what was known as the Sea Shot in the
west. Part of the field to the east of Scotland Road was still agricultural
in the 1830s but by that time most of the old town field was labelled as
'brick fields' on the town plans; ironically the field was used to supply
the bricks for the very houses which eventually overwhelmed it, and
agriculture left the boundaries of the old royal borough for ever.

The conquest of the air was, in a rather haphazard fashion, achieved
in the eighteenth century. In 1785 Vincenzo Lunardi, the famous
Italian balloonist, announced his intention of making a demon-
stration flight from the North Fort at Liverpool. On the day appointed
a great crowd assembled to witness the event, but the weather was wet
and the winds were variable – the flight looked like being a non-starter.
Lunardi was a great showman, however, and when the weather cleared
in the afternoon he determined to press on with the flight and started

to inflate the balloon, announcing that he would make his ascent at five in the afternoon.

The crowd waited patiently, five o'clock came and went, but there was no sign of the balloon. It took Lunardi until six o'clock to fill his balloon to a respectable size and a gun was fired to warn the impatient and long-suffering crowd that something was going to happen. The balloon was still some way off maximum inflation and he therefore threw two boxes of ballast out of the basket, followed by his pistols, his speaking trumpet and his life-saving cork jacket. Was there sufficient lift to get him airborne? The balloon hovered first one way and then the other. The suspense was excrutiating. Then, very slowly, it began to rise.

'For a moment an awful silence took place', said the *Liverpool General Advertiser*, 'but this immediately gave way to loud and reiterated bursts of applause'. All was quiet and still again with a hushed awe at the ascent and Vincenzo Lunardi saluted the spectators gracefully, waving his hat from high above them in the basket. There was more drama and suspense as the wind took the aeronaut, without his cork jacket, in the wrong direction and out over the sea. Lunardi was equal to the occasion. He saluted the crowd again and threw out his hat, coat and waistcoat which fluttered down to the ground – he apparently stopped short of throwing out his trousers. The wind shifted. An hour and twenty minutes later, suffering from cold and exposure without the bulk of his clothing, he landed in a wheatfield at Simonswood.

In July 1835 a Frenchman, Alexis de Tocqueville, came to visit Liverpool on his way to Ireland. He wrote down his first impressions:

> Liverpool. Town destined to become the centre of English trade. A fisherman's harbour three centuries ago. A small town sixty years ago. The slave trade, basis of its commercial greatness. It carried slaves to the Spanish colonies at better prices than all the others. The foundation of the United States, the manufacturing development of Manchester and Birmingham, and the spread of English trade over the whole world, have done the rest.
>
> Liverpool is a beautiful town. Poverty is almost as great as it is at Manchester, but it is hidden. Fifty thousand poor people live in cellars. Sixty thousand Irish Catholics.[5]

De Tocqueville went to see the French Consul, M. Laine. The conversation which followed was between two Frenchmen discussing the trade of Liverpool, what was going to happen to the town, and how things in general compared to the situation in France.

> Q. Is there much trade between France and Liverpool?
> A. Very little to speak of. In trade one needs, above all else, exchanges. Now our tariff is so fixed that we can buy nothing from England; so they look for nothing from France.
> Q. And our wines?
> A. The English reduced their duties on our wines: the result was one very difficult to foresee: the consumption of wine went down rather than up. I think the reason was that the lowering of the tariff allowed horrible French wines to be introduced. The taste for French wine has always been a fashion. Naturally, the English prefer the warm wines of the South and strong spirits. The lowering of the price and the introduction of bad French wine has almost killed that fashion . . .

The conversation turned to brandy, trade in general, and ship-

building.

Q. Liverpool is growing the whole time?

A. Incredibly fast. Everything goes at a run. The railway will further speed up the rate at which London can be bypassed as a seaport. Already London deals almost only with European trade, and soon the trade of Northern Europe will pass through Liverpool, Hull and Derby. Probably in ten years Liverpool's commercial power will be greater than that of London.

Q. Is the consumption of cotton going up?

A. Immensely. It is only limited now by the production of the raw material. Almost all the cotton grown in the world comes to Europe: 200,000 bales a year go to France; 700,000 – 800,000 to England. A bad year in America would make Europe go entirely short, and suddenly send prices up. You have seen for yourself that all the South of the United States is covered with cotton-fields: it cannot be planted in America as quickly as it is consumed in Europe. Little iron ships have just been made which can go up the smallest American streams, and go to fetch the cotton everywhere it grows . . . [From 1820-50 Liverpool handled at least 80% of the UK's raw cotton imports.]

Q. Are railways still proving profitable undertakings?

A. Yes. They go on paying 9 per cent, and you can see that they are prospering by the great works the Company is undertaking. For instance the passenger tunnel which is going to go under almost the whole town and arrive near the port, having gone a mile-and-a-half underground.

What were these railways which the French found so interesting? In 1835, when this conversation took place, the railway was a very novel form of transport which had existed for several years in Liverpool. It all started in the previous decade, and the story of how it began deserves a chapter of its own.

A delightful drawing of Chisenhale Street bridge on the Leeds and Liverpool Canal in 1802. The River Mersey can just be seen to the right of the bridge. When the first length of canal was opened as far as Parbold in 1774, it ran through the original Liverpool townfield and open countryside to the terminus at Liverpool. The whole area quickly became built up, of course, and it is interesting to compare this picture to the one on page 179, which shows a later Chisenhale Street bridge on the same site. (L.R.O. DP 175).

Above: *Laying of Foundation Stone, Birkenhead Docks. (by Edward Duncan).*

The bill for the Birkenhead Docks was passed by the House of Commons on 14th March 1844 and construction began soon afterwards. We can see from the painting that the laying of the foundation stone was a great event, attended by a large gathering of all classes of society. In 1855 the docks became part of the Mersey Docks and Harbour Board.

Right: *A detail from the fascinating aerial view of the mid-1840s by Ackerman. There are at least two separate versions of this view (see also pages 140-1). In this version, the docks are portrayed much more realistically. Note that in this view the centre of the Albert Dock has not yet been completed and filled with water. Although the perspective, especially of the ships in the estuary, leaves a lot to be desired, the general impression is accurate and, read in conjunction with Ordnance Survey maps of the same date, gives a wealth of invaluable information. Note the Customs House, the churches, the Goree Piazzas, and the baths in the foreground.*

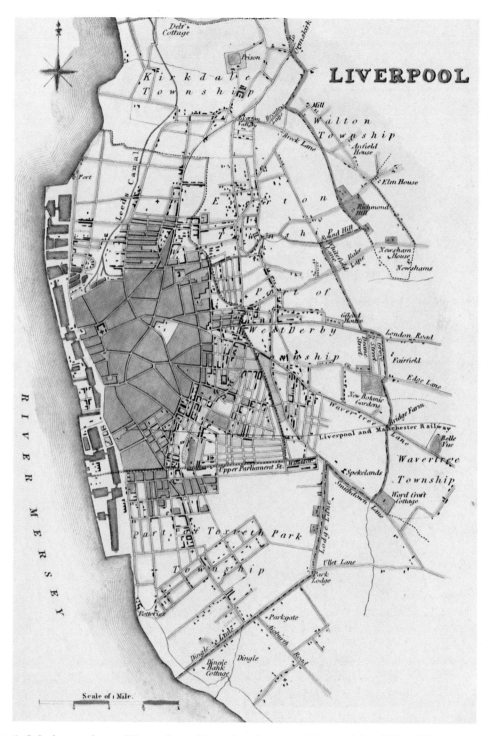

Plate 1: *Only the central part of Liverpool can claim to have been part of the town before 1835, and this map shows the street plan at that time. The high-class developments in the area around Rodney Street can easily be identified. Kirkdale, Everton, part of West Derby and Toxteth Park all came within the boundary when it was extended in 1835 – these were the abodes of the wealthy and were all still very rural at this time.*

Plate 2: *A watercolour by Herdman showing St Nicholas' Church, Tower Buildings and a footbridge across part of the dock system, drawn from George's Dock in 1868. A scene of maritime activity before the docks were closed off from public access.*

Plate 3: *New Baths, George's Parade 1829. by Messrs Pyne (engraved by Robert Wallis).*
The baths at the Pier Head were a feature of Liverpool for many years, and Eyes plan of 1766 shows the location of the earlier baths on the sea front. Both baths and docks were a great attraction in Georgian and Regency Liverpool. In fact, George's Dock and several other docks had parades to seaward, designed for promenaders. In this picture the shipping in George's Dock can be seen behind the baths, with the spire of St Nicholas' rising above.

Plate 4: *Entrance of the Liverpool and Manchester Railway at Edge Hill, looking from the Moorish Arch. A lively scene drawn by Bury and Ackermann in 1831, shortly after the opening of the new railway. The train on the right is just emerging from the tunnel which led from Crown Street Station, the original passenger terminus, while the considerably longer tunnel in the centre led down to the docks at Wapping.*

Plate 5 *(Below): The Moorish Arch which crossed the railway. It was not simply for decoration, however, since the twin castellated towers contained the winding engines which pulled the trains up through the tunnel from Wapping. Near here was where the trains, either from Wapping or Crown Street Station, were coupled to a locomotive for the journey out towards Manchester. Not shown on this picture are the twin chimneys (in the form of classical columns) which rose high above the towers to carry away the smoke from the steam engines.*

Plates 6 & 7 *(Overleaf): Bury and Ackermann's superb drawings of the trains which could be observed on the Liverpool and Manchester Railway. From top to bottom we see the engine* Jupiter *pulling a train of top-hatted and crinolened first-class passengers (note the coach, complete with footman, on the last carriage); the* North Star *drawing 'a train of the second class, for outside passengers'; the* Liverpool *passing a water point with a train of 'waggons with goods &c.'; and, finally, the* Fury *pulling a train with terrified cattle and pigs.*

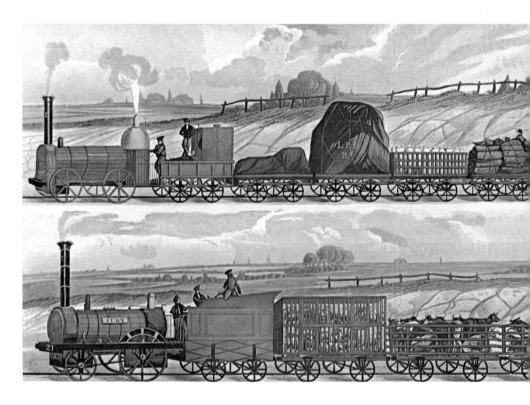

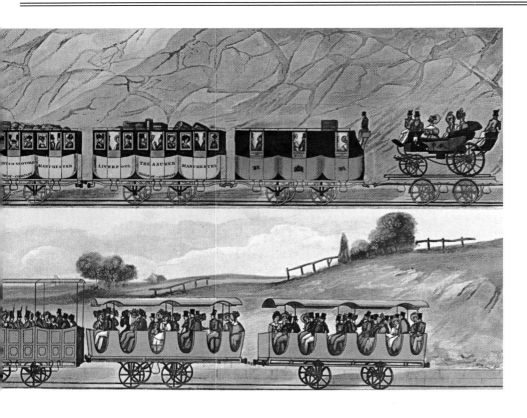

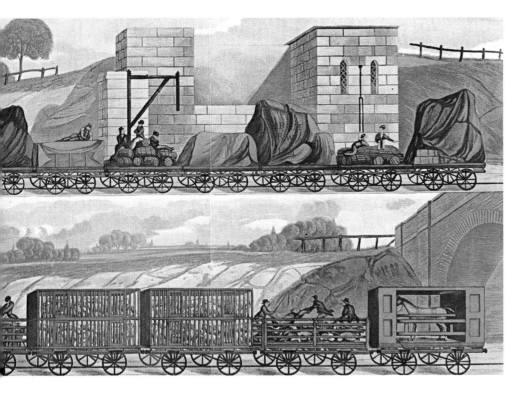

Plate 8: *(Opposite, top) 18th-and 19th-century Liverpool attracted many artists to capture on canvas the highly attractive views to be had of shipping in the Mersey. This picture, by Samuel Walters, shows the* Frankfield *and at least nine other sailing vessels, with Liverpool in the background.*

Plate 9: *(Opposite, bottom) Also by Walters, this painting shows a sailing vessel being towed out of the estuary.*

Plate 10: *(Left) A stormy day in the Mersey is captured by F. Calvert (1827-44).*

Plate 11: *(Below) Some of the most visually striking and beautiful paintings are by Robert Salomon (1775-post 1842). This one, 'American Ships in the Mersey off Liverpool' is particularly fine.*

Plate 12: *Samuel Walters has captured the scene off St George's Pier beautifully. Entitled 'Returning to Ireland', it shows crowds of people waving goodbye as vessels carry passengers out to the waiting ships.*

Plate 13: *A modern view from the very top of the Liver Building looking south along the Mersey, with the Albert Dock prominent in the foreground.*

Chapter Nine

Riding on the railway

HERE was a saying, 'Liverpool Gentlemen, Manchester Men'. It was an atrocious piece of snobbery based on the fact that Manchester was a manufacturing centre with mills and smoking chimneys, whereas Liverpool was a healthy place with clean sea air, populated by wealthy merchants who merely took a percentage cut of the manufactured goods as they passed through for export. The saying did not endear some of the Liverpolitans to the Mancunians, but there were other things on which they agreed entirely, and one of them was the problem of the transport of goods between the two places.

Bales of cotton were frequently left on the dockside for weeks on end waiting for transport to Manchester, and the cynics pointed out that the cotton sometimes took less time to get from America to Liverpool than from Liverpool to Manchester. The canal companies were unable or unwilling to solve the problem, and the merchants of both towns therefore began to look around for an alternative solution.

The idea of building a railway was talked about before 1820, but the first people to take any action on the matter seem to have been Joseph Sandars, a Liverpool corn merchant, and William James, who came from West Bromwich. Sandars visited the Killingworth Colliery in Northumberland where he saw steam locomotives in action. He met George Stephenson and saw the Stockton and Darlington Railway under construction.

When the idea of a railway between Liverpool and Manchester was suggested, there was no difficulty in finding money and support. The first Bill came before Parliament in 1825 but was thrown out by one vote at the committee stage. Railways were associated in the public mind with black coaldust and collieries and some of the main opponents of the Bill were two Liverpool gentlemen, the Earl of Derby and the Earl of Sefton, who strongly objected to anything as common as a public railway passing near their country estates. A new Bill for a longer and more difficult route was put forward in 1826. The new route was well south of Knowsley and Croxteth and this time the Bill was carried. George Stephenson was appointed engineer and construction began straight away.

Plenty of railways existed before the Liverpool and Manchester;

some of them carried passengers as well as coal, and some used steam traction to haul the trains. Because of the scale and massive investment of the Liverpool and Manchester Railway, however, it was the first true passenger line. The whole world knew that the project was a milestone in railway history and an event which would change the world if it succeeded in its purpose.

The sheer grandeur of the projected railway, the thirty-one miles of double track, the earthworks and the cuttings, the bridges and embankments, the great tunnels connecting the terminus at Edge Hill with the docks and the classical architecture of the stations and railway buildings, were all executed on a massive scale which had never previously been envisaged.

The artists Bury and Shaw were commissioned to draw views of the new line, some of which are reproduced on pages 118-120. A triumphal 'Moorish Arch' was built at Edge Hill to represent the gateway in and out of Liverpool. A great underground tunnel had to be excavated connecting Edge Hill with the docks at Wapping. When completed, the tunnel was whitewashed and lit by gas. It became one of the sights of the town for visitors and fashionable promenaders and it even had the names of the streets above written up at appropriate points on the tunnel wall.

The Olive Mount cutting, blasted out of the solid rock in order to keep the gradients within reach of the primitive locomotives, was a long chasm up to seventy feet deep and, when first constructed, only twenty feet wide.

During 1828 a considerable controversy erupted among the directors as to how to power their railway. Some favoured horses, and a considerable lobby grew in favour of Benjamin Thompson's patented system of 'reciprocal working', using stationary steam engines. Others, including the Stephensons, argued that locomotives were now sufficiently well advanced in design to meet the challenge. A delegation was duly sent to view all the various systems in use around the country and reported back – in favour of stationary engines for the Liverpool and Manchester. However, George Stephenson and his assistant, Joseph Locke, submitted a contrary report in favour of locomotives. The dilemma grew and in 1829, when the works were well in hand, the directors decided to hold a competition for steam locomotives to see if an engine could be found to meet the exacting requirements of the new railway.

This most unusual competition was a challenge to the leading engineers of the day. There was to be a locomotive trial, with a prize of five hundred pounds for the best engine and the directors issued a set of rules for all entrants. The engine must consume its own smoke, it had to draw twenty tons at ten miles per hour for a distance of seventy miles with a boiler pressure not exceeding fifty pounds to the square inch. It must have safety valves and a steam gauge. It must be mounted on springs. It must not weigh more than six tons fully laden. It had to be ready for trial on the first of October 1829.

A course was laid out at Rainhill, with a stand to accommodate the fashionable society. Flags and bunting fluttered in the breeze and the expectant crowd was entertained by a brass band playing the popular tunes of the day. Crowds of people arrived from miles around, some from very far afield. The gathering at Rainhill had all the atmosphere of the racecourse, but the spectators were to witness a much rarer and historic event to be fought out between mechanical horses. There were five runners:

Rainhill Trials, 6th October 1829

1. *The Novelty*, made by Messrs Braithwaite and Ericsson of London;
2. *The Sans Pariel*, made by Mr Timothy Hackworth of Darlington;
3. *The Rocket*, made by Mr Robert Stephenson of Newcastle-on-Tyne;
4. *The Cycloped*, made by Dr Brandreth of Liverpool;
5. *The Perseverence*, made by Mr Burstall of Edinburgh.

Burstall's machine encountered an unfortunate accident and overturned on its way from Liverpool to Rainhill, and poor Burstall did not arrive until the competition was over. Dr Brandeth's machine, the only entry to be built in Liverpool, was a blatant breach of the rules. It consumed oats rather than coal, and was powered by a horse in a treadmill – but as he was a major shareholder the directors humoured the eccentric doctor and during some of the many delays, as the engineers struggled to get their engines to perform, he was allowed to entertain the crowds with an exhibition of his retrograde step in technology.

Timothy Hackworth's *Sans Pariel* was a solid engine built around a large black boiler. It had vertically mounted cylinders and a tall smokestack. The trimmings were smartly painted in green and yellow but the *Sans Pareil* was overweight and it had no springs. It therefore failed the requirements but the judges generously decided to let it show its paces anyway. Hackworth was struggling with a leaky boiler and begged more time to prepare his machine for the ordeal.

The great favourite was the *Novelty,* a light locomotive gaily painted in bright blue, fitted with a traditional leaf-spring suspension and with

One of the famous Bury and Ackermann lithographs, showing the skew bridge over the Liverpool and Manchester Railway at Rainhill. It was near here that the famous Rainhill Trials were held to find out if a locomotive could operate successfully on the new line and, if so, which one.

Braithwaite and Ericsson's Novelty, *the early and popular favourite with the crowds at Rainhill. Until it suffered damage to the mechanical bellows which fanned the fire, the* Novelty *seemed to be on course for a famous victory, managing speeds of up to thirty miles per hour.*

The Sans Pariel, *built by Timothy Hackworth of Darlington. Weighing in at nearly 4½ tons, this was the heavyweight entry. It had no springs and thus was not eligible to run the trial, but the judges allowed Hackworth to show the* Sans Pareil's *paces anyway. Although the machine struggled on the day, the Company must have been impressed by its performance, for they bought the machine afterwards.*

Only the fact that its designer, Dr Brandreth of Liverpool, was local and a major shareholder of the company, allowed the Cycloped *to compete at all. Perhaps the judges thought that watching this retrograde step in technology show its paces would entertain the crowd. Note the oatbox for the horse.*

Robert Stephenson's Rocket *was well equipped for the long-distance endurance test which the Company had set at Rainhill. With a new-fangled tubular boiler and a steam blast to draw the air across the flames, the* Rocket *was easily able to fulfil the requirements of the test, and carried away the £500 prize.*

Mr Burstall's Perseverance *overturned on the way to the competition and, when it did eventually arrive, 'creaked away like an old Wickerwork pair of panniers on a cantering Cuddy Ass'. It received a £25 consolation prize, however.*

Bury and Ackermann's depiction of the tunnel which connected Edge Hill station with the docks at Wapping. When completed it was whitewashed, lit by gas and became a major tourist attraction – nothing quite like it has ever been seen before.

The impressive Olive Mount Cutting, near Liverpool. When it was first excavated, it was only twenty-feet wide and over sixty-feet deep, though it was later widened considerably. As can be seen, men are still working on it, with picks, shovels, scaffolding, baskets and pulleys. Even today, the cutting is an impressive engineering feat. In all, some 480,000 cubic yards of stone and other material were removed.

a pair of mechanically driven bellows to force air over the fire. To the uninitiated it was not at all obvious which end of the *Novelty* was supposed to be the front and which end was supposed to be the back, but at one end was a highly polished copper boiler and water tank, while at the other end was a homely wicker basket of coals and two vertical cylinders just visible above one set of wheels. The spectators, most of whom hadn't the faintest idea of what a locomotive should look like, thought the *Novelty* the smartest and best-looking vehicle in the competition. It certainly had a great turn of speed and when it showed its paces by racing past them at nearly thirty miles an hour a great cheer went up to gladden the hearts of the top-hatted engineers on the footplate. But, alas, there was a sudden dull explosion and smoke and sparks were emitted from some-where in the bowels of the engine. Messrs Braithwaite and Ericsson discovered that the mechanical bellows which fanned the fire had burst. The engine had to be repaired before it could complete its trial.

On the morning of the 8th the Stephen-sons' entry weighed in at four tons and two hundredweight, well within the permitted maximum. It was a smart little engine with the boiler clad in wood and brightly painted in yellow and black. The smoke stack was nearly as tall as the engine was long. Two gleaming pistons were angled to drive the

forward wheels which were placed to carry most of the weight. Behind was a matching yellow tender carrying coal and a large barrel feeding water to the boiler.

The Stephensons had worked hard at their locomotive and it was the unseen features which were the most advanced. Inside was a novel tubular boiler, giving a greater heating surface for the fire and a steam blast to draw the air across the flames. As the *Rocket* let off steam through her safety valves the wagons were attached with their test loads of stone. The timekeepers stood by with their watches.

It is thought that George and Robert Stephenson, father and son, nursed the *Rocket* through the famous trial themselves. The train had to make ten runs in each direction over the course of one and a half miles. A break was allowed to refuel and take on water, then another ten runs had to be completed. The time for every run was noted down. The Stephensons kept their machine well inside its capabilities and only on the last three runs did George open up the throttle. The time taken was one hour, forty-eight minutes for the first half and two hours and three minutes for the remainder – it was an excellent performance and well within the times set by the rules of the competition. The little engine had more than met the requirements; it was a great triumph for the Stephensons, and one which they undoubtedly deserved.

Both the *Novelty* and the *Sans Pariel* were allowed to have a second attempt. Both were capable of meeting the running requirements, had they been more fortunate on the day, but neither could match the overall performance and reliability of the *Rocket* – there was no doubt about the winner. George Stephenson attached a coach to his engine with thirty passengers and ran them along the line at the breathtaking speed of 24 to 30 miles per hour. From that time onwards no other locomotive could match the *Rocket* for fame and popularity.

Crown Street Station, the original terminus for passengers. The railway's offices were also housed here. When the line from Lime Street was opened in 1836 this station was relegated to being a goods and maintenance yard.

The result of the Rainhill trials was nowhere better summarised than in a letter from John Dixon of Darlington, one of Timothy Hackworth's team. He wrote to his brother James about the event:

> . . . The Rocket is by far the best engine I have ever seen for blood and bone united . . .
>
> Timothy has been very sadly out of temper ever since he came for he has been grobbing on day and night and nothing our men did for him was right, we could not please him with the Tender or anything; he openly accused all G.S.'s people of conspiring to hinder him of which I do believe them innocent, however he got many trials but never got half of his 70 miles done without stopping. He burns nearly double the quantity of coke that the Rocket does and mumbles and roars and rolls about like an Empty Beer Butt on a rough pavement and moreover weighs above 4 Tons consequently should have had six wheels and as for being on Springs I must confess I cannot find them out . . . She is very ugly and the Boiler runs out [of water] very much, he had to feed her with more Meal and Malt Sprouts than would fatten a pig . . .[1]

Dixon also witnessed the late arrival of the *Perseverance* from Edinburgh. Burstall's story was very similar to Hackworth's. 'Burstall from Edinbro upset his [locomotive] in bringing from L'pool to Rainhill', he continued, 'and spent a week in pretending to Remedy the injuries whereas he altered and amended some part every day till he was last of all to start and a sorrowful start it was; full 6 miles an hour creaking away like an old Wickerwork pair of panniers on a cantering Cuddy Ass.'

The future of steam locomotion was assured, but certain of the local gentry were still scathing and grumpy about the idea of a railway. Partly as an attempt to win them over, they were invited to partake in a ride over the completed section of track. One of the fortunate ones to receive an invitation was Thomas Creevey, the journalist and Member

The goods depot at Wapping. The line to Wapping was built to connect the railway with the docks and thus cater for the overland cargoes which the Manchester traders were so keen to have delivered efficiently. It was built underground on the insistence of the town council, who were uneasy about having locomotives running through the centre of the town. Note the turning platform in the foreground.

of Parliament, who was related to the Earls of Sefton. He agreed to participate in the excursion but as a politician he was incapable of admitting that he was wrong about the railway, and he remained faithful to the jaundiced Knowsley and Croxteth view of the undertaking:

> . . . To-day we had a lark of a very high order. Lady Wilton sent over yesterday from Knowsley to say that the Loco Motive machine was to be upon the railway at such a place at 12 o'clock for the Knowsley party to ride in if they liked, and inviting this house to be of the party. So of course we were at our post in 3 carriages and some horsemen at the hour appointed . . . But the quickest motion is to me frightful: it is really flying and it is impossible to divest yourself of the notion of instant death to all upon the least accident happening. It gave me a headache which has not yet left me. Sefton is convinced that some damnable thing must come out of it; but he and I seem more struck with such apprehension than others . . . The smoke is very inconsiderable indeed, but sparks of fire are abroad in some quantity: one burnt Miss de Ros's cheek, another a hole in Lady Maria's silk pelisse, and a third a hole in someone else's gown. Altogether I am extremely glad indeed to have seen this miracle, and to have travelled in it. Had I thought worse of it than I do, I should have had the curiosity to try it; but, having done so, I am quite satisfied with my first achievment being my last.[2]

There were others, however, who were far more open minded and unbiased about the new form of transport. In the summer of 1830 when the railway was nearing completion there was talk of little else in Liverpool, but for a short time some of the public did allow their minds to run on other matters. A popular new actress was appearing for the first time in Liverpool at the Theatre Royal. 'Fame ran before her, like the morning star', wrote the *Liverpool Albion.* The young lady was only twenty-one. She was appearing as Juliet in the famous Shakespearean tragedy associated with that name. Fanny Kemble was the niece of Sarah Siddons, whom the Liverpool audiences always loved and appreciated, and the theatre-goers were eager to see Miss Kemble's performance. It was, however, impossible for Fanny to live up to the reputation of her aunt and the high expectations of the audience.

'On Monday night a young lady, whose figure is good, but whose features are not very expressive, made her appearance in the character of Juliet. She sustained the part with as much ability as could reasonably be expected from her youth and her short appearance on the stage', wrote the poker-faced critic of the *Liverpool Albion.* But Fanny was much more than an actress. Her beauty, her vivacity, her girlish charm and youthful intelligence enabled her to win over any circle of society, but it is not for her acting abilities that Fanny Kemble is loved and remembered in Liverpool. When it was suggested that the acting company should take a ride on the railway Fanny was thrilled at the prospect. Her account of the engine would do credit to an engineer, for few people in any profession could have matched her descriptive passages and her glowing enthusiasm:

> We were introduced to the little engine which was to drag us along the rails. She (for they make these curious little fire horses all mares) consisted of a boiler, a stove, a small platform, a bench and behind the bench a barrel containing enough water to prevent her from being thirsty for fifteen miles – the whole machine not bigger than a common fire engine. She goes upon two wheels, which are her feet, and are moved by

bright steel legs which are called pistons: these are propelled by steam, and in proportion as more steam is applied to the upper extremities (the hip-joints I suppose) of these pistons, the faster they move the wheels: and when it is desirable to diminish the speed, the steam, which unless suffered to escape would burst the boiler, evaporates through a safety valve into the air. The reins, bit and bridle of this wonderful beast is a small steel handle which applies or withdraws steam from its legs or pistons, so that a child might manage it. The coals which are its oats, were under the bench, and there was a small glass tube affixed to the boiler, with water in it, which indicates by its fullness or emptiness when the creature wants water, which is immediately conveyed to it from its reservoirs.[3]

The engine was none other than the *Rocket* and the driver was none other than George Stephenson himself. The passengers sat pale and apprehensive in the carriage behind and wondered what perils awaited them. The engineer invited Fanny to join him on the footplate. She gathered her skirts and climbed nimbly up beside him.

> . . . This snorting little animal which I felt rather inclined to pat, was then harnessed to our carriage, and Mr Stephenson having taken me on the bench of the engine with him, we started at about ten miles an hour. The steam horse being ill adapted for going up and down hill, the road was kept at a certain level and sometimes appeared to sink below the surface of the earth and sometimes to rise above it. Almost at starting it was cut through the solid rock, which formed a wall on either side of it, about sixty feet high. You can't imagine how strange it seemed to be journeying on thus, without any visible cause of progress other than the magical machine, with its flying white breath and rhythmical, unvarying pace, between these rocky walls, which are already clothed with moss and ferns and grasses; and when I reflected that these great masses of stone had been cut asunder to allow our passage thus far below the surface of the earth, I felt as if no fairy tale was ever half so wonderful as what I saw. Bridges were thrown from side to side across the tops of these cliffs, and people looking down upon us from them seemed like pygmies in the sky.

Fanny thrilled again as the locomotive puffed out into the countryside and climbed to the dizzy height of forty-five feet on the Broadgreen Embankment. The apprehensive passengers trundling nervously behind had seen enough, and Stephenson uncoupled their carriage to be collected later. He took his young passenger on to see more marvels. He shovelled on the coal to raise a good head of steam and the engine accelerated to a breathtaking speed of thirty miles an hour. The fire glowed red in the belly of the brave little *Rocket,* the white steam hissed and escaped from her cylinders and flew in a great plume from the top of the chimney stack.

They made a curious pair on the footplate as they sped through the Lancashire countryside. The old, white haired, Geordie ex-collier with his tall hat and coat tails, and the slim, London society girl, educated at a French finishing school, grasping tightly to the handrail. Fanny removed her bonnet and drank in the air:

> The wind, which was strong, or perhaps the force of our own thrusting against it, absolutely weighed my eyelids down. When I closed my eyes this sensation of flying was quite delightful, and strange beyond description; yet strange as it was I had a perfect sense of security, and not the slightest fear.

They slowed and stopped at the Sankey Viaduct. The engineer

Bury and Ackermann's evocative drawing of the Sankey Viaduct on the Liverpool and Manchester Railway. Nine bold arches, each with a clearance of sixty feet, span the valley to carry the railway far above the Sankey Brook Navigation below. Building the viaduct this high up meant that considerable embankments had to be built on the approaches to the viaduct itself. Quite a sight for Fanny Kemble!

offered a horny hand to the actress, and they both scrambled down the embankment so that he could show her how he had carried the metals high over the Vale of Sankey on nine great stone arches. He also told of the problems encountered in building the viaduct, the geology of the land, the laying of the railway across Chat Moss, and the many other difficulties involved with building the level road. 'He explained to me the whole construction of the steam engine', said Fanny, 'and said he could soon make a famous engineer of me'.

The Liverpool and Manchester Railway was George Stephenson's crowning achievement, but it had thrown up all sorts of technical, financial, political and personnel problems. It warmed his heart to find one so young and attractive who appreciated all he had achieved.

> Now for a word about the master of all these marvels, with whom I am most horribly in love. He is a man from fifty to fifty-five years of age; his face is fine, though careworn, and he bears an expression of deep thoughtfulness; his mode of explaining his ideas is peculiar and very original, striking and forcible, and although his accent indicates strongly his north-country birth, his language has not the slightest touch of vulgarity or coarseness. He has quite turned my head.

The opening day of the new railway was set for the following month and Fanny was determined to be back in Liverpool for the occasion. As the time came near, more and more visitors arrived in the town, and a week before the great day Liverpool was packed to overflowing, with the private carriages of the wealthy parked all night in the streets because there was insufficient space in the stable yards. People arrived from all over the country and from the continent. Some had travelled from across the Atlantic to witness the opening of the railway. It was estimated that there were half a million people in the town the night before the opening day, and nobody talked of anything else but the railway. 'So intensely were the lower orders absorbed in the anticipations of the day', reported the *Liverpool Courier*, 'that if by common consent a holiday had not been talked of, few, very few, would have had sufficient resolution to pursue the toils of the day whilst the novel spectacle was exhibiting'.

On the early morning of the fifteenth, vehicles of every description and crowds of 'gay and happy pedestrians' were heading for the best vantage points. The heights above the cutting were crowded with 'a dense body of individuals, all striving to obtain a glimpse of the preparations that were in progress in the deep chasm below . . . Along the entire line, as far as the eye could reach, the heights and slopes on each side of the road, were thronged with individuals all in their holiday suits and gayest attire . . . Every elevation and building around was converted into an observatory, from which many an eager eye was bent; and female hearts seem to have forgotten their timidity in anxious expectation, enlivening the housetops with their fair and smiling faces.' According to one spectator, even the Quakers threw aside their gravity, they 'looked as gay as larks, and joined in the general joyousness'.

All the way to Manchester crowds lined the route. Special stands were built at Sankey to allow people to watch the cavalcade of trains pass over the viaduct. At Manchester a crowd of a hundred thousand had assembled by noon, with every vantage point in the vicinity of the railway covered by men, women and children anxious to see the first trains arrive. Numbers of people stood on the roofs of the buildings, with others standing on water tubs which had been brought and converted for the purpose. Several elegantly dressed ladies, 'at the risk of despoiling their flounces and fubelows', stood near the top of a building in Water Street where part of the roof had been stripped off to give them a better vantage point. On the whole line from Ordsall-Lane to Eccles the multitude was assembled. The fields adjoining the railway and all the various bridges were crowded with spectators.[4]

The procession consisted of seven short trains, each with four or five carriages and hauled by the latest locomotives. The *Northumbrian* led the procession pulling the Duke of Wellington's carriage and an open car carrying a band. The Duke's carriage was thirty-two feet long and eight feet wide. With a lofty canopy of crimson cloth resting on eight carved and gilt pillars and with ornamental gilt balustrades, it looked rather like a hearse and it was the height of vulgar taste but, like the emperor's new clothes, everybody was expected to admire it.

The leading train was followed by the *Phoenix*, the *North Star*, the *Rocket*, the *Dart*, the *Comet*, the *Arrow* and the *Meteor* each pulling their own train of brightly coloured carriages. At twenty to eleven a gun was fired and the procession was under way through the great Moorish Arch and into the rocky walls of the Olive Mount cutting. 'Masses of densely packed people lined the road, shouting and waving hats and handkerchiefs as we flew by them', said Fanny Kemble. 'What with the sight and sound of these cheering multitudes and the tremendous velocity with which we were borne past them, my spirits rose to the true champagne height and I never enjoyed anything so much as the first hour of our progress.'

The procession must have been the grandest ever beheld, whether we consider the triumph of mechanical art which it exhibited, the engines moving 'like things of life', or the brilliant display of rank and talent, beauty and fashion which it contained. The splendour of the cars; the brilliance of the coaches and carriages; the neat elegance of the humbler vehicles in the form of open cars; the gay appearance of the variegated flags which fluttered in the breeze; the beauty of the engines, the men and boys who worked them dressed in the new blue livery of the company, faced with red . . . above all, the beauty, the variety and the extent of the cortege must have presented a most enchanting spectacle as it rolled majestically onwards.[5]

Fanny Kemble was in high spirits until she found that her mother, who was travelling in the same carriage, was frightened to death and 'intent upon nothing but devising means of escaping from a situation which appeared to her to threaten with instant annihilation herself and all her travelling companions'.

Everything went according to plan until the trains reached Parkside where the locomotives were scheduled to stop and take on water. Then everything began to go drastically wrong. Some of the passengers got out of the trains and wandered over the tracks, quite oblivious to the danger of their position. William Huskisson, an MP for Liverpool and former President of the Board of Trade, stepped across the tracks to speak to the Duke of Wellington when the *Rocket* was seen bearing down on him. Others, seeing the danger, yelled at Huskisson to get clear of the line but the MP hesitated, became confused, and fell just as the engine was upon him. His left leg was crushed by the wheels of the locomotive and the accident proved fatal. The Prime Minister wished to return to Liverpool after the confusion brought about by the accident, but the people of Manchester had waited a long time for the trains to arrive and the Boroughreeve of Manchester pleaded with him to continue with his journey.

The massacre of Peterloo was still fresh in the minds of the

When moving forward to take on some water, the Rocket *ran over the leg of William Huskisson MP, administering fatal injuries which marred the opening day for the brave, new railway. This drawing shows the water point at Parkside where the unfortunate accident occurred.*

Manchester people, however, and the Duke of Wellington was not the most popular person to visit them on their home ground. There were demonstrations, too, against the plight of the handloom weavers whose livelihood was being destroyed by the factory system and by the introduction of machinery into the mills. The trains managed to reach Manchester amid great disturbances and demonstrations, but they had not been there long before the police and company officials asked the Duke to leave for fear of the disturbances getting out of hand. The Duke of Wellington never left his carriage, and the return journey was a shambles, with the railway company's carefully laid plans thwarted by the unscheduled departure and with engines on the wrong side of the tracks. Engines and coaches were joined together in one long train. One of the couplings broke and had to be lashed together with ropes. At one point a wheelbarrow was found across the rails. It was not until ten o'clock in the evening that the weary travellers arrived back at their point of departure.

The need for the demonstrators to make their point to the Prime Minister was natural and understandable, but it was a great shame that a fatal accident and political demonstrations had ruined what should have been a great occasion for Manchester. In terms of posterity, however, the events of the day would be remembered far longer than the political issues which were current at the time and the world's first true railway was an unqualified success. 'At first it was comparatively slow', wrote the Rev Edward Stanley of the departure from Liverpool, as he captured the sense of history in the making, 'but soon we felt that we were indeed *going*, and then it was that every person to whom the conveyance was new, must have been sensible that the adaption of locomotive power was establishing a fresh era in the state of society; the final results of which it was impossible to contemplate.'

On the fifteenth of September 1830 the railway age had begun. The Liverpool star had reached its zenith.

Railway Station, Lime Street 1838, by Lacey of Bold Street.
The magnificent frontage of Lime Street Station, with classical arches and Corinthian capitals, soon after it was opened for passenger traffic. A good example of the civic pride with which Victorian towns held their main line stations.

A rural view of Lime Street in 1818 by J. T. Eglington, showing haycarts and a stagecoach departing down the London Road, long before the railway terminus was built. Known formerly as Lime Kiln Lane, the name is derived from some lime kilns belonging to William Harvey which stood on the site of the station; they were removed in 1804.

Below: *A good example of Herdman's work, showing the pillars of St George's Hall on the left and the frontage of the original Lime Street Station, designed by John Fowler, on the right. The two columns were of polished red granite, later removed to Sefton Park and replaced by stone lions.*

Chapter Ten

Passage to America

N JULY 1815 a very strange vessel appeared in the Mersey. She was only forty-tons burden, and she had travelled from the Clyde via the Isle of Man and was anchored in George's Dock. The curious thing about the *Elizabeth* was that she could make headway without the help of wind or sails, a feat which was somehow achieved by puffing out clouds of dark smoke and white steam from a tall chimney, and causing two great wheels mounted with sets of paddles to rotate and thrash at the water.

> On Wednesday last, about noon, the public curiosity was considerably excited by the arrival of the first Steam Boat ever seen on our River. She came from the Clyde, and on her passage called at Ramsey in the Isle of Man, which place she left early on the same morning. We believe she is intended to ply between this port and Runcorn; or even occasionally as far as Warrington. Her cabin will contain about one hundred passengers.[1]

For a time the owner, Colin Watson, used the *Elizabeth* to provide a ferry service between Liverpool and Runcorn, but she was sold off the following spring and the pioneer steamship company was dissolved. Steam vessels had arrived to stay, however, and the next year they were being built on the banks of the Mersey, the first being the *Duke of Wellington,* of sixty tons, shortly followed by the *Prince Regent* of 58 tons, both built at Runcorn in 1816. The *Princess Charlotte,* was built by Mottershead of Liverpool in the same year and the double-hulled *Aetna,* built by Dawson of Liverpool, appeared in the following year.[2]

Many traditionalists refused to ride in the steamboats because of the great volumes of smoke and steam which they emitted, a fact which convinced nervous passengers that the boats were about to blow themselves up at any minute. 'The steam boats make a rather laughable appearance', wrote Ellen Weeton, 'they go puffing and blowing, and beating their sides, and labouring along with all their might'.

But the thrashing of the paddles was a sign of the future. The steamboats were successful as ferries; they also proved to be very useful as tugs, particularly in situations where oar power was the only previous alternative. Before long the steamers began to ply on the open sea routes and in 1819 the *Liverpool Mercury* described a new steam packet to Belfast, called the *Waterloo,* built in John Scott's yard at

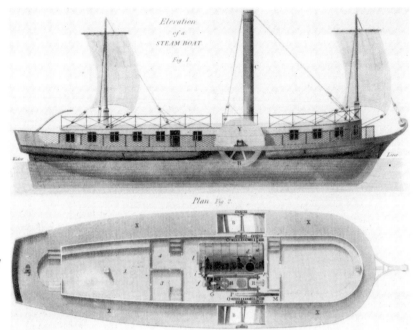

A typical Clyde steamer of the 1810s. Glasgow was quite a centre for the manufacture of pioneering steamboats and the Mersey's first steamboat, the Elizabeth, *came from there in 1815. Not unlike the boat in this picture in appearance, the* Elizabeth *was 58-feet long and built by Wood & Co. She was one of the first steamships able to operate a regular timetable regardless of the state of the tide.*

Greenock on the Clyde and with a displacement of 210 tons:

> New Belfast Packet. Yesterday a beautiful Steam Packet arrived at this port from Belfast after a passage of only 24 hours. She is called the Waterloo, and is a fine well-built vessel, burthen 201 tons, length 98 feet, breadth on deck 37 feet, and has two highly finished engines of 30 horse-power each, which work without noise or vibration, and are on the low-pressure construction, perfectly safe from accident. They are attended by two experienced engineers. The vessel is also provided with two masts with sails and rigging. Her interior accommodations are as complete and elegant as skill and experience can make them. She has a handsome dining room, capable of accommodating all the cabin passengers; a separate and neatly-decorated cabin for ladies; twenty-two well furnished beds well accommodated with light and air; and a comfortable place for steerage passengers . . .[3]

The fares were £1 11s 6d for cabin passengers and 10s 6d for those travelling steerage; tickets could be obtained from Mr John Crowther at the Salthouse Dock. It was necessary to stress the safety of the engines and also the sail assistance, without which no steamboat would dare to venture out to sea.

Some idea of the hazards and unreliability of the early steam ferry service is given in a letter from Mrs Thomas Holt, who describes a journey from Chester undertaken by her husband and son in the winter of 1824. The travellers encountered a violent storm with hail 'as large as bullets', which caused the leading horses to turn completely round and nearly overturn their coach. For the Mersey crossing they boarded the steamer *Vesuvius* which subsequently broke down in the middle of the river and, after waiting half an hour, they were transferred to another steamer called the *Abbey*. After another hour and a half the *Abbey* reached the Liverpool landing stage but because of the heavy weather the ferry was unable to get near the steps to

Double launch of steamers at Liverpool.

Paddle steamers were built on both sides of the Mersey from before 1820, and as they grew in size the launching became something of an event. A double launch, as shown here, was clearly an even greater local event. Note that engines and paddles have yet to be fitted. For many years steamers like this served as ferries, tugs and tenders in the Mersey.

disembark her passengers. Eventually a rope was flung ashore and caught by some sailors on the stone pier. The boat was then hauled up to the pier but the passengers were obliged to scramble up the wall to safety. 'They were both starved and very much fatigued when they arrived home', wrote Mrs Holt, meaningfully.[4]

In 1819 another steamship arrived in the Mersey which created quite a sensation for it had actually travelled from across the Atlantic. *The Savannah* was built along the classical lines of a three-masted sailing ship, but she was also fitted with an engine, a curious bent smokestack and a set of paddle wheels amidships. It was not a true crossing by steam power, for the ship could easily have crossed from America without using the engines at all and in fact they were only used for a fraction of the voyage, but the ship still made a great impression – more especially when it was seen how easily she could manoeuvre herself into dock by use of the paddle wheels:

> Among the arrivals yesterday at this port we were particularly gratified and astonished by the novel sight of a fine steam ship, which came round at half after 7pm, without the assistance of a single sheet, in a style which displayed the power and advantage of the application of steam to vessels of a largest size, being of 350-tons burden. She is called the Savannah, and sailed from Savannah the 26th of May and arrived in the Channel five days since: during her passage, she worked the engine for 18 days. Her model is beautiful, and the accommodation for passengers elegant and complete; this is the first ship on this construction that has undertaken a voyage across the Atlantic.[5]

The more difficult crossing, in the opposite direction, from England to America, was not achieved under steam until 1838. The engineer Isambard Brunel designed the steamship *Great Western* of 1,321 tons to carry passengers from Bristol to New York in what he saw as an extension of his recently opened Great Western Railway. When the shipowners of London and Liverpool heard of the challenge they too decided to enter the competition. The London men chartered the *British Queen* to make the passage, a slightly larger ship than the *Great Western,* and in Liverpool the 1,150 ton *Liverpool* was prepared for the race. Neither London nor Liverpool was able to get its first choice of vessel ready in time to sail before the *Great Western,* however. The Londoners had to charter the smaller *Sirius* of 703 tons and the Liverpolitans chartered the 617-ton *Royal William* for the race.

The *Sirius* was the first to sail, and was soon followed by the much larger *Great Western,* breathing hard on her heels. The *Sirius* arrived off New York on April 22nd. Rumours that she steamed the last few miles by burning her cabin furniture and everything inflammable on the ship were quite untrue, but she only had fifteen tons of coal left on arrival and had sacrificed four barrels of resin. The *Great Western,* in spite of an engine-room fire which nearly killed her designer, arrived only a day later with plenty of fuel to spare, having made a faster passage in fifteen days and five hours from Bristol. The Liverpool entry was an ignominious third, and did not stagger into New York until the following July.

The *Royal William* was simply not ready to sail in time to meet the challenge, but when she did manage to cross the Atlantic her times were impressive, with eighteen days and twenty-three hours outward, and only fourteen days, nineteen hours for the return passage. She was the first steamer to make the crossing from Liverpool and the local people appreciated her efforts. 'When in Bootle Bay', said the *Liverpool Mercury* on her return, 'she threw up blue lights and fired guns. Soon afterwards she passed Clarence [Dock] and the Prince's Pier amidst loud cheering and cast anchor off George's Pier where the passengers landed.'

The lucrative transatlantic mail contract was worth sixty thousand pounds and Brunel hoped to win it with his successful new steamship, but Liverpool managed to secure the contract with the Cunard steamship *Brittania,* built in 1840, and which was able to guarantee fifteen crossings a year in each direction. The *Brittania* was one of the first Cunard liners, 207-feet long and carrying 115 passengers. She made forty crossings in all, including the passage made by Charles Dickens on his visit to America in 1858. Brunel went on to build his *Great Britain* at Bristol and the *Great Eastern* on the Thames at Millwall, but both these ships came to be based in Liverpool, which was the most profitable port from which to operate them. Liverpool was the only port with the facilities to handle the magnificient *Great Eastern,* a vessel many years ahead of its time and, at 18,914 tons, the largest vessel afloat for thirty years.

By the middle of the century, the Liverpool docks system had grown almost out of all recognition. Major changes began in 1811 when an Act of Parliament was obtained to fill in the Old Dock which had become almost an inland dock after the recent new developments to seaward. Dock space was at a premium and shipping was still using the Old Dock until 1826, but Regency Liverpool had no sentiment for the past and the following year one of the earliest wet docks in the world was drained and filled in. The prime site was used to build the fifth customs house, a classical building designed by John Foster the younger, which took eleven years to complete. When finished, it was one of the most impressive buildings in Liverpool and one which rivalled the town hall in grandeur, but it did not impress Brunel, who described it as of 'very inferior stone' and 'an extravagant waste of strength in massive corners and spires'.

How much better Albert Dock looks with tall ships in it. The lightness, airiness and height of the masts contrasts and complements the solidity and heaviness of the warehouses. Here we see three American ships tied up together.

Great Fire of 1833.
'Fourteen warehouses and nine dwelling-houses burnt down in Lancelot's Hey, New Quay &c, being the most destructive fire since that in the Goree [1800]; damage estimated at – warehouses £28,000, dwelling-houses £2,000, merchandise £168,000. On this property insurance was effected to the amount of £150,000.' (Gore, 1833). A very dramatic view of the fire as seen from George's Dock.

Customs House.
A view of the Customs House from Canning Dock.

In 1824 a Yorkshireman called Jesse Hartley was appointed as engineer to the docks. He was a man of powerful vision who arrived at the right time to carry out his grand concepts of dock development and with the strength, solidarity and skill needed for the new shipping era. Hartley worked in granite and cast iron, materials in which he could express his own genius and the spirit of the age. The first of his works was Brunswick Dock and a half-tide basin built to the south of the docks. It was a development on a massive scale, with twelve acres of water enclosed for the dock and another two acres for the basin. Opened in 1832, the dock was built for the timber trade and the eastern quay was sloped to facilitate unloading. Two large adjacent graving docks were added later.

Jesse Hartley went ahead with Clarence Dock, which opened in 1830. Designed for the new steamers, these docks were constructed some distance to the north of Prince's Dock to avoid the risk of fire. Clarence Dock was the first to incorporate continuous covered sheds, a facility which was found to be so successful that it was later provided around many of the older docks. Waterloo Dock was reconstructed as an inner and outer dock and the Victoria and Trafalgar Docks completed the development between Clarence Dock and Waterloo. These new docks were also designed to accommodate powered vessels, owing to the great increase in the number of steam vessels being used for commerce at this time.

In 1839 Hartley produced his bold designs for the Albert Dock, to be built on the river side of Salthouse, and parliamentary sanction to begin construction was given in 1841. Albert Dock was opened by the Prince Consort in 1845. Sandon Dock was opened in 1849. Huskisson Dock followed in 1852 and was extended eastwards in 1860. Canada Dock was opened in 1859 with extensive timber yards and there seemed no end to the steady expansion of the dockside waterfront.

It was a truly cosmopolitan waterfront, with produce imported from and exported to all parts of the world. Manufactured goods stood on the quays waiting for export – iron and steel, cotton goods from Lancashire, woollen garments from Yorkshire, machinery and metal manufactures made in the Midland factories. Bales of raw cotton could be seen unloading from the southern states of America. Beef, mutton, bacon and ham came from the meat-exporting countries. Raw wool and grain arrived from Australia, and timber from the wooded slopes of a score of countries throughout the world. There were cargoes of tea from India and China mixed with the aroma of spices from the Orient. The repeal of the Corn Laws in 1846 opened up the grain trade with Russia, while the Cotton Famine of the 'sixties had one bright lining in that it opened up a cotton trade with Alexandria and other parts of Egypt. There was the smell of brimstone, coffee, ginger, cowhides, jute, molasses, palm oil, pepper, rice, rum, saltpetre, sugar, tallow, tobacco and turpentine. The waterfront was a magical mixture of textiles and spices, tar and soot, ropes and rigging, sails and smokestacks, horses and carriers, kegs, casks and barrels, and ships flying the flags and colours of every nation.

Liverpool was a sailors' town. Dockside pubs were everywhere. The sound of boisterous revelling and powerful sea shanties was heard from the tavern doorways as the sailors spent their few days' leave and their hard-earned money on beer, women and song. Prostitutes

Overleaf: Central Liverpool as Liverpudlians would never have seen it before. An aerial view by Ackerman, perhaps based on the Ordnance Survey that was completed in the early-1840s, but perhaps undertaken from actual observation from a balloon. In any event, it is a fascinating glimpse at the town at an important point in its growth and development.

roamed the streets and solicited the mariners for custom – the sailor could choose from brash Liverpudlian whores, fat and buxom floosies to green-eyed Irish lasses, petite dark-haired Chinese street walkers, and dusky exotic eastern maidens, all prepared to sell him their favours at the right price. The brothels stood alongside the beer houses on the dockside roads.

In 1839 arrived Herman Melville, a wide-eyed cabin boy who had sailed from New York. He described the Liverpool dockside street scene in some detail:

> In the evening, especially when the sailors are gathered in great numbers, these streets present a most singular spectacle, the entire population of the vicinity being seemingly turned into them. Hand-organs, fiddles and cymbals, plied by strolling musicians, mix with the songs of the seamen, the babble of women and children, and the groaning and whining of beggars. From the various boarding houses, each distinguished by gilded emblems outside – an anchor, a crown, a ship, a windlass or a dolphin – proceeds the noise of revelry and dancing; and from the open casements lean young girls and old women, chattering and laughing with the crowds in the middle of the street. Every moment strange greetings are exchanged between old sailors who chance to stumble upon a ship-mate, last seen in Calcutta or Savannah; and the invariable courtesy that takes place upon these occasions, is to go to the next spirit vault, and drink each other's health.[6]

The great value of Melville's writing is that he saw Liverpool not from the viewpoint of the traveller or the merchant but from the dockside as a humble sailor from the lower decks. His comments are not always flattering, but they are honest and full of character.

> . . . of all sea-ports in the world, Liverpool, perhaps, most abounds in all the variety of land-shark, land-rats and other vermin, which make the hapless mariner their prey. In the shape of landlords, bar-keepers, clothiers, crimps and boarding-house loungers, the land-sharks devour him, limb by limb: while the land-rats and mice constantly nibble at his purse.
>
> Other perils he runs, also, far worse; from the denizens of notorious Corinthian haunts in the vicinity of the docks, which in depravity are not to be matched by anything this side of the pit that is bottomless. And yet, sailors love this Liverpool; and upon long voyages to distant parts of the globe, will be continually dilating on its charms and attractions, and extolling it above all other seaports in the world., For in Liverpool they find their Paradise – not the well-known street of that name – and one of them told me he would be content to lie in Prince's Dock till he *hove up anchor* for the world to come.

Herman Melville was fascinated by the Liverpool dock system, which was far superior to the wooden jettys and ramshackle piers on the waterfront he had left behind:

> Surrounded by its broad belt of masonry, each Liverpool dock is a walled town, full of life and commotion; or rather it is a small archipelago, an epitome of the world, where all the nations of Christendom, and even those of Heathendom, are represented. For, in itself, each ship an island, a floating colony of the tribe to which it belongs.
>
> Here are brought together the remotest limits of the earth; and in the collective spars and timbers of these ships, all the forests of the globe are represented, as in a grand parliament of masts. Canada and New Zealand send their pines; America her live oak, India her teak; Norway her spruce and the Right Honorable Mahogany, member for Honduras and

Campeachy, is seen at his post by the wheel. Here, under the beneficient sway of the Genius of Commerce, all climes and countries embrace; and yard-arm touches yard-arm in brotherly love.

A Liverpool dock is a grand caravansary inn, and hotel, on the spacious and liberal plan of the Astor House [a grand hotel on Broadway]. Here ships are lodged at moderate charge, and payment is not demanded till the time of departure. Here they are comfortably housed and provided for, sheltered from all weathers and secured from all calamities.[7]

Herman Melville went to explore the town. In his hands he carried *The Picture of Liverpool or the Stranger's Guide and Gentleman's Pocket Companion*, an old guidebook bound in green morocco which had belonged to his father. The book was first published in 1796, though Herman's copy was the enlarged second edition of 1808. It was over thirty years old and Liverpool was a town that had greatly altered since the time when Allan Melville had dined with William Roscoe. To his dismay poor Herman could hardly find anything mentioned in his father's guidebook. The Old Dock had been filled in, Riddough's Hotel where his father stayed in Lord Street had been demolished, and all that remained of the Old Fort on the North Shore was a public house built from the stones of the fort when the walls were pulled down.

It was Herman Melville who was unwittingly responsible for spreading the fiction that Liverpool was named after an extinct fowl called the Liver Bird. He was not the originator of the myth; he copied the story in good faith from his guidebook and published it in his novel *Redburn*. The novel was widely read in America and was also popular in Britain; it became an American classic and the story of the extinct Liver Bird was soon being repeated and established as a 'fact'.

The New York waterfront was catching up with Liverpool very quickly and by 1850 New York had a greater volume of shipping, though it had less total commerce. The New York based American Black Ball Line helped Liverpool to break into the passenger trade across the Atlantic, a trade which was previously monopolised by London and Bristol. In 1816 the Black Ball Line ran ships twice a month in each direction. The passage from New York to Liverpool was scheduled for twenty-three days with forty days for the crossing from England to America.

In 1825 the British Government acknowledged that there was an unemployment problem and that the country was overcrowded. Accordingly, the anti-emigration laws were relaxed to make it easier for people to emigrate to America. The trade in passenger traffic expanded rapidly and soon many shipping lines were competing for custom. The Red Star Line was established in 1821, the Swallow Tail Line and others followed thick and fast until the shipping lines became so numerous that to list them becomes a mere catalogue.

A new breed of shipowner began to appear. John Bibby, who started by running packet ships between Parkgate and Dublin, was typical of the new race of self-made men. He expanded his service to Alexandria and later to America. Enoch Train's White Diamond Line traded between Liverpool and Boston. William Brown, founder of Brown, Shipley and Co., was an American who became colonel of the Liverpool Volunteers and received a knighthood for his services. The White Star Line was started by Wilson and Pilkington in the 1840s.

William Lamport and George Holt founded their company in 1845, Charles MacIver set up business in 1851 with one ship sailing to the Mediterranean. He was joined by Samuel Cunard, a Quaker from Halifax, Nova Scotia, and George Burns – between them they created the Cunard service to the Levant. A Scot called Sir Donald Currie founded the Castle Line to Calcutta in 1862 and later ran ships to South America before the company became part of the Union Castle Line. The Australian Black Ball Line was founded by James Baines, born behind a cake shop in Upper Duke Street, who rose to control eighty-six ships and three thousand seaman. He is reputed to have died bankrupt in a common lodging house.

The emigration movement reached its peak in the 1840s and 1850s. Many of the emigrants came from England, Scotland and Ireland, but they also came from the countries of the European continent where economic forces and political disturbances caused people to search for a new life in the new world. On the quayside were Germans, Scandinavians, Poles, Hungarians, Czechs, Romanians, Austrians, Greeks, Italians and even the occasional Chinese who for some reason chose to emigrate via Liverpool.

It was a sad sight to see the emigrants, many of whom came from remote and rural villages and hamlets, lost in a strange and busy sea port, sitting on their humble boxes of belongings, waiting on the quayside until they could find a berth to take them to begin a new life and cast away the last remains of the old, open to theft and deceit from unscrupulous 'runners' and the notorious gang of thugs known as the Forty Thieves.

Before they could find a berth the emigrants had to find their way through the maze of emigration officialdom, and run the gauntlet of the many swindlers and conmen purporting to be officials. They were pounced upon by gangs of runners calling themselves porters who carried their luggage and refused to release it until they were paid an exorbitant fee for carriage. Golden sovereigns were exchanged for very dubious American dollars. Non-existent passages to America were promised, with boarding-house accommodation provided until the ship was ready. The accommodation was usually in the poorest part of town, in a damp cellar with only straw mattresses to sleep on. The corrupt lodging-house keepers pocketed the money and the promised passages did not materialise.

Between 1819 and 1859 an estimated five-million emigrants sailed to the United States and about half a million to Canada – about two thirds of these emigrated through Liverpool. The great majority travelled steerage, with up to a thousand people crammed in below decks, most of whom had never been to sea before. They were thrown into an unknown world of ropes, sheets, yards, sailors oaths, wet and tossing decks and miserable food.

The passengers were allowed no naked lights. They were obliged to rise at 7am. They had to roll up their own beds, sweep the decks and throw dirt and rubbish overboard. On Sundays they mustered at 10am for divine service. They brought their own food with them and had to cook it themselves. It was because of a cooking fire or a lighted match that the 1,300 ton *Ocean Monarch* caught fire in 1848, with 338 emigrants aboard. The fire started in the Mersey and by the time the ship was in the open sea the flames were out of control and had spread

'Farewell to England'

MIGRATION to the American colonies began in the seventeenth century and grew steadily throughout the eighteenth. Liverpool did not become heavily involved until long after the Americans had gained their indepedence but when emigration reached its peak in the mid-nineteenth century the majority of emigrants sailed from Liverpool. Crowded and emotional scenes took place by the dockside as emigrants prepared to leave their homelands behind to begin life afresh in the New World. Most of them were destined for the United States, but many sailed for Canada and some as far away as Australia. The majority travelled 'steerage' and were accommodated in very basic conditions on the sailing ships of the times. Later in the century the steamers, such as those of the Allan Line shown below, provided better conditions, but steerage accommodation was still very primitive by later standards.

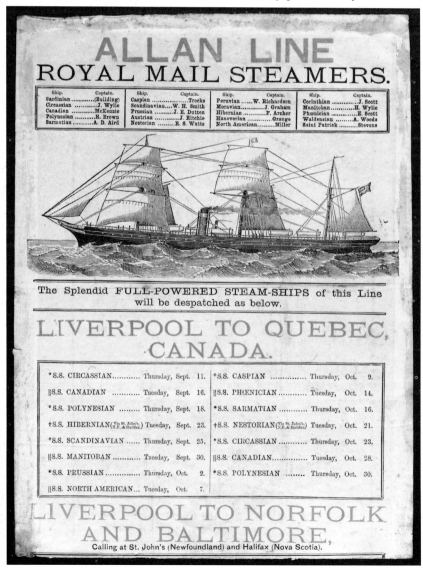

ALLAN LINE
ROYAL MAIL STEAMERS.

Ship.	Captain.	Ship.	Captain.	Ship.	Captain.	Ship.	Captain.
Sardinian	(Building)	Caspian	Trocks	Peruvian	W. Richardson	Corinthian	J. Scott
Circassian	J. Wylie	Scandinavian	W. H. Smith	Moravian	J. Graham	Manitoban	H. Wylie
Canadian	McKenzie	Prussian	J. E. Dutton	Hibernian	F. Archer	Phœnician	E. Scott
Polynesian	R. Brown	Austrian	J. Ritchie	Hanoverian	Grange	Waldensian	A. Woods
Sarmatian	A. D. Aird	Nestorian	R. S. Watts	North American	Miller	Saint Patrick	Stevens

The Splendid **FULL-POWERED STEAM-SHIPS** of this Line will be despatched as below.

LIVERPOOL TO QUEBEC, CANADA.

*S.S. CIRCASSIAN	Thursday, Sept. 11.	*S.S. CASPIAN	Thursday, Oct. 9.
‖S.S. CANADIAN	Tuesday, Sept. 16.	‖S.S. PHŒNICIAN	Tuesday, Oct. 14.
*S.S. POLYNESIAN	Thursday, Sept. 18.	*S.S. SARMATIAN	Thursday, Oct. 16.
†S.S. HIBERNIAN(Via St. John's, N.F. & Halifax)	Tuesday, Sept. 23.	†S.S. NESTORIAN(Via St. John's, N.F. & Halifax)	Tuesday, Oct. 21.
*S.S. SCANDINAVIAN	Thursday, Sept. 25.	*S.S. CIRCASSIAN	Thursday, Oct. 23.
‖S.S. MANITOBAN	Tuesday, Sept. 30.	‖S.S. CANADIAN	Tuesday, Oct. 28.
*S.S. PRUSSIAN	Thursday, Oct. 2.	*S.S. POLYNESIAN	Thursday, Oct. 30.
‖S.S. NORTH AMERICAN	Tuesday, Oct. 7.		

LIVERPOOL TO NORFOLK AND BALTIMORE,
Calling at St. John's (Newfoundland) and Halifax (Nova Scotia).

Left: The emigration movement continued until the twentieth century. Here a group of fledgling Americans leave their hostel in Great George Square for their ship, the Lucania, and the next leg of the long journey to the New World. In all, it has been estimated that around nine million people made the same hopeful voyage from Liverpool in search of a better life.

Opposite: An advertisement for the Allan Line service to Canada. The number and frequency of sailings are clearly demonstrated, with no fewer than six trips leaving Liverpool during September alone.

Right: Atkinson Grimshaw's evocative painting of the docks at night. This would have been the kind of damp, misty sight that would have been many emigrants' last reminder of home.

Below: 'Farewell to England'. A uniformed policeman and a dock official survey the congregated humanity aboard an emigrant ship in the late-nineteenth century, shortly before sailing time.

to the whole vessel. The passengers and crew were forced to choose between death by fire or by water as the *Ocean Monarch* began to sink about six miles off the Great Orme's Head. Her fate was witnessed by several other ships who could only get to the scene in time to pick up a few survivors. Witnesses described the horror of the sinking. They saw the passengers climbing out like ants onto the jib with the whole ship an inferno of flames. The burning foremast fell onto the crowded jib, which crashed into a heavy sea with the people still clinging to it. A few moments later the *Ocean Monarch* disappeared beneath the waves. The death toll was 178.

On top of the perils of the high seas the emigrants had to run the risk of disease and shipboard fever, which claimed many more lives than accident and shipwreck. Dysentry and typhoid fever were common on the emigrant ships. The worst outbreak was in 1847 when the fever reached epidemic proportions; all the quarantine beds in New York were full and the United States refused entry to any ship carrying the fever. Exhausted immigrants had to beat back to sea again and head for the St. Lawrence, where thousands of Irish immigrants died only days after seeing the coast of their hopeful new world.

The United States Government, concerned and dismayed with the endless tide of penniless immigrants, insisted that the newcomers had a bond to show that they had enough money to support themselves on arrival. Finally, having at last made it tired and exhausted to America, the long-suffering immigrants had to run the gauntlet of thieves and conmen all over again. Runners in Liverpool had tipped off their fellows in New York with names and personal details of the new arrivals. Unscrupulous tricksters, posing as friends of the family, milked the emigrants afresh for any money which their English counterparts had left on them.

The whole business of emigration, which should have been a romantic and moving episode in the life of the new Americans, was marred by the corruption and the dishonesty of the runners and the thieves at both ends of the passage.

It would be wrong, however, to pass by the whole episode as nothing but corruption. There were many fair dealers and the honest agents who did not make the headlines. As the emigrant ship was ready to sail the orange sellers, cap merchants, Everton toffee sellers, vendors of ribbons and lace, nuts, gingerbread and sweetmeats swarmed all over the decks until the moment of departure. There was the search for stowaways and the roll call of those on board by the mates who knew an appealing rhyme for every name: Paddy Bile, come here awhile; Joseph Brown, come on down; William Jones, show your bones.

Romantic paintings of the times show the fond farewells and the emotions raised in the hearts of those who left their country of birth behind them. As the ship got underway the emigrants, thrown together in common circumstances and sharing the same small world below decks and the same monotonous meals, gossiped and befriended each other. They talked fondly of their villages and birthplaces which they left behind and of the new life which they hoped to find across the Atlantic. Many made their own music. They sat around the stove and sang songs of their homelands between the swaying and creaking of the wooden decks and they danced and made merry by the light of the swinging oil lamps.

The rounded hulls and square decorated sterns of the traditional three-masters were gradually replaced by taller and longer sleek-lined ships. There were fully rigged Baltimore clippers, brigantines and schooners with frames of live oak, sleek three-masted barques, clipper ships arriving from the Far East with four masts carrying mainsails, royals, sovereigns, topsails and topgallants on every one. They appeared on the horizon as a great stack of swelling canvas leaning before the wind as they hauled their way to the Mersey Bar after the long voyage across the oceans of the world.

It was the halcyon days of sail. The Black Ball ship *Yorkshire* was the fastest packet ever built and crossed to America under sail in an astonishing sixteen days. One of James Baines sailing ships, the *Lightning,* logged an incredible 436 miles in a day's run on the first day of March 1853, a record which still holds for a sailing vessel. Sailors like Herman Melville knew and understood the romance of the high seas and the companionship enjoyed by seamen of all nations:

> I know not how many hours I spent in gazing at the shipping in Prince's Dock, and speculating concerning their past voyages and future prospects in life. Some had just arrived from the most distant ports, worn, battered, and disabled; others were all a-taunt-o–spruce, gay and brilliant in readiness for the sea.
>
> Every day the Highlander had some new neighbor. A black brig from Glasgow, with its crew of sober Scotch caps, and its staid thrifty-looking skipper, would be replaced by a jovial French hermaphrodite, its forecastle echoing with songs, and its quarter-deck elastic from much dancing.
>
> On the other side, perhaps, a magnificent New York Liner, huge as a seventy-four, and suggesting the idea of a Mivert's or Delmonico's afloat, would give way to a Sydney emigrant ship, receiving on board its live freight of shepherds from the Grampians, ere long to be tending their flocks on the hills and downs of New Holland.[8]

Samuel Walters' evocation of the great gale of January 1839 with several ships in difficulties amid a very heavy sea off Liverpool.

Chapter Eleven

Annals of the poor

T IS NOT until the nineteenth century that facts and figures become available which tell of the terrible conditions of the poor and underprivileged members of society. In the first decades of the century the wealthy moved out of the town centre and left it to be inhabited by the growing masses of the poor and destitute. At this time there were few places in the world where the contrast between rich and poor was as marked as in Liverpool and, even by the harsh standards of the time, Liverpool consistently had Lancashire's worst record of bad housing and endemic poverty.

The problem was eased, but by no means cured, by the work of the many Churches and by the charitable societies created in the early-nineteenth century. The number of places of worship had increased many fold since St Nicholas' was first joined by St Peter's in 1704. St George's dated from 1734, St Thomas' from 1748, St Pauls from 1769. These were followed by St Anne's (1773), St James (1774), Trinity (1784), Christ Church (1799), St Mary's and St Mark's (1803), St Luke's (1811), St Andrew's (1815), St Philip's (1815), St Michael's (1816), a church for the school of the blind (1818), and even a floating chapel in a converted ship anchored in the valuable mooring space of the Salthouse Dock. Baines gives an interesting description:

> This large nautical sanctuary was formed out of the ship William, of 447 tons, which was purchased by the *Seaman's Friend Society and Bethel Union,* on the 6th of October 1821, for the sum of £940, and the expense of the ship, and fitting it up as a neat and commodious chapel, after deducting the money received on the sale of the original stores was £1,051. Accommodation is here afforded to upwards of 1,000 persons, and ever since the chapel was opened, on the 16th of May, 1822, the attendance has been satisfactory to the benevolent individuals to whose piety and zeal the seamen are indebted for this accommodation.[1]

The dissenters' meeting houses from the early part of the eighteenth century became the churches of St Stephen's (1792) and St Matthew's (1795). The number of different religious denominations was legion, and by 1824 when Baines compiled his directory there were places of worship for Nonconformists, Calvinists, Scottish Presbyterians, the Society of Friends, Wesleyan Methodists, New Connection Methodists, Primitive Methodists, Welsh Methodists, Armenian Welsh,

Opposite:

St Nicholas' Church from George's Basin, 1840, by W. H. Bartlett. A very fine and authentic study from the dockside and full of atmosphere. Note the chaise, the new gaslighting, and the sailor heaving on a rope.

St Peters, 1910. One of the best loved of the old churches of Liverpool, dating from 1704 when it was built "over the pool". In its last few years the church was used as the pro cathedral of Liverpool and it was the place where people gathered on New Year's Eve to welcome in the new year.

St Georges, 1734.

St Thomas, 1748.

St. Georges Church.

St. Thomas's Church.

The east side of Irwell Street, looking towards George's Dock, showing the Mariners' Church in the dock, painted around 1869 by Herdman.

Welsh Calvinists, Welsh Independents, and five Roman Catholic churches which included St Anthony's, St Patrick's and St Peter's.

Supplementing the social work of the Churches was a prodigious number of charitable societies and allied establishments, many of which were efficiently organised by the wives of the members of the gentlemen's clubs. There was the Female Penitentiary, 'for reclaiming an unfortunate class of females', the Ladies' Charity 'to relieve poor married women in child-bed with medical assistance', the Ladies Benevolent Society which visited distressed women in their homes and the Dorcas Society which made garments for the poor. There was the Stranger's Friend Society, the Liverpool Charitable Society, the Catholic Orphan's Society, The Society for Bettering the Condition and Increasing the Comfort of the Poor, and the Charitable Institution House to name but a few.

The Marine Humane Society was formed to reward boatmen and fishermen who were prepared to go to the assistance of vessels in distress. The society placed six sets of resuscitating apparatus at various situations around the docks and had two 'newly invented pumps for drawing poisonous liquors, or ardent spirits, from the stomach, when taken to such excess as to produce suspended animation'. Members were given a set of detailed directions for restoring drowned persons, but some of the well-meaning instructions may well have misfired – 'Tobacco-smoke, or the smoke of myrrh or frankincense, is to be thrown gently into the fundament, with a proper instrument, or the bowl of a pipe covered, so as to defend the mouth of the assistant'.

The provision of schooling for the poor made great strides in the first decades of the nineteenth century. Prior to 1800 there were few schools other than the old Grammar School and a charity school for forty boys and ten girls founded in 1709 by Bryan Blundell, who became mayor of Liverpool in 1721. Blundell's school was known as the Blue Coat School and from 1717 it was housed in an attractive Queen Anne style building which was typical of the Liverpool of that period and which, unlike much of the private housing of the time, happily survived the turbulent changes of the following centuries.

Figures given by Baines show that twelve Anglican church schools were established by 1824, with seven Methodist schools, fifteen belonging to the Sunday School Union, another six Sunday schools and four day schools supported by the union and five which did not owe affiliation to any religious sect at all. Of these only four, the Blue Coat School, Hunter Street School, the Welsh Calvinists in Pall Mall and the Manesty Lane School, claimed to have existed before 1800.

The old Grammar School closed in 1810 when John Baines, the last of the schoolmasters, died. The number of children attending day school in 1824 was given as 7,165 but when the Sunday school figures were added the total increased to 11,866. At this time the Sunday schools provided a very valuable service for the poor, and for children whose parents could not afford the day-school fees they were the only place where the elements of reading and writing could be acquired.

In London Road was the School for the Blind, one of the first of its kind in the country, founded originally as the Blind Asylum in 1791. The enlightened founder, Mr Pudsey Dawson, soon discovered that the blind children had many talents, and he converted the asylum into a school. The school was soon attracting blind children from every part of the British Isles and children from abroad, regardless of birth or creed. A new, fully residential building was opened in 1808, with places for a hundred pupils.

The pioneering work of the Blind School can hardly be overrated and it was soon contributing to local industry and making a substantial income of £1,800 per annum. 'The principal occupation of the pupils', said the committee in their report of 1823, 'is spinning, hamper, and basket making; the plaiting of sash-line; the weaving of worsted rugs for hearths, carriages, and doors, of linen, and of floor cloth, and sacking; the making of sacks, and list and worsted shoes; the manufacturing of rope-twine, pack-thread, log-lines, clothes-lines, and fish-lines, of stair carpeting, and of foot-bears, points and gaskets from old ropes, and the learning of music; in the last department the attention of the committee is principally directed to qualifying the pupils for the office of organist.'[2]

As the trickle of emigrants to the New World increased to a mass exodus, the problem of Liverpool's poor and homeless increased with it. Under the new Reform Bill the old borough council was superceded in 1835 by the new more representative and democratically elected council. The boundaries of the borough were extended to include Kirkdale, Everton, part of West Derby and Toxteth Park, with Dingle Lane as the new boundary – this brought all the middle-class areas into the boundary and the council thus had the powers to raise local taxes to help with atrocious social problems which were developing in the older areas around the docklands.

In its first decade the efforts of the new council met with some measure of success, but in the 1840s came a problem so severe that no council could possibly have solved it. The problem originated in Ireland, where the terrible ravages of the Potato Famine forced many families to leave the land and seek their livelihoods elsewhere. America was the obvious place for them to go, but many could not raise the money for the fare across the Atlantic and they came instead to Liverpool where they hoped to find employment and to earn the cost of their passage across the Atlantic.

The exodus from Ireland grew from thousands to hundreds of thousands and in 1847, when it reached its peak, the figure usually quoted for the number arriving in Liverpool is three hundred thousand. 'Houses of the lowest class were so crowded during this period that it was common to see every apartment of the dwelling occupied by several families, without a partition or curtain to separate them', reads the report of the Domestic Mission, 'Every tide floated in a new importation of Irish misery, and the snow was loosened from our doors by hordes of bare-footed beggars'.

The immigrants did not all remain in Liverpool. Many did succeed in finding a passage to America, while others came and moved on to other parts of England. But those who had no money for their passage, those in the worst and lowest state of poverty, remained perforce to swell the misery of the Liverpool slums. The census returns show a population of 223,003 in 1841 rising to 376,065 in 1851. The greater part of this huge increase was in the lower social classes, many of whom were the unfortunate victims of the famine in Ireland.

There are plenty of depressing accounts of the problems of the poor. The annual report of the Domestic Mission run by the Reverend John Johns revealed 'Mothers newly become such without a garment on their persons, and with infants nearly as naked, lying upon straw or shavings, under a miserable covering, without fire or food, or the means of procuring them; children taken from their schools, in order to earn by begging . . . infirm or aged people, who were shivering out their last hours of life in absolute want'.[3]

Sailors arriving at the docks were greeted with scores of beggars lining the dock walls, who knew that the sailors went ashore for their meals at twelve noon and this was the time when they congregated on the kerbsides to accost them. Herman Melville described the scene outside Prince's Dock in about 1840:

> Every variety of want and suffering here met the eye, and every vice showed here its victims. Nor were the marvellous and almost incredible shifts and stratagems of the professional beggars, wanting to finish this picture of all that is dishonourable to civilisation and humanity.
>
> Old women, rather mummies, drying up with slow starving and age; young girls, incurably sick, who ought to have been in the hospital; sturdy men, with the gallows in their eyes, and a whining lie in their mouths; young boys, hollow-eyed and decrepit; and puny mothers, holding up puny babes in the glare of the sun, formed the main features of the scene.
>
> But these were diversified by instances of peculiar suffering, vice, or art in attracting charity, which, to me at least, who had never seen such things before, seemed to the last degree uncommon and monstrous.
>
> I remember one cripple, a young man rather decently clad, who sat huddled up against the wall, holding a painted board on his knees. It was

a picture intending to represent the man himself caught in the machinery of some factory, and whirled about among spindles and cogs, with his limbs, mangled and bloody. This person said nothing but sat silently exhibiting his board. Next to him, leaning upright against the wall, was a tall, pallid man, with a white bandage round his brow, and his face cadaverous as a corpse. He, too, said nothing; but with one finger silently pointed down to the square of flagging at his feet, which was nicely swept, and stained blue, and bore this inscription in chalk:–

'I have had no food for three days;
My wife and children are dying'[4]

In 1846 the council appointed the country's first medical officer of health, William Henry Duncan, to help with the problem. Dr Duncan estimated that about half of the working classes were living in crowded, insanitary courtyards, usually referred to simply as courts, a practice which had been condemned forty years earlier by Doctor James Currie, the opponent of the slave trade, but about which nothing had been done. The courts were the standard type of foul-smelling inner-city dwelling with inadequate sewers and no proper drainage, where the many residents shared a single contaminated water supply. They were the breeding ground of diseases like typhoid fever and cholera.

In 1847 the council spent £67,000 on poor relief, of which it claimed to have given over twenty thousand to the Irish poor and to have assisted a total of 47,194 paupers. The following year the figure had risen to £117,000. The health committee under Doctor Duncan inspected 14,085 cellars and found that 5,841 of them had wells of stagnant water beneath the floor. A total of 27,123 people were found to be living in cellars and five thousand of them were given marching orders because their abodes were pronounced unfit for human habitation. It is not obvious how they were rehoused.[5]

Of course, as Ebenezer Scrooge pointed out, there was always the workhouse. The workhouse on Brownlow Hill was rebuilt in 1842 at a cost of £25,000 and was designed to hold 1,800 inmates. The number grew until it eventually held several thousand people, enough to populate a good-sized Victorian town. In the 1850s ladies were not encouraged to visit the workhouse, but there were many better-off women who were very concerned about the conditions of the poor and they became the leading lights in the charity efforts.

Mrs Josephine Butler was one lady who successfully obtained access to the workhouse and she was shocked by the special wards, by the bridewell for women and the dingy sheds where the oakum work was done. Josephine Butler provided a home of rest for the sick and incurable poor and an industrial home to house some of the waifs and strays of the Liverpool slums.

Some of the most detailed descriptions of the scene in the 1850s come from the pen of the American writer, Nathaniel Hawthorne, who arrived in 1853 to take up the position of United States Consul in Liverpool. Hawthorne's first impression of the slums was very depressing:

I should not have conceived it possible that so many children could have been collected together, without a single trace of beauty, or scarcely of intelligence, in so much as one individual; such mean, coarse, vulgar features and figures, betraying an unmistakably low origin, and ignorant and brutal parents. They did not appear wicked, but only stupid, animal and soulless. It must require many generations of better life to elicit a soul in them. All America could not show the like.[6]

As his last sentence implies, Hawthorne was not quite an unbiased observer. He was a prime example of the transatlantic traveller of his times, common in both England and America, intensely patriotic but seeming to find fault with the other nation. Hawthorne wanted to find poverty in the old world and he had no problem in finding it. He actually admitted that he preferred the poorer streets of Liverpool to the more fashionable ones, and his passages are not entirely unsympathetic:

> Almost every day, I take walks about Liverpool; preferring the darker and dingier streets, inhabited by the poorer classes. The scenes there are very picturesque in their way; at every two or three steps, a gin-shop; also [fil]thy in clothes and person, ragged, pale, often afflicted with humors; women, nursing their babies at dirty bosoms; men haggard, drunken care-worn, hopeless, but with a kind of patience, as if all this were the rule of their life; groups stand or sit talking together, around the door-steps, or in the descent of a cellar; often a quarrel is going on in one group, for which the next group cares little or nothing.
>
> Sometimes, a decent woman may be seen sewing or knitting at the entrance of her poor dwelling, a glance into which shows dismal poverty. I never walk through these streets without feeling as if I should catch some disease; but yet there is a strong interest in such walks; and moreover there is a bustle, a sense of being in the midst of life, and having got hold of something real, which I do not find in the better streets of the city. Doubtless, this noon-day and open life of theirs is entirely the best aspect of their existence; and if I were to see them within doors, at their meals, or in bed, it would be unspeakably worse. They appear to wash their clothes occasionally; for I have seen them hanging out to dry in the street.

Nathaniel Hawthorne was such a sharp observer that he noticed and recorded the smallest details which bring an immediacy and realism to his writings. He had no need to mingle among the slums; his job and position in society enabled him to mix with the wealthy and to attend the mayor's soirées in the town hall, but he still continued with his rambles and recorded the minutae of street scenes:

> Further items of street rambles – little grey donkeys, dragging along disproportionately large carts; the anomalous aspect of cleanly dressed and healthy looking young women, whom one sometimes sees talking together in the street, – evidently residing in some contiguous house; the apparition, now and then, of a bright, intelligent, merry, child's face, with dark, knowing eyes, gleaming through the dirt like sunshine through a dusty window pane; at provisions-shops, the little bits of meat, ready for poor customers, and little heaps of selvages and corners, snipt off from points and steaks; the kindliness with which a little boy leads and lugs along his little sister; – a pale hollow-cheeked, large-eyed girl of 12, or less, paying a sad, cheerless attention to an infant; – a milkwoman, with a wooden yoke over her shoulder, and a large pail on each side; in a more reputable street, respectably dressed women going into an ale and spirit-vault, evidently to drink there; – the police men loitering along, with observant eye, holding converse with none, and seldom having occasion to interfere with anybody; – the multitudinousness and continual motion of all this kind of life. The people are as numerous as maggots in cheese; you behold them, disgusting, and all moving about, as when you raise a plank or log that has long lain on the ground, and find many vivacious bugs and insects beneath it.

The poorest areas of the town were the narrow, cramped streets and dingy alleyways around the docks. Abraham Hume, the vicar of Vauxhall, was a clergyman who was very concerned about the social welfare of the people in his parish. In 1858 he produced a map which he called *Liverpool Ecclesiastical and Social,* and upon which he marked out what he called pauper streets, semi-pauper streets, and streets of crime and immorality.

He identified two of the poorest areas. One was between Netherfield Road and the northern dock system and the second was bounded by Park Lane, St. James Street, Windsor Street, Northumberland Street and the southern docks. He was able to show that these were the two

DISEASES.	Jan.	Feb.	March	April	May	June	July	August	Sep.	October	Nov.	Dec.	Total.
Fever.	5	6	6	3	4	10	9	9	10	5	8	8	83
Mortification.				1									1
Pleurisy.	2				2								4
Inflammation of the Bowels								1	1				2
Sore Throat.		1											1
Rheumatic Fever.		1	4	1									6
Teething.	1			1		1				2		1	6
Worm Fever.								1	1				2
Small Pox.	13	13	9	4	18	16	19	25	27	29	32	14	219
Measles.			2			4	5	3	1	1	1		17
Consumption.	25	26	28	33	34	35	29	30	27	27	29	35	358
Apoplexy.	2	2	4	1	3	3	1				1	3	20
Palsy.	2	1	4		2	3	3		1		1	2	19
Convulsions.	13	9	16	19	15	4	7	7	14	4	8	4	120
Asthma.	2	9	4	4									19
Chincough.				1	1	1	2	4		7	22	7	45
Colic.							1				1		2
Purging and Vomiting.	1												1
Decay of Age.	5	8	3	2	1	1	1	4	3				28
Dropsy.	2	4	1	2	1	2	1	2	1	1			17
Jaundice.						1							1
Cancer.			2		1								3
Lying-in.	3	1		1	1	1	1	1	1		1		11
Drunkenness.	1									1			2
Want.	1						1				1		3
Casualties.	1		2			1	2	3	1	2	3	2	17
Total	79	80	84	74	83	83	81	87	92	81	110	73	1007

Infirmary 11
Still-born 25
Unknown Diseases 42

1085

Table of Mortality, as printed by Enfield.

358 died of consumption, 219 from smallpox. Two died of drunkenness, three of want, one of a sore throat. Eighteenth-century bills of mortality provide fascinating reading.

Top: *The Blue Coat Hospital.*

As late as the eighteenth century, the word hospital was still used to describe a hospice.

The picture shows the Blue Coat Chambers as they appeared in 1770. Now a grade-one listed building, this is the oldest and one of the very few eighteenth-century buildings which still survive in central Liverpool. The architect is unknown; the style is Queen Anne, with painted stone quoins and a cherub's face on the keystone over every window.

Centre: *The Poor House, 1770.*

It may look a grim establishment, but by the standards of the times it was an efficient and comfortable home for the poor of the parish. A new workhouse was opened on Brownlow Hill only two years after this engraving was made.

Bottom: *Sailor's Hospital.*

The hospital was opened in 1752, originally as an appendage to the General Infirmary. Seamen paid sixpence a month out of their wages to support it. On the right of the picture is the Townsend Mill.

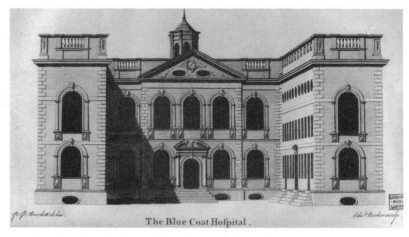

The Blue Coat Hospital.

most heavily infected areas from the cholera epidemic of 1849.

Hume drew two circles on his map, each representing a radius of five hundred yards. One was centred on his own deprived parish of Vauxhall, and the second on the Junction of Hope Street and Myrtle Street which contained the middle-class housing of Rodney Street and Abercromby Square. His first circle embraced twelve churches which served a population of 35,000 people, nearly three thousand people per church. The second circle contained twenty-seven churches and served a population of only 10,000 people, less than four hundred souls per church.

Abraham Hume concluded that Church life bore a direct relationship to social conditions in Victorian England, but to improve the conditions unfortunately required a lot more than the mere building of more churches – it required many generations of work and large numbers of dedicated social workers.

When Nathaniel Hawthorne came to visit the workhouse at West Derby, we might expect some descriptions which would turn the stomach enough to make Dickens' accounts of the workhouse look almost bearable. But Hawthorne, not for the only time in his journals, surprises us with a glowing account which makes the workhouse seem a caring and tolerable place in which to live.

> I went yesterday with Mrs Heywood and another lady, and Mr Mansfield, to the West Derby Workhouse, which Mrs Heywood, with some charitable purpose or other, had a desire to inspect. We were first shown into a room where paupers are received on their first arrival; and the superintendent of this room was a bright, cheerful old woman, between eighty and ninety years old. She has been a good many years in the workhouse, and has learned to knit since she was seventy; and kept her fingers busily employed all the time she was talking to us . . .
>
> In the next room, was the domicile of an old man and his wife; for the authorities sometimes allow old married people to live together, when there is no risk of their increasing the population of the Work-House. In another room, there was an old lady, alone, and reading; a respectable looking, intelligent old soul, with rather more refined manners than the others; so I took off my hat in her room. There was a row of books on the mantlepiece, mostly religious but with a romance amongst them . . .
>
> We went into various other rooms, into which the women were variously classified; and everywhere there were comfortable coal-fires in the open fire-places, and the women sitting quietly about them, all knitting as fast as their fingers would go. They looked well-fed and decently clothed in blue-checked gowns, all of one fashion; but none of them had a brisk cheerful air, except two or three very old persons, to whom a childish vivacity seemed to have returned with their extreme age.
>
> In one room (where there were at least a dozen women) was an old lady in bed who declared herself to be more than a hundred years old, and the Governor said a hundred and four. She was positively the cheerfulest and jauntiest person in the house; it was as if she had long ago got through with all the real business of life, and had nothing else to do but to be as merry as she could for the little while she stays here; – and so she seems to make herself a kind of old pet, whom people talk to as if she were a child, and she gives wayward, childish, half-playful answers. . .

Of the many well-meaning Victorian families who sought for a method of improving the care of the sick and the poor, few achieved as much as the Rathbones of Liverpool, who were still remembered for their efforts in the abolition of the slave trade. Mrs Rathbone was responsible for the first public baths where the poor could wash themselves and she supported a movement which led to Kitty Wilkinson converting a cellar into a public washroom where the clothing and bedding of cholera victims could be washed and cleaned before being re-used. When his wife became ill William Rathbone was very impressed by the nursing skill she received and he asked the nurse involved to treat some of the poor at his own expense. The nurse agreed to the request but 'accustomed though she was to many forms of sickness and death, she was not able to endure the sight of the misery which she encountered amongst the poor'. She asked to be released from her contract, but William Rathbone talked her round and persuaded her to stay. With an admirable sense of vocation the nurse eventually devoted the rest of her life to helping the underprivileged.

By employing a nurse to visit the sick in their homes William Rathbone started a movement which grew to become the District Nursing Society, and which eventually became a national body. He needed help and experience to further his aims and in 1861 he wrote to Florence Nightingale for advice. Miss Nightingale replied with the idea that a school be established in Liverpool for training the nurses and she suggested the means of setting up the school and gaining the support of the local authorities. Rathbone took her advice and at his own expense he founded the Liverpool Training School and the Home for Nurses.

The only way in which a hospital of the times was likely to cure a patient was through the patient's sheer determination to get out of the place once they came to realise the squalor which they had been brought into. Florence Nightingale noted that the floors of the wards were usually made of bare untreated wood, which became 'saturated with organic matter, which when washed gave off the smell of something quite other than soap and water'. Walls and ceilings were of plaster and became 'saturated with impurity'. Heating was supplied by a single fire at one end of the ward and in winter the windows were kept closed for warmth. It was sometimes months at a time before the air was changed and in some hospitals half the windows were boarded up for the whole of the winter months. After a time the smell became sickening, the walls streamed with moisture and 'a minute vegetation' appeared growing on them. The remedy was to scrub the walls with lime and scrape off the growth but the workmen employed to clean the walls frequently became seriously ill from the noxious nature of the work.[7]

William Rathbone wanted to introduce proper nursing care into the hospitals. He chose to start with the Liverpool Workhouse Infirmary which was, by the standards of the times, reasonably well administered – but the condition of the sick was miserable and there were about twelve hundred ill paupers to be cared for. Most of the nurses were recruited from among the inmates, and although they were known by the title of nurses, they must not be confused with the post-Nightingale nurse, for the job was not considered a calling or a vocation of any kind. No training was given; the nurses merely had to help with day-to-day manual tasks of looking after the inmates. Many nurses were drunkards and some were prostitutes, and no self-respecting woman would consider taking up the job as a career.

There existed a small number of paid workers, untrained parish officers, who were said to wear kid gloves in the ward to protect their hands from infection and disease. The head nurse of a large London hospital did not even attempt to defend the reputation of her staff. In the course of her long experience she claimed she had 'never known a nurse who was not drunken, and there was immoral conduct practised in the very wards, of which she gave me [Miss Nightingale] some awful examples'. Liverpool was no better. Drink was continually being smuggled into the wards. How the inmates were able to afford it is a mystery, but there were common scenes of drunken violence and on some of the wards a policeman had to patrol all night to keep order.

> The wards were an inferno, the hordes of pauper patients more degraded than animals. Vicious habits, ignorance, idiocy, met her on every side. Drunkenness was universal – thirty-five of the pauper nurses had to be dismissed for drunkenness in the first month. Immorality was universal. Filth was universal. The patients wore the same shirt for seven weeks, bedding was only changed and washed once a month, food was at starvation level, spirits entered the infirmary freely.[8]

William Rathbone, by William Smith.

The Rathbones first came to Liverpool from Cheshire in the early-eighteenth century. They quickly established themselves as respectable and successful timber merchants. No family in Liverpool has earned greater public respect than the Rathbones in their efforts to improve the conditions of the poor and underprivileged.

William Rathbone wished to improve conditions in the infirmary and Florence Nightingale suggested another nurses' training school based at one of the Liverpool hospitals. One problem was that the workhouse was managed by a committee known as the Vestry and their permission was required before anything could be done. Rathbone asked Florence Nightingale to use her influence and management abilities to win over the workhouse management to his ideas. It was a battle which lasted for about a year but Rathbone and Nightingale finally won and in 1865 the redoubtable Miss Agnes Jones arrived at the workhouse infirmary, smartly attired and ready for business with her team of twelve qualified nurses.

Florence Nightingale described Miss Jones as 'pretty and young and rich and witty, ideal in her beauty as a Louis XIV shepherdess'. The governor of the workhouse, with whom she soon quarrelled, described her as 'too strict, a stiff-necked Prebyterian Irishwoman from Ulster with a hot Irish temper'. Relations between the inflexible Agnes and the management quickly became strained – much to the dismay of William Rathbone, who predictably rushed off to London on the next train asking Florence Nightingale to help with her tact and diplomacy.

Gradually things improved, as Agnes became less rigid in her approach, while the inmates and visitors could hardly help but notice the immense improvements which she had effected and eventually even the governor had to concede that the new and efficient nursing staff had actually brought down the cost of running the hospital. When

Miss Margaret Beavan, by John A. A. Berrie.

The first woman Lord Mayor, Miss Beavan was known affectionately as 'the little mother of Liverpool'. She is still remembered for her work with children's hospitals. In 1928 she shook hands with the Mayor of Birkenhead (clad in oilskins and gumboots) under the Mersey when the pilot tunnels first met.

Josephine Butler visited the hospital she was most impressed at the new high standards of care and by the excellent work of Agnes Jones and her trained nursing staff.

Rathbone, in a speech to the House of Commons, argued that large towns like Liverpool attracted the poor and the homeless from other areas, that the burden on the rates was too large and the poor should be seen as a national problem with the bill to be footed by the whole of the community. His ideas were too far ahead of their time and it was not until the twentieth century that some of the burden was removed from the local to the national budget.

William Rathbone was an austere, unselfish, high-principled and tender-hearted man. He was outwardly dry and unemotional but he became totally captivated by his contact with Florence Nightingale and there existed a mutual respect and close relationship between them. There is little doubt that Florence admired him and his work, but his respect for her bordered on idolatory. 'In any matter of nursing Miss Nightingale is my Pope and I believe in her infallibility', he wrote. He declared himself 'proud to be one of her journeyman workers', and when she moved house to South Street (London) he presented her with a stand filled with flowering plants, which he paid to have renewed every week right up to the end of his life.

Of the many thousands who have a claim to hold a place in the history of Liverpool there are none who deserve be remembered more than men and women such as William Rathbone, Agnes Jones, Kitty Wilkinson, and William Duncan and Josephine Butler. Their work was continued by Father Nugent, Canon Major Lester and in the twentieth century by the work of Eleanor Rathbone and Margaret Beavan. They did not and could not solve the impossible problems they were faced with in their times, but they dedicated their lives to the underprivileged. They left things far better than they found them, and they eased the burden of human suffering as much as it was within their power to do. They have many successors among the hospital and social workers of twentieth-century Liverpool, among the Church workers, among the police and the teaching professions and among those whose work is with the poorer classes and the socially deprived.

Chapter Twelve

Gateway to the Empire

FOUR-DAY music festival was held every three years in the church of St Peter. The city fathers expect us to believe that it was for this reason that they built the massive architectural pile which they called Saint George's Hall. The music festival was in fact the catalyst which stimulated plans for a grand concert hall, and a competition was held for the best design. At much the same time the Corporation arranged a second competition for a new assize court. The winner of both competitions was Harvey Lonsdale Elmes, a gifted architect who was only twenty-three years old at the time. The Corporation then changed their plans and asked Elmes to design a building which would accommodate the concert hall and the assize court together under one roof. The architect readily obliged.

The foundation stone was laid in 1838 to mark the occasion of Queen Victoria's coronation. This was a token gesture to honour the new queen, for Elmes' designs were not yet complete. Building commenced about four years later and a superb classical edifice of Darleydale stone began to appear. Huge columns of red granite supported a mighty tunnel vault combining massive Roman features with the more delicate Greek columns. Engineering problems had to be solved, such as hollow blocks to lighten the load of the vaulting over the great hall, and the air conditioning system whereby the air was passed over jets of water to clean it before being driven along the heating ducts by steam-powered fans.

The young architect did not live to see his work finished. He died 'a martyr to architecture' in 1847 and Saint George's Hall was completed under the guidance of Professor C. R. Cockerell who, among other things, was responsible for the superb interior design of the concert hall. Saint George's Hall was inaugurated on the 18th of September 1854 and when Queen Victoria first saw it she was sufficiently impressed to declare it to be 'worthy of ancient Athens'. The architectural world thought very highly of Elmes' design and the architect Richard Norman Shaw spoke for many when he called it 'one of the great edifices of the world'. It was by any standards a magnificent and impressive structure.[1]

Lime Street and St John's Gardens became the fashionable parade for Victorian Liverpool and other civic buildings to complement Saint

Overleaf, top: The soot-blackened Victorian heart of Liverpool, showing St. George's Hall, surely one of the grandest buildings in the north of England, together with the Central Libraries, Picton Reading Room and Walker Art Gallery in the background on William Brown Street. The roof of Lime Street Station can just be seen, bottom right.

In the foreground is the North Western Hotel, opened in 1871 to the designs of Alfred Waterhouse, well known as the architect of Liverpool University and Manchester Town Hall. This solid and beautiful Victorian building is now in great danger of being demolished.

Overleaf, bottom: Sir James Allanson Picton, by William B. Boadle.

James Picton, one of Liverpool's greatest historians. His Memorials of Liverpool *appeared as two volumes in 1873, followed by his selections from the municipal archives published in 1883 and 1886. He is remembered by the Picton Reference Library, where he laid the foundation stone in 1875.*

George's Hall were constructed in the second half of the nineteenth century, so that by late-Victorian times a superb collection of neo-classical architecture graced this part of the city centre.

The William Brown Library, with a portico of six Corinthian columns, was built in 1860, its original purpose being to house the natural history collection of the 13th Earl of Derby which was bequeathed to the town in 1851. William Brown was a wealthy merchant who offered to defray much of the cost and was rewarded with a street name and a library named after him.

The Picton Reading Room was built between 1875 and 1879, designed by Cornelius Sherlock and modelled on the reading room at the British Library in London. The library was named after the historian James Picton, knighted in 1881, who wrote the most comprehensive history of Liverpool ever undertaken.

The Walker Art Gallery was opened in 1877, built to designs by H. H. Vale, with impressive statues of Raphael and Michelangelo positioned on each side of the main entrance and with friezes to portray local events such as the granting of the first charter by King John. Above the portico was a matronly figure representing Liverpool herself, crowned with a laurel wreath and holding a trident in one hand and a ship's propellor in the other.

Outside the Art Gallery was the Steble fountain with the bronze centrepieces representing the four seasons. It was erected in 1879, the gift of Colonel R. F. Steble, a former mayor of Liverpool. In 1884, Sessions House was added to the group, a classical design by F. and G. Holme. The frontage of five bays was designed with a portico of four paired Corinthian columns and with the coat of arms of Lancashire County Council located in the pediment. Inside, an Italian Renaissance-style staircase gave access to the upper floors.

No self-respecting Victorian centre was complete without a memorial to the Duke of Wellington's victory at Waterloo and in Liverpool a column was inaugurated in 1863. Designed by George Anderson Lawton of Glasgow, it was an exact replica of the Melville monument in Edinburgh, with a fluted Doric column, 132-feet high, of Darley-dale stone with reliefs on the base showing the grand charge at Waterloo. The Duke's statue was cast from the metal of French guns captured after the battle. On the west side iron pegs marked out the Board of Trade standard measurement table.

On the other side of Lime Street was the railway station completed in 1836, the major terminus for Liverpool. The railway companies competed to produce the best in station architecture, and when the Liverpool, Crosby and Southport line was extended from Waterloo to Tithebarn Street in 1850 the new terminus, which also served the line to Ormskirk and Preston, was described in typically exaggerated terms as 'A magnificent structure built at enormous expense . . . second in architectural effect to none in Liverpool'. It lasted less than forty years before it was found to be too small and was replaced by Exchange Station in 1884-88.

On the Cheshire side of the Mersey the Chester and Birkenhead Railway opened in 1840 and the Hoylake Railway carrying commuter traffic followed soon afterwards. It was obvious that a tunnel beneath the Mersey would be of great value to the traffic between Liverpool and the Wirral, but the drawbacks of steam traction for an underground railway were very obvious and in 1866 the Mersey Pneumatic Railway was proposed, with trains travelling at great speed along sealed and partially evacuated pneumatic tubes. This advanced idea was too far ahead of its time, and it was not until 1880 that shafts and trial

William Brown, by Sir John Watson Gordon.

Remembered by William Brown Street, which was formerly known as Shaw's Brow, Brown was a wealthy merchant who paid for the building of the William Brown Library and Museum, the museum being built originally to house the natural history collection of the thirteenth Earl of Derby.

headings were built for a tunnel. The first contractor of the Mersey Tunnel Railway failed, but Major Samuel Isaac took up the challenge and had successfully completed the work by 1886. It was a very great engineering achievement for the times. Gore described the grand opening ceremony by the Prince of Wales. He was more concerned about the royalty and the pomp of the reception at the Town Hall than in the engineering works:

> His Royal Highness the Prince of Wales, accompanied by his two sons, Prince Albert Victor of Wales and Prince Edward George of Wales (guests for the time being of the Duke of Westminster), left Eaton Hall and journeyed, via Chester and Birkenhead, through the Mersey Tunnel Railway to James Street Station, Liverpool. On alighting, they were received by his Worship the Mayor, David Radcliffe Esq. JP, the Lord Lieutenant of the County and Lady Sefton, Lord Claud and Lady Hamilton, and others. His Royal Highness then declared the Mersey Tunnel Railway open. The Royal Party proceeded to the Town Hall, where an address was presented to H. R. H. by the Corporation – this was followed by a dejeuner. His Worship the Mayor availed himself of the opportunity of presenting H. R. H. Prince George with a handsome sword, indicative of his rank as Lieutenant RN, and H. R. H. Prince Albert Victor with an elegant volume, containing photographic views of Liverpool &c. Their Royal Highnesses then left by Lime Street Station for London.[2]

It was the twentieth of January, and in the afternoon the tunnel was opened and several thousand members of the public were allowed the novel experience of walking under the river to the other side. It was Major Isaac's crowning achievement, and his name was perpetuated on the company's first locomotive, but the strain of building the tunnel was too much for his health and he died soon afterwards.

Liverpool has always been very progressive when it came to trying out new forms of transport, and only seven years after the tunnel opened another pioneering railway was built along the dockside. The Electrical Overhead Railway was an elevated structure, built above the roadway to carry passenger traffic and dock workers. Elevated railways were popular in some of the American cities, but the Overhead was the only experiment of its kind in Britain.

From the start the Overhead was a big tourist attraction, for when the line was completed it provided a superb view of the whole of the Liverpool Docks and passengers could view shipping from all over the world in full operational order – an exciting and novel sight to visitors from the inland towns. Liverpool had by this time sacrificed all of its coastline to commerce but it was still a popular tourist area, partly because of the grandeur of the civic centre and partly because of the popularity of the growing seaside resort of New Brighton, which holidaymakers reached by means of the ferry from Pier Head.

The railways provided a local transport system for some of the outlying areas. Other suburbs were served by a network of horse-drawn omnibuses which ran from 1830, with tramlines first appearing in the 1860s. As with most urban transport systems the first routes were operated by a number of local companies, often competing for the same custom. In 1898 the Corporation was able to purchase the whole of the tramway system, which had grown to over a hundred miles of track and they started to convert to electrical traction. The main tram termini were at Pier Head, St George's Crescent, and the Old

Opposite, top: The Overhead Railway under construction, around 1890. A span of the deck is lowered into position by Ives' Patent Gantry. It appears that prefabricated sections of the Overhead were brought along the existing deck and progressively lowered into position. One report has it that the Overhead was so well built that the firm contracted to demolish it in the 1950s went bankrupt because it was taking so long to pull it down!

Opposite, bottom: The Overhead Railway and Dock Road at the Pier Head. This view dates from before the war when mixed traffic still included many horse-drawn vehicles. The hoardings are full of interest, particularly the one advertising the popular trips to view the docks and the liners. Note the tangle of overhead tram wires.

A fascinating painting by John Pride of the Goree Piazzas in 1939, just two years before they were destroyed by the Luftwaffe in the Blitz. Underneath the Overhead Railway is another train and, just discernible in front of it, by the second pillar from the right, is the man whose sole job was to walk ahead of the train with a red flag to warn of its approach – an amazing and seemingly pointless exercise, since at this date (faster and quieter) electric trams were operating along something like eighty miles of track without the services of such an 'early warning system'. Local folklore still perpetuates the unlikely story that slaves were once chained to the iron rings in the arches of the Goree and in the cellars of Tom Hall's pub on the corner.

Haymarket.

There was another important transport development which was not so popular in Liverpool. It was the Manchester Ship Canal, first proposed in 1825, the same year as the first proposal for a Mersey Tunnel. As with the tunnel, it was not until the 1880s that the technology and the resources to build the canal became available. A Bill came before a House of Commons Select Committee in 1885 and the canal was constructed between 1887 and 1894.

Unlike the railway sixty years earlier, it was not to be 'the Liverpool and Manchester' Canal. Liverpool provided a few speculative shareholders but the city as a whole strongly opposed the idea. The Manchester manufacturers were tired of their dependence on Liverpool and of the fact that they were forced to pay port dues on all their imports and exports. The idea of a canal to bypass Liverpool was one which greatly appealed to them, and the ship canal was a big financial success, with everywhere except Liverpool benefiting from it. The prophets of doom forecast the total collapse of trade through Liverpool, but, as with the abolition of the slave trade which the very old could still remember, the Jeremiahs were wrong again. Deep sea vessels were growing contantly in size and the facilities at Manchester were necessarily expensive and limited. The trade through the Port of Liverpool was checked by the opening of the ship canal, but it recovered very quickly.

In 1857 control of the docks passed from the town council into the hands of the Mersey Docks and Harbour Board, which was created on the recommendation of the Board of Trade. The board controlled not only the docks on the Liverpool frontage but also the Birkenhead Docks. There were twenty-eight board members, four of whom were nominated by the Mersey Conservancy Commissioners (i.e. by the First Lord of the Admiralty, the President of the Board of Trade, and the Chancellor of the Duchy of Lancaster), and the other twenty-four were democratically elected by all persons paying rates on goods or ships of more than ten pounds per annum. Members were obliged to live within ten miles of the port or borough boundary, a rule which was probably aimed at keeping the Manchester party off the committee.

The number of vessels plying in and out of Liverpool grew slowly in the latter half of the nineteenth century, increasing by only ten per cent in fifty years and even decreasing in some years. The volume of trade, however, increased by a factor of five over the same period, and this was because the average size of the ships increased tenfold as steam increasingly gained ground over sail and as facilities to handle larger ships became available. The figures for the registered shipping show the distribution of sail and steam during this period:

Shipping registered in Liverpool, 1850-1906[3]						
YEAR	SAIL		STEAM		TOTAL	
	No. of Ships	Tonnage	No. of Ships	Tonnage	No. of Ships	Tonnage
1850	1,750	503,224	93	11,411	1,843	514,635
1860	2,228	933,723	223	67,885	2,451	1,001,608
1870	2,155	1,156,566	456	280,807	2,611	1,437,373
1880	1,824	999,809	667	555,062	2,491	1,554,871
1890	1,352	916,726	967	1,006,713	2,319	1,923,439
1900	1,018	614,968	1,073	1,713,506	2,091	2,328,474
1906	914	410,251	1,305	2,401,432	2,219	2,811,683

Liverpool was no longer challenging for the place of second port in the kingdom – it was challenging for the title of first port, with London itself as the only rival. London at this time had fifty per cent more ships than Liverpool, but as we have seen the number of ships was not a fair measure of the amount of trade. The Mersey could handle larger ships than the Thames and the average vessel on the Mersey was twice the size of the average vessel on the Thames, so that the tonnage registered in Liverpool was one third greater than in London.

In terms of trade, the London cargoes were more valuable, at £261 million in the year 1905, compared to £237 million at Liverpool – all of which shows that the unscrupulous statistician can use the figures to prove whatever he wishes by choosing figures for ships, tonnage or trade.

Trade figures from the same source for the rest of the world show £221 million for New York, £196 million for Hamburg, £147 million for Antwerp and £86 million for Marseilles – all of which helped to prove Liverpool's claim to be the second city of the British Empire and the leading seaport of the world's leading maritime nation.

To the connoisseur of ships London was definitely an inferior port to Liverpool, with smaller ships, a shallow river and no watery horizon for the sun to set into. John Masefield, future poet laureate, was born in a southern county, but Masefield understood Liverpool and spent some of his formative years there – he knew what was at the heart of

Opposite, top: The massive hulk of the Great Eastern *beached at New Ferry in 1888 before her demolition. She was the largest ship afloat for thirty years.*

Opposite bottom: The Princes' Landing Stage photographed some time before the First World War, with passengers waiting to board a White Star liner.*

Left: A luxury liner, the Brittanic, *at a crowded Princes' Landing Stage.*

Below: An excellent view of Salthouse Dock in around 1907. Begun in 1734, Salthouse was one the earliest docks to be built; Albert Dock, just visible on the right, was built to seaward about a hundred years later. Wapping is on the left.

the city and when he came to live at Greenwich he could not help but compare the Thames to the Mersey:

> It is a wretched river after the Mersey, and the ships are not like the Liverpool ships, and the docks are barren of beauty. But the sailor-town is yet the one human part of London, and I hope I shall find happiness . . . in wandering about among the crimps, by the marine stores, with a sailor as a comrade, and a quid of jacky in my cheek. But it is a beastly hole after Liverpool; for Liverpool is the town of my heart and I would rather sail a mud-flat there than command a clipper ship out of London.[4]

In the autumn of 1891, John Masefield came as a young boy of thirteen to join the training ship *HMS Conway,* an old wooden-walled sailing vessel moored in the River Mersey. One of the first sights which young Jack witnessed was the four-masted barque *Wanderer* leaving the Mersey in full sail. It was a sight so fine that nearly forty years later Masefield wrote about it in both verse and prose.

John Masefield was an average apprentice. He did his stanchions and brass work well and when he did the sweeping up he did not try and hide the dust in an odd corner, but he failed miserably at manning the pumps – 'He is no good on the bilge pump. He lost us half our butter that time. He doesn't even know the tucks of an eye-splice yet.' But John Masefield had a genius for words which has seldom been equalled in the English language and he loved to use that gift to describe the ships and the sea. He regretted the passing of the age of sail and he described his memories of the Mersey and of the many ships and colleagues he remembered from his youth:

> Though I tell many, there must still be others,
> McVickar Marshall's ships and Fernie Brothers',
> Lochs, Counties, Shires, Drums, the countless lines
> Whose house-flags all were once familiar signs
> At high main-trucks on Mersey's windy ways
> When sunlight made the wind-white water blaze.
> Their names bring back old mornings, when the docks
> Shone with their house-flags and their painted blocks,
> Their raking masts below the Custom House
> And all the marvellous beauty of their bows.

Ships were built and, more especially, repaired in Liverpool, though Lairds of Birkenhead far outstripped her in building steamships during the boom of the 1860s and 1870s. Engineering firms and foundries were large employers, but unlike the cotton towns inland Liverpool had few factory operatives and therefore few job opportunities for women and children in the nineteenth century. Import processing remained important, as seen from the high investment in chemicals, sugar refining and tobacco. Glass and, increasingly, soap manufacture employed many Merseysiders and work became more and more diverse. Liverpool remained very distinctively a sea port, however, and because most of her industries were related directly or indirectly to the prosperity of the port, the town and its casually-employed dockers were highly vulnerable to recession.

In Victoria's long reign two new charters were granted. The charter of 1880 at last recognised the fact that Liverpool was a great world trading centre and raised it to the status of a city. In the same year a bishopric was created, which meant that plans could begin to be made to build a cathedral. In 1893 there followed a second charter which, among other concessions, allowed the first citizen to be called by the title of Lord Mayor. Two years later there was another boundary extension which almost trebled the land area of the city by taking in West Derby, Wavertree, Toxteth and Walton. The time when Liverpool had been part of West Derby manor and Walton parish was forgotten by all except the historians. Figures from the 1901 census show that the population inside the new city boundary was 684,947.

In keeping with the cultural life of Liverpool was the Philharmonic Orchestra which became the Royal Liverpool Philharmonic and which had its home in the Philharmonic Hall built between 1846 and 1849. The Historic Society of Lancashire and Cheshire was founded in 1848, and technical education was provided by the Mechanics Institute which had existed as early as 1825.

The Liverpool Academy of Arts was another nineteenth-century foundation, and the theatre and performing arts were always well supported. The Victoria Building on Brownlow Hill was built between 1887 and 1892 to the designs of Alfred Waterhouse and housed the University College. It was this building which became the head-quarters of the University of Liverpool in 1903. Strictly speaking, the long-awaited university was an Edwardian rather than a Victorian foundation, but the neo-gothic architecture of red brick and terracotta was genuine Victorian and very typical and symbolic of the new universities founded in the great industrial cities of the North and the Midlands and which quickly achieved very high academic standards – they became known as red-brick universities.

The Pier Head developed into an important centre. It was a busy stop on the Overhead Railway and a major tramway terminal, but the main reason why it became a centre of activity was as the embarkation point for the Mersey ferries; for the pleasure steamers connecting the seaside resorts of Lancashire, Cheshire and North Wales; for the packet boats to Ireland and the Isle of Man; and also for the tenders serving the glamorous ocean-going liners of the late-nineteenth century.

The George's landing stage, a floating stage very near the dock of the same name, was opened in 1847, partly to serve the growing emigrant traffic. The Prince's landing stage, opened in 1876, was a much larger affair. It was half a mile in length and was therefore capable of serving ferries, pleasure boats, tenders and packets all at the same time.

In the early years of the twentieth century George's Dock suffered the same fate as the Old Dock a hundred years earlier and was drained and filled in – this enabled the land at the Pier Head to be redeveloped. The offices of the Mersey Docks and Harbour Board were completed in 1907, an impressive block with a fine classical frontage, with cupulas on each corner of the roof and a high church dome dominating the centre of the building. Soon after its completion a new and larger office block was planned on the site of the dock just to the north.

The new structure became the best-loved and most famous building of the Liverpool waterfront and the Atlantic seaboard. The Royal Liver Building, built to house the head offices of the Royal Liver Friendly Society, was designed by Aubrey Thomas as one of the world's first reinforced-concrete structures. The main office block, decorated in the ornate fashion of the times, rose to a height of ten deep storeys and was adorned with a dome at each corner and two elaborate towers rising in stages to a height almost as high again as the main block. The towers were situated centrally at the east and west ends of the building and housed a clock, affectionately known as Great George, which was completed in 1911 and set in motion at the precise moment of the crowning of King George V in Westminster Abbey. The crowning feature of the Royal Liver Building itself was a stroke of great genius – the famous mythical Liver Birds were perched on top of the towers at a height of over three hundred feet above the ground.

The original Liver Bird was an eagle, the ancient symbol of Saint John which was later adopted by King John and used on his coinage. The first depiction of the eagle, carrying a sprig of foliage in its beak, appears on a seal from 1352, but it is impossible for any ornithologist to deduce the species of this degenerate medieval bird without some inside information on the matter. When the Borough of Liverpool was granted a coat of arms in 1797, the bird became a tall and graceful cormorant which carried a small bunch of seaweed in its beak, representing the 'laver' or 'lever' part of the placename. When the new bishopric of Liverpool was granted arms in 1882, the eagle was correctly restored to the arms, but the Liver Birds have entered into the realms of popular mythology, where they will always remain watching over the Mersey waterfront from their high perch.

A few years later a third building completed the trio at the Pier Head. It was the office of the famous Cunard Steamship Company. The age of the luxury liner had arrived and the contrast between the ocean-going passenger vessels which first appeared in the eighteen-nineties and those which made the passage across the Atlantic fifty years earlier could hardly have been more marked. Standards of comfort and safety had improved beyond all recognition.

The shipping lines claimed that their vessels were stately homes at sea and the claim was nothing short of the truth. The *Luciana,* built in 1893 for the Cunard Line, offered spacious passenger lounges, reading rooms, saloons with wooden wainscoat panelling, open coal fires and the new electric light. The decor and interior furnishings were the elaborate upholstery, draperies, mirrors and chandeliers of the late-Victorian age. The dining room with its Ionic pillars, long banqueting tables and richly patterned tablecloth could do justice to a town hall and every meal was good enough for a civic reception. Six bakers, three confectioners and four butchers were constantly preparing food and the cooking stoves in the saloon galley were twenty-five feet long and four feet wide. Even the second- and third-class passengers were provided with berth cabins of various sizes. The *Luciana* carried 450 passengers first class, 300 second class and 700 in third class or steerage. With a crew of 400, she was a floating town which plied back and forth across the Atlantic.

Even the lavish *Luciana* could not compare in grandeur to the four-funnelled *Lusitania* which was launched in 1907 and could carry up to three thousand passengers. When the *Lusitania* left the Mersey on her maiden voyage to New York in 1907, she was the largest and most luxurious ship afloat. The banks of the Mersey were thronged with hundreds of thousands of people who had turned out to see her leave for New York; the river was crowded with tugs and ferry boats flying flags and bunting, fussing about to try and get a better view of the departure and to give her a rousing send-off.

The *Lusitania* was the most powerful vessel ever built and was to challenge for the Blue Riband awarded to the fastest crossing of the North Atlantic. It was dusk and nine o'clock on a September evening when the great ship sounded her hooter and sent a flock of seagulls flapping and screaming across the Mersey Estuary. The electrical generator was started and the ship became a romantic floating fairy palace of a thousand glittering lights, shimmering and reflecting in the waters below. She made the fastest crossing ever and brought New York less than five days' sail from Liverpool. Only two months later she was joined by a sister ship, the *Mauretania,* which sailed for New York on November the 16th to an equally rapturous send-off.

For many years these floating palaces were the most luxurious liners on the Atlantic; the ill-fated *Titanic* would have been their only serious challenger. They evoked a sense of awe and wonder wherever they went, and their arrival in New York and Liverpool was an event frequently reported by the local press. The *Lusitania* was sunk by a German submarine during the First World War, but the *Mauretania* was still operational in the 1920s and the two Cunarders held the coveted Blue Riband between them for more than twenty years. Franklin D. Roosevelt did not normally enjoy sea voyages, but his impressions of the *Mauretania* caused him to modify his opinions:

> Every ship has a soul. But the *Mauretania* had one you could talk to. At times she could be wayward and contrary as a thoroughbred. To no other ship belonged that trick of hers – that thrust and dip and drive into the seas and through them, which would wreck the rails of the Monkey Island with solid sea, or playfully spatter salt water on the Captain's boiled shirt as he took a turn on the bridge before going down to dinner. At other times, she would do everything her Master wanted of her with a right good will. As Captain Rostron once said to me, she had the manners and deportment of a great lady and behaved herself as such.[5]

Another of the passengers, Theodore Drieser, described something of the decor, the catering and the formal dinner:

> There were several things about this great ship that were unique. It was a beautiful thing all told – its long cherry-wood panelled halls . . . its heavy porcelain baths, its dainty state-rooms fitted with lamps, bureaux, writing desks, wash stands, closets and the like. I liked the idea of dressing for dinner and seeing everything quite stately and formal. The little be-buttoned call-boys in their tight-fitting blue suits amused me. And the bugler who bugled for dinner! That was a most musical sound he made, trilling the various quarters gaily as much as to say, 'This is a very joyous event, ladies and gentlemen: we are all happy; come, come; it is a delightful feast.'

It was in the days when Liverpool held the luxury passenger traffic across the North Atlantic that the Adelphi Hotel was rebuilt. The first Adelphi dated from 1868-9. It was built on the site of the White Horse Tavern and was owned by the Midland Railway Company. Charles Dickens described the Adelphi as the best hotel in the world. The turtles for the famous turtle soup were kept in a tank in the basement. The new hotel, built in 1912 to the designs of Frank Atkinson, was even grander than the building it replaced and catered for the first-class transatlantic passengers from the luxury liners.

In 1901 an architectural competition for the new cathedral was held and the young architect Giles Gilbert Scott was the winner with a design which incorporated a pair of twin towers. Scott later revised his design to give a massive central tower and although the time taken to build the cathedral did not compare to the medieval cathedrals it was not until 1942 that the central tower was completed. The cathedral has often been criticised as an out-dated example of Gothic revival architecture, but seen in the perspective of the nineteenth century when the bishopric of Liverpool was created, the architecture was the only style possible and it readily embodies the spirit of the late-Victorian era. It does not pretend to be a medieval creation. Seen in its own right it is a magnificent structure that is symbolic of the age in which it was created and a worthy addition to the Liverpool skyline.

The twentieth century has made many other additions of various merit to the architecture of Liverpool, but it also removed many valuable buildings from previous ages. The church of St Peter's, built in 1704, before the time of the first dock, and the oldest building in Liverpool before it was demolished in the 1920s, was deemed to be redundant when the cathedral was under construction. Much of the best civic architecture of Victorian Liverpool, however, happily survived to give the city centre a sense of style and character to be enjoyed by posterity. What did not and could not survive were the last tall ships of the great days of sail. The masts, yards and ropes and rigging, the sheets and sails and swelling canvasses were remembered with nostalgia by the *Conway*'s most famous cadet:

Opposite, top: The Mauretania, *sister ship to the ill-fated* Lusitania, *sunk by a German U-boat in 1915 with the loss of 1,201 lives. The* Mauretania *was still operational in the 1920s and was highly praised for the unashamed Edwardian luxury in which (first-class) passengers were entertained during the crossing.*

Opposite, bottom: A far cry from the early trans-Atlantic passenger vessels which first carried travellers and emigrants to the New World – and, indeed, a far cry from modern air travel today!

Real windows with curtains instead of portholes, beautifully crafted marble wash-stands, luxurious beds and decor – no expense is spared to pamper the travellers in this first-class cabin.

These splendid ships, each with her grace, her glory,
Her memory of old song or comrade's story,
Still in my mind the image of life's need,
Beauty in hardest action, beauty indeed,
'They built great ships and sailed them' sounds most brave
Whatever arts we have or fail to have;
I touch my country's mind, I come to grips
With half her purpose, thinking of these ships
That art untouched by softness, all that line
Drawn ringing hard to stand the test of brine,
That nobleness and grandeur, all that beauty
Born of a manly life and bitter duty,
That splendour of fine bows which yet could stand
The shock of rollers never checked by land.
That art of masts, sail-crowded, fit to break,
Yet stayed to strength and backstayed into rake,
The life demanded by that art, the keen,
Eye-puckered, hard-case seaman, silent lean,
They are grander things than all the art of towns,
Their tests are tempests and the sea that drowns,
They are my country's line, her great art done
By strong brains labouring on the thought unwon,
They mark our passage as a race of men,
Earth will not see such ships as those again.[6]

Right: *Liverpool University, painted in 1949 by A. P. Tankard. The University was an important institution in the city and is still one of the most popular with students today. It has now been joined by Liverpool Polytechnic.*

Below: *One of the best-known and best-loved waterfronts in the world. The Pierhead with its three grand buildings and the floating landing stage packed with people; this view from the 1930s shows the Goree Piazzas which were bombed in the Blitz. In the background can be seen the tallest chimney in Liverpool, belonging to Musgrave's chemical works; the chimney was used as a navigational aid by sailors.*

Opposite, centre left: *Negro tipster, Aintree 1901. As a Liverpudlian character, with policeman's uniform and sergeant's stripes, this takes some beating.*

Opposite, centre right: *a dark inner-city court, on Burlington Street, with a 'Mary Ellen' fruit cart in the middle. Most of these courts had two toilets and a single water tap for all its residents.*

Opposite, bottom left: *Chisenhale Street Bridge on the Leeds and Liverpool Canal. Factories and mills used water for cooling purposes and returned it to the canal considerably warmer than before. This not only meant that the canal was less likely to freeze over, but that children often swam in it. The original canal terminus at Leeds Street was built over in the 1960s and access is no longer allowed onto the canal in the city centre. Compare the same view in 1802 on page 111.*

Opposite, bottom right: *A public wash-house, where housewives would go to do the weekly wash and chat with friends and neighbours. Liverpool's first wash-house was in Cornwallis Street.*

Left: St. Nicholas' Church in the background marks where the original shoreline of Liverpool used to be. All of the foreground, including the line of the Overhead Railway, the Princes' Landing Stage and all of the docks are on reclaimed land. Nearly all early photographs show this area to have been thronged with people, with all kinds of street performers out to make a penny or two from the passers-by.

Right: *The Walker Art Gallery forms part of one of the most attractive ranges of public buildings in the country.*

Centre left: *The Town Hall in around 1890. A magnificent public building that, unfortunately, cannot be opened to the public on a general basis. Here we see it with cabs waiting for fares and a horse-drawn tram complete with gentlemen on the roof. Horse trams were gradually replaced with electric ones from 1898 to 1901.*

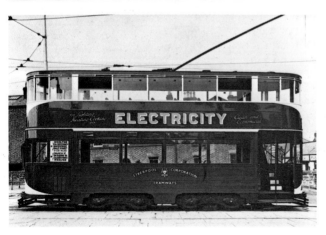

Chapter Thirteen

War and Depression

HE Liverpool birth rate, in spite of a steady decline throughout the Victorian period, was still very high and was quoted as 31.7 per 1,000 in 1907, compared to the national average of 26.3. The death rate was given as 32.5 per 1,000 in 1861-70. Falling to 20.4 by the period 1901-7, it stood at about 26 per 1,000 during the first three decades of the century, but William Farr's statistical work showed that much higher death rates of up to 39 per 1,000 had existed in the 1840s and even as late as 1870 in some of the poorer parts. Another source put the death rate in 1837 at a staggering 71 per thousand! The improvement at the start of the new century was commendable but still a long way above the figure of 17 per 1,000 which Farr took to be indicative of poor surroundings in his times.

The Victorians gave us the first photographic record of our towns and cities to lend visual support to the findings of the official health reports. Pioneers like Francis Frith and Arthur Priestley depicted the great civic buildings and main thoroughfares, while Thomas Burke and C. F. Inston concentrated on the back streets, the slums and the ordinary people. Parts of Liverpool, it would seem, were little changed from the scenes described by Hawthorne and others in the 1850s.

The Great War of 1914-18 did nothing to improve the social and living conditions of the great majority of people. Some 13,500 Liverpudlians are reckoned to have died in foreign fields while, back home, the sheer scale of the conflict meant that far more people were involved than in any previous war. With so many men away at the front, there were moves in 1916 to break the traditional male monopoly at the docks and to employ women as porters but these were defeated by the dock labourers' union and women were left to find what work they could in the expanding sectors of retailing and the other traditionally male occupation of office work. The docks remained buoyant, the quantity of merchandise shipped through the port during the war was high, but indications of hard times ahead came when it appeared that in 1918 the number of ships using the port was scarcely half of the pre-war total.

With regard to the war at sea, after the Battle of Jutland the Germans concentrated their efforts on submarines and U-boats, with a policy of destroying as much merchant shipping as possible. In the middle years

Opposite

Centre right: Tilling-Stevens petrol-electric motor bus, 1915.

An excellent picture of one of the earliest Liverpool motor buses, complete with driver, conductor and passenger. The outside staircase is just visible at the rear. With such a well developed tram network, motor buses only really came into their own in the late '50s.

Bottom left: A new tram photographed in 1933 at the Woolton terminus. On the 10pm trams you could even post a letter on board.

Bottom right: The last 'Green Goddess' seen in Liverpool, now a museum piece. Between 1934 and 1939, 362 new, modern trams like this were introduced in Liverpool, providing a more comfortable service than before. Lines were gradually extended to the suburbs and, when the line to Kirkby Industrial Estate was completed in 1943, a journey of nine miles was possible to the Pier Head. By 1945 over 90 miles of tramlines were in use and a tram enthusiast could go as far as Stockport or Rochdale, by changing to other operators' vehicles. By the mid-1950s, the trams were seen as obsolete and phased out, so that by September 1957 they had ceased to be a feature of the Liverpool streetscene.

Family Group, by C. F. Inston.
  An emotive study by one of the great pioneering photographers at work in Liverpool. The family are poor but proud, the children are well shod and show no signs of poverty in their faces.

Fishwives, around 1900, by C. F. Inston.
  Liverpool may have long outgrown its fishing-village origins, but the fishwives still remain, perhaps the (second?) oldest profession in town.

of the war hardly a day went by in Liverpool without a report coming through of a merchant vessel sunk at sea.[1]

The Germans did not draw the line at the sinking of naval and merchant vessels. On the 7th of May 1915 a German submarine torpedoed the passenger liner *Lusitania* on her voyage from New York to Liverpool. The luxury liner sank about ten miles off the Irish coast near the Old Head of Kinsale, with a death toll of 1,201 out of the 2,661 on board. The whole world was so shocked by the incident that there were riots in the streets of London. 124 of the drowned passengers were American civilians and the sinking of the *Lusitania* played a very influential part in the decision of the United States to enter a war in which she did not wish to become involved.

The Mersey ferries played their part in the Great War when the Wallasey boats *Iris* and *Daffodil* were used to transport landing parties of Royal Marines to Zeebrugge for an attack on a German U-boat base. The marines fought well and no fewer than eleven VCs were awarded to those who took part in the action. The raid was considered to be a success but casualties were very heavy, with 176 dead and 472 injured. The ferries themselves suffered extensive damage but they both returned to the Mersey still afloat. In recognition of their part at Zeebrugge they were allowed the prefix 'Royal' before their names.

Life in the 1920s and 1930s was hard. Unemployment (and underemployment) had always been a feature of life on the docks. While the wage rates for those in work were good and consistently higher than those in the cotton towns, much of the work was casual, with no guarantee of employment from one day to the next. Many dockers were fortunate to average three days' work a week and there was little chance for wives to supplement the family income by working. At its worst, over a quarter and sometimes as many as a third of the insured labour force was out of work and, while this was not as high as in some cotton towns, it stubbornly refused to fall and in 1939 the unemployment rate was still double the national average. More worrying still was the mounting problem of long-term unemployment, particularly among young men.

Housing presented a seemingly even more daunting challenge than the lack of steady work. Liverpool Corporation was actually a pioneer of council house building. It began a modest programme as early as 1869, and expanded it considerably at the turn of the century so that by 1915 some 2,900 flats and houses had been constructed. 20,000 'insanitary' houses had been demolished since 1864 and only(!) 2,770 back-to-back houses remained to blight the city centre. In fact, the housing situation was worse after the Great War than before it. Despite the construction of a further 35,000 council homes, there was such a shortage of houses that the moderately well-off were obliged to live in expensive slums, a fact noted by George Orwell among others. Overcrowding was terrible in the old areas and the new council estates themselves had many disadvantages. They were built out in the suburbs and were thus expensive to travel to; the houses were often expensive to rent; estates like Huyton and Norris Green were built without proper facilities like bus or tram services, shops or pubs; and, as we now know all too well, the new estates could so easily become soulless and unattractive.

Perhaps one of the best overall views of the city during the 'twenties and 'thirties is provided by the writer J. B. Priestley, who was a regular visitor and had a detached outsider's view. Priestley wrote at length about his impressions in the 1930s during a time of depression and high unemployment. He visited Chinatown where he was served with 'good china tea', though he thought the number of Chinese was rapidly declining. He shopped at Paddy's Market and the Irish quarter and he wrote at some length about the problems of the Irish in Liverpool. With the help of old friends and journalists from the *Liverpool Daily*

Street Urchins on the Steble Fountain.

A superb example of the photographic work of C. F. Inston, who must be given the credit for the smiles on the faces. Taken in about 1895, to own a pair of shoes was the exception rather than the rule.

Post, he was able to meet up with an elderly vicar whom he described as 'a sturdy figure, and as downright as a bo'sun'. The vicar called his parish the queerest in England. It contained as cosmopolitan a selection of children of all races as could be found anywhere in the world. Priestley described an infants' school which the vicar showed him:

We hurried off to the local school that all these half-caste children attended. By the time we got there the little ones were leaving, and my companions singled out several of them, who answered his smiling questions very softly and shyly. All the races of mankind were there, wonderfully mixed. Imagine an infant class of half-castes, quadroons, octaroons, with all the latitudes and longitudes confused in them. I saw there things, baby-size, neatly put away in cupboards; and this they had done themselves. They could have been pictured in the act, not as a Liverpool infants' class but as the human race, which is probably still a baby, trying to tidy up.

On the floor above a class of older children had not yet been dismissed, and the vicar marched me in to look and listen to them. There cannot be a queerer class anywhere in the world. The woolly curls of the negro, the smooth brown skin of the Malay, the diagonal eye of the Chinese, they were all there, crazily combined with features that had arrived in Lancashire by way of half a dozen different European countries, from Scandinavia to Italy. Nor did their appearance tell the whole tale; indeed it could be oddly deceptive. A boy could look pure Liverpool and prove to be three-parts Chinese. The negro influence was the most obvious. One little girl looked ready to bud into another Florence Mills. A handsome

Above: Liverpool Court, 1913.
Thousands lived in courts like these. Court life varied greatly, from abject poverty to the friendly and supportive neighbourliness which seems to be evident in this picture.
In 1846 Liverpool's first medical officer of health reckoned that about half the working population was living in crowded, insanitary courtyards, often sharing just a single water supply and a couple of toilets. By the twentieth century conditions had improved but they were still bad enough for wholesale demolition to be considered the only viable option after the war.

Left: Court with washing, 1913.
Showing ash bin, washing, gas lamp on bracket, graffiti, and occupants. Thought to be No. 9 court, off Mason Street.

sturdy lad, with a fine head, proudly carried and big flashing eyes, was the grandson of an African chieftain . . .[2]

Such cultural integration was rare, however, as each religious and racial group lived predominantly within its own community. A large Irish community lived around Scotland Road; the Welsh quarter was centred around the nearby 'Flower' streets off Stanley Road; the Jews kept their businesses in Islington and many lived in Allerton and attended a synagogue in Queen's Drive; the Chinese lived in the south around Pitt Street. Protestants and Catholics lived and even worked separately – Protestant dockers in the south, Catholic in the north.

Some people even today look at the separate communities and claim that this has contributed to harmonious race relations. The reality, especially from the viewpoint of the ethnic minorities themselves, was – and is – rather different. There has always been a powerful strain of racial prejudice in Liverpool, as elsewhere.

Religion produced even more community strife, especially before the Second World War. As early as the 1860s the Orange Order, introduced by the not insignificant contingent of Protestant Irish from Ulster, was fanning the flames of anti-Popery, a cause enthusiastically endorsed by many within the ranks of Anglicanism and Toryism. Local politics were used by some to further sectarian interests and there were allegations that the Church hierarchies actually encouraged the extremists on either side or at best did little to restrain them. The Protestant/Catholic divide was very real – the Protestant Party won elections in small wards right up until 1973, while T. P. O'Connor held Liverpool Scotland for the Nationalists for many years at the beginning of the century; Sinn Fein even won the Exchange seat in 1918! People who lived in inter-war Liverpool well remember the anxiety, the tension and occasionally the pitched battles which took place on July 12, echoing similar riotous assemblies which had taken place in Liverpool on that day right from the early years of the nineteenth century.

Helen Forrester remembers her reaction when she arrived in Liverpool at the age of twelve, in the middle of the Depression with an unemployed father hoping to find work:

> Liverpool looked a dreadfully dismal place to my untutored eyes. Water swirled along the gutters, carrying a horrid collection of garbage. Across the road, the fine Corinthian pillars of St George's Hall looked like a row of rotting teeth, and to my right, down William Brown Street, marched a series of equally large, black buildings. When I peeked farther out of the station I could see the entrance of a big theatre, the Empire, and farther along at the corner was a public house, the Legs o' Man, near which a number of seamen stood laughing and joking, oblivious of the rain. Much later on, a sailor told me that sooner or later everybody in the world passed the Legs o' Man and if you waited long enough you could meet there anybody you cared to look for; certainly it was a great meeting place.
>
> Along the pavement men in shabby cloth caps shuffled from litter-bin to litter-bin to sift through the garbage for food and cigarette ends. In the gutter stood four unemployed Welsh miners, caps held hopefully out while they sang over and over again in sad tenor voices 'Land of our Fathers' and 'All through the Night'.[3]

J. B. Priestley wandered down to the docks at Wapping and down to the dark, foggy banks of the Mersey with his friend the vicar. He tried to capture the atmosphere of a seaport in the Great Depression of the 'thirties:

> It was deep dusk. There were some last feeble gleams of sunset in the shadowy sky before us. Everything was shadowy now. The warehouses we passed seemed empty of everything but shadows. A few men – far too few – came straggling along, their day's work over. We arrived at the edge of the Mersey, and below us was a long mudbank. The water was a grey mystery, a mere vague thickening of space. Something hooted, to break a

silence that immediately closed up afterwards to muffle the whole spectral scene. We walked slowly along the waterfront, from nothing, it seemed, into nothing; and darkness rose rather than fell; and with it came a twinkle of lights from Birkenhead that reached us not across the river but over a gulf that could not be measured. I have rarely seen anything more spectral and melancholy. It was hard to believe that by taking ship here you might eventually reach a place of sharp outlines, a place where colour burned and vibrated in the sunlight, and that here was the gateway to the bronze ramparts of Arabia, to the temples and elephants of Ceylon, to flying fish and humming birds and hibiscus. With our hands thrust deep in our overcoat pockets, we trudged along and talked about Liverpool's trade, a fitting topic for the time and place.[4]

There was worse than unemployment to follow the Depression of the 'thirties and a war broke out which was even longer and more terrible than the Great War of the previous generation. The people might have been forgiven for thinking that the world had come to an end.

By 1940, when the pace of the war had quickened, the Luftwaffe were systematically bombing all the major seaports in the kingdom, and the war brought death and chaos right into the streets and backyards of the people. The cold statistics give a total of 3,875 killed during the blitz from Liverpool, Bootle, Birkenhead and Wallasey, with 7,144

One of a series of superbly sharp and detailed photographs showing the war damage in the town centre after the May Blitz in 1941.

This photograph was taken from atop the Victoria Monument in Derby Square, one of the few buildings in the area to be unscathed. Ironically, this was the exact site of the medieval Liverpool Castle – when he founded the castle, King John could hardly have expected war ever to be like this!

Right: Damage to Bluecoat
Hospital, 1942. Photo W. H.
Tomkinson.
   Cherubim faces remain
intact on the east wing of the
Bluecoat Hospital, but the glass
has gone from most of the
windows. It was fortunate that
the damage to central
Liverpool's oldest building was
repairable.

Below: Overhead Railway
damaged in air-raid.
   The Overhead survived the
war, but not without many
incidents like this one. The rails
still span the gap but no deck
remains to support them.

seriously injured. About half of the dead and injured were casualties of
what became known as the May Blitz of 1941 when the bombardment
from the German bombers was almost continuous every night
throughout the whole of May and through the first two weeks of June.
The number of times the sirens sounded out the air raid warnings was
509 and the number of actual bomb raids was 79. The damage to

private property was exceptionally high. It was estimated that 184,840 homes out of a total of 282,000 were damaged by the raids and 10,840 houses were destroyed.

In some of the early raids the Germans dropped landmines, one of which fell on a shelter at Durning Road Junior Technical School in the small hours of a November morning in 1940. There were about three hundred people in the shelter. The air raid warden was Mrs F. B. Taft, a middle-aged woman who displayed magnificent courage and composure throughout what Churchill described as 'the worst single incident of the war'. The number of people who lost their lives was given as 166. An eye-witness described the incident:

> If anyone deserves a medal it is that woman. She was magnificent in her courage and common-sense. Even as we heard groans from the dying, some of them children, she never cracked up. None of us thought that we would ever get out alive, but Mrs Taft kept cheering up everyone. When people said 'We'll never get through', she just replied, 'They'll get us out all right'. A direct hit was made on the shelter just after my wife and myself had entered. The shelter lights fused, a boiler burst and a fire started at one end. The mass of people made it almost impossible to move about. The roof came through under the enormous weight of the debris and the best we could say was that we believed the victims' end was instantaneous. The horror of it all did not rob the people of their courage. None of the women screamed. Nobody fainted. For the first few seconds we did not realise that we had been buried. We tried to scramble for the exits. Mrs. Taft said, 'Keep calm and try the emergency exits'. They were jammed too. We all thought we were lost. Then, to add to our troubles, a fire started somewhere in the main section. I could see it over the brickwork. It wasn't apparently very large but smoke poured into our part and people nearly choked with fumes. Water from the burst boiler and the broken water main slowly flooded the floor of the shelter. It rose to our knees. We didn't know where it was coming from or where it would stop, and wondered if we should be drowned. Then Mrs Taft shouted, 'I can see a light'. She had found a small window leading out of the shelter which had not been blocked by the terrific amount of debris. She raised a cry for volunteers to dig a way through. Four men came forward. They flashed a torch and someone outside saw it. Rescue work began.[5]

During the May Blitz hardly a day passed without a major fire breaking out from incendiaries and bombing. For more than a month the whole city seemed to be afire. The flames and the red sky over Liverpool could be seen from towns many miles to the north and from the coast of North Wales.

In Huskisson Dock the *S. S. Malakand,* a steamer of the Brocklebank line, was loading supplies of ammunition from the Kirkby factory when a blazing barrage balloon fell onto the deck. The fire was extinguished in spite of the danger, but incendiaries were falling all round the dock and one of them set fire to the dockyard sheds. The dry timber of the shed soon became an inferno of flames and in spite of the efforts of the fire service the flames began to envelop the *Malakand* with her highly explosive cargo. Efforts were made to scupper the ship before the cargo exploded, but by that time the fire was too much out of control. The explosion which followed was one of the greatest of the war. It destroyed the whole dock; a four-ton anchor was blown a hundred yards away; some of the debris was found over two miles from the explosion and a great gap was made in the Overhead Railway and the nearby station.

Enemy U-boats were creating havoc with the essential supply lines of food and provisions across the North Atlantic. In 1941 the centre for counter measures against the U-boats was switched from Plymouth to Liverpool where it was located in the basement of Derby House. In what became known as the Battle of the North Atlantic the positions of 2,200 convoys were tracked throughout the war, an average of around a thousand radio reports came in every day and the positions of all convoys were carefully monitored.

Between seven and eight thousand merchant ships made the crossing during the war years. The men who manned them faced a danger comparable to the soldiers on the front line and they played an essential part in the war effort. Captain F. J. 'Johnny' Walker, a popular naval officer who had served at Dunkirk, was the man responsible for the protection of the convoys. Walker frequently worked around the clock with no sleep. He lived long enough to see his battle won and his last convoy arrive inside the Mersey Bar, but he suffered a stroke brought about by exhaustion and he died in the old Royal Naval Hospital at Seaforth at the age of forty-seven.

The number of human stories of bravery and suffering during the war years is sufficient for a specialised study which could fill many volumes. In 1942 the last all-clear sounded, but it was still three more years of all-out effort before peace came back again to an exhausted England. Among the public buildings lost was the church of St Nicholas, gutted by fire, with only the walls and tower left standing. The Corn Exchange was reduced to a pile of rubble, and the Customs House was damaged so badly that it was decided to pull it down. The Goree Piazzas, which had survived fire and storm throughout the whole of the nineteenth century, finally succumbed to the blitz. It was remarkable that in spite of the extensive damage to the docks the Liver Building and its neighbours were unharmed. The Cathedral also escaped almost unscathed. There was damage to the central libraries and one incendiary actually came through the roof of St George's Hall but prompt action by the fire service kept the extent of the damage to a minimum.

The inexpressible relief when at last the war was over was something which only those who lived through it could appreciate. Things gradually got back to normal. League football was played again and in 1947 Liverpool won the first post-war Football League Championship – it was not forgotten that Everton had been the champions in the last season before the war began. There was no league football during the war because it was considered unwise to have large regular gatherings of people, but this did not prevent many friendly fixtures from being played. In times of war and peace the sportsmen of Goodison Park and Anfield did more than any other individuals in the city to keep up the spirits of the Dicky Sams and the Scousers.

The origins of Association Football, like many other institutions in Liverpool, belong to Victorian times. At the grass roots of the community the working man first began to find more time and leisure in the 1870s, when some had a little time and money to spare at the end of the long working week. When the Lancashire Football Association was formed in 1878 it was dominated by clubs from the manufacturing towns of the textile belt and had no representation from Liverpool. By 1882, however, a number of local football clubs had appeared and the

Liverpool and District Football Association was formed.

The early clubs were church organisations such as the teams from St Mary's, St Peter's, St Benedict's and the St Domingo's Methodist Church team created in 1878. By 1886 the popularity of the sport had mushroomed so much that the number of clubs had grown to 151. The leading clubs of the day were Bootle, Liverpool Caledonians and Liverpool Ramblers, plus the St Domingo club which changed its name to Everton the year after its formation – the players became known locally as the 'Moonlight Dribblers' because of their nocturnal training habits.[6]

By the 1880s soccer had become a very popular spectator sport, and in 1886 the Bootle-Everton clash, the first round of a local cup-tie, was interrupted by a disorderly crowd. By the time the Football League was formed in 1886 Everton, who had wasted no time in signing professional players in the previous year, was the leading club in Liverpool and became a founder member of the League. Dicky Sams flocked from all parts of the city to support their team, and the first home match in the Football League drew a gate of nine thousand against Accrington, whom they beat by two goals to one. Professional soccer had come to stay.

The Everton club went from strength to strength and in the third season of league football, much to the dismay of Preston North End and Blackburn Rovers, Everton carried off the league championship. The earliest Everton colours were blue and white stripes, but before settling on the traditional blue strip Everton experimented with black shirts and red sash, also ruby shirts with blue trimmings, while their prettiest garb was probably the trendy salmon jerseys worn with long blue knickerbockers which reached below the knees.

In 1882 there appeared on the scene one John Houlding who became president of the Everton FC in the 1882-83 season. Houlding was a self-made man who started life as an errand boy in the Customs House and worked himself up to be the owner of a brewery which he called 'Houldings Sparkling Ales' – he was dubbed 'King John' by the local press. In 1884 Houlding was instrumental in moving the Everton club to premises in Anfield Road, on a site previously owned by another brewer. He quarrelled with the club over a proposal to purchase some adjoining land and the Everton members refused to support King John. They resolved to take their club elsewhere and purchased a plot of land on the north side of Stanley Park for the sum of £8,090. A limited company was formed and the Goodison Park ground was ready for the opening of the 1892-93 season.[7]

King John gave notice to quit. He managed to retain some of the Everton players and with the aid of John McKenna he set up a new professional club from scratch, which he tried to register as the 'Everton Football Club and Athletic Grounds Company Limited'. The Football Association refused to allow another club with the name of Everton, but Houlding was unperturbed and registered his club under the name of Liverpool instead. For the remaining ten years of his life King John ran the new club with astonishing shrewdness from the boardroom chair, and it quickly became acknowledged as a serious rival to the club on the other side of Stanley Park.

Football soon became a way of life for players and spectators. The players were local heroes and their autographs on the popular

Goodison Park, 1922.
A view of the Everton ground as it was in the 1920s before the completion of two-tier stands on all four sides.

schoolboy market were worth those of two peers of the realm. In the early days Everton had a number of middle-class players in their team, but the game was soon dominated by ordinary working men. To become a professional player was a great opportunity for youths from the poorer walks of life, and from early days both sets of players lived a lifestyle far removed from their origins. In 1894 the Everton players held their pre-season training at a hotel in Hoylake whilst the Liverpool team went to Hightown. Players' salaries in the 1890s were typically three pounds a week, but many players were earning more than this and by the end of the century the Football Association resolved on a maximum wage of four pounds a week because they thought the situation was in danger of getting out of hand.

The first meeting between Everton and Liverpool was a Liverpool cup fixture which Liverpool won by the only goal, but tables were turned in the first league match between the two teams in 1894 when Everton won 2-0 before a crowd of 44,000. Most of the spectators paid sixpence for admission and the gate money of over a thousand pounds was a huge sum for the times. Admission charges were raised to a shilling after the First World War, but local derby games rarely drew less than fifty thousand and both clubs played before an average gate of 35,000 for league matches.

Both clubs were wealthy from the high gate money. They were powerful forces on the transfer market and they were consistently successful. In 1906 Liverpool won the league championship and Everton won the FA cup. Liverpool won two successive league championships in the 'twenties, Everton won in 1928, managed to get themselves relegated soon afterwards, but went on to win two more league titles and the FA cup in the 'thirties. The outstanding Everton personalities were Tommy Lawton and Dixie Dean, a goal-scoring legend who scored 379 goals in thirteen seasons, including 82 in

1927-8. His great rival at Anfield was Elisha Scott, the Liverpool goalkeeper, a man whose local standing may be judged by the fact that his autograph was valued at the same as Dixie Dean's.

The partisan supporter appeared very early in the history of Everton and Liverpool. Local schools found they were faced with a problem when supporters would not allow their sons to play for the school soccer team if it meant wearing the colours of the rival club. Indeed in some areas, with green and orange also barred because of the Catholic and Protestant factions, the choice of colours available became very limited.

Oddly enough, the religious associations of Liverpool and Everton were not as strong as one might have imagined and certainly not as divisive as in Glasgow. That is not to say that people did not take the game seriously. For many supporters the football club was a second religion that dominated their lives; for them the success of their club more than compensated for lower standards of living and unemployment. They revelled in the atmosphere of a cup tie or a local derby. They packed the close double-decker stands of Goodison Park where fifty thousand fans shared the tight arena or they joined the great mass of surging humanity on the Kop at Anfield. They enjoyed the good-natured scouse witticisms voiced from behind the goal. They joined in the chants and the songs of the terraces. They chatted with the knowledgeable supporters who could reel off teams and scorers from the cloth-capped decades before the war.

An athletic Dixie Dean rises above an opponent. In the inter-war years, Dixie Dean was the city's most famous footballing personality, scoring 379 goals in thirteen seasons with Everton.

They came to witness the game itself, with its fast, exciting and flowing football; the quick thrust down the centre of the field and the groan as a shot hits the side netting and waves of humanity ripple down the Kop to be broken by the barriers; the delicate midfield play with ball passed quickly and accurately weaving patterns from man to man; the applause following a diving fingertip save by the goalkeeper; a great gasp at an interception and sudden reversal of the direction of play; the disbelieving silence when the away team scores a goal; the chanted name of a local hero growing ever louder as he moves nearer the goal with the ball at his feet. And at last the rapturous unbridled joy of a home goal with the ever-expectant atmosphere lifted ever higher for long afterwards and with the cheering heard from the other side of the city.

Chapter Fourteen

The Mersey Sound

FTER the First World War one of the main topics of conversation on Merseyside was the idea of a road tunnel to carry the vastly increased volume of road traffic between the two sides of the river. Work on the Mersey Road Tunnel began in December 1925 when Princess Mary, Viscountess Lascelles, turned a golden key to start the excavating machinery. By April 1928 pilot tunnels had been driven from both Lancashire and Cheshire shores to meet in mid river. Miss Margaret Beavan, the first lady Lord Mayor of Liverpool, shook hands with Alec Naylor, the Mayor of Birkenhead, through a hole which had been ceremoniously broken through the thin wall of rock dividing the two tunnels. Clad in oilskins, hats and gumboots the mayors still managed to wear their chains of office for the offical photograph of what was an historic event.

The tunnel was a long and arduous excavation, and it was another five years before the public was allowed to walk through for the first time, when over seven thousand pounds was raised for charity from the sixpences paid by 300,000 people. When King George V and Queen Mary arrived for the official opening in 1934 the Mersey Tunnel was considered to be one of the greatest tunnelling feats of the times and a million people lined the route of the grand opening parade.

The new tunnel, with underground junctions and two exits at each side of the river, was the longest and most complex underwater road tunnel in the world. It was one of the wonders of an age which still appreciated the monumental labours of the navvies and the knowledge and skills of the civil engineers. The following account is a child's view of the tunnel after the war. It describes the feelings of many who experienced the wonder of a trip through for the first time:

As a small child I remember standing at the tunnel entrance and watching the traffic pay at some green and cream toll booths for the right to enter the dark mouth of the tunnel entrance. I was told what I took to be a children's fairy tale, that the tunnel went all the way under the river to the distant Cheshire shore. It was true that there was traffic coming out as well as going in but I assumed that the whole story was a fiction in the same mould as the Santa Claus story and that in fact there must be some kind of underground car park beneath the ground.

When I was about seven years old the Sunday school organised a coach outing to Raby Mere. The excited chatter of the children in the coach

Mersey Tunnel, Dock entrance 1935.

A view of the dock entrance to the Mersey Tunnel, with St Nicholas' Church and the Overhead Railway in the foreground. The Mersey Tunnels were both great feats of civil engineering and improved access across the river immeasurably. With hindsight, however, the fact that they deposited huge amounts of traffic right in the city centre can be seen as a mixed blessing that has created many traffic problems right up to the present day. Scotland Road, for one, has never recovered from the shock.

became hushed when it plunged into the mouth of the tunnel and entered the Halls of Hades below. The daylight faded away behind us and was replaced by a long line of dim yellow lights lining the walls for as far ahead as the eye could see. There was a strange loud roaring of traffic and sharp eerie echoes of lorries changing gear somewhere far away in the distance. We came to a set of traffic lights where lorries from the docks joined our stream of traffic, and it seemed that there was a whole system of roads in this hollowed out world beneath the ground. The road in front seemed to reach a dip and start to climb upwards, but the dip was an illusion caused by the downward slope meeting the level section at the lowest point of the tunnel. Somebody said the roaring in our ears was the sound of the river above and that it could break through the walls at any moment.

After what seemed an age another change in slope was seen ahead; this time it signified a true upward ramp, and we came to another set of traffic lights. The coach changed gear and ground on until at last a distant bright glare of sunlight was seen ahead of us. The children breathed a sigh of relief, small fists were unclenched as the coach came out into daylight again. We covered our eyes against the glare of the sunshine, a dazzling brightness after the dim lighting of the tunnel.[1]

The Mersey Tunnel did not put the ferries out of business. The floating landing stage at the Pier Head was the point of departure for boats to Birkenhead, Seacombe, Wallasey and New Brighton, with the departure point for the Isle of Man steamer just downstream from the ferries.

Except for the curious survival of a Punch and Judy show on Lime

THE NEW PIER AT NEW BRIGHTON, CHESHIRE.—

Street, Liverpool's early aspirations towards becoming a seaside resort were long forgotten, but on the Cheshire bank of the Mersey New Brighton had developed into a classic seaside resort with photographers' booths, saucy postcards, penny slot machines, pier entertainments, fortune tellers, fairground rides and an open air swimming pool. In the first decades of the century it even boasted a tower taller than the one at Blackpool and of a design quite different to Eifel's

Parisian landmark. New Brighton had sand and rocks, a light-house, and a fort built of red sandstone to guard the entrance to the Mersey Estuary. The factor which distinguished New Brighton from other resorts was that few day trippers arrived by train, and nearly all the holidaymakers arrived at the landing stage by ferry from Liverpool.

Liverpudlians in the northern suburbs found the seaside resort of Southport to be easier of access by train. Good planning and good fortune made Southport into one of the few seaside towns which successfully managed to segregate the needs of residents and holiday makers. It was a place where Liverpool merchants and Manchester businessmen lived peaceably next door to each other and it provided a much-needed sense of style and elegance to the heavily industrialised county of Lancashire. In the summers of the late 1940s the journey from Southport to New Brighton was made via train, overhead railway and Mersey Ferry:

Opposite, top: New Pier at New Brighton. Built in 1866-67 to the designs of Eugenius Birch, New Brighton Pier was a classic example of the flambuoyant pier designs of the time, with pavilions, lookout towers, and plenty of space for promenading. Many Liverpudlians will recall the exploits of the one-legged diver from the end of the pier.

Opposite, bottom: A superb period piece, showing smartly dressed Victorians embarking on the ferries at the Princes' Landing Stage.

> At Southport we had not yet graduated from the children's rides of Peter Pan's Pool to the wonders of Pleasureland, so that all the rides in Liverpool seemed to be constructed on a giant scale. The trams carried posters back and front which depicted a pair of eyes and enabled them to stare at the world as they clanked along. They were tall green vehicles, full of eccentric character with stairs at both ends and a trolley which hissed and sparked as it trailed over the junctions in the overhead cables. Upstairs were toast-rack seats such that the passenger could choose to face forwards or backwards. Even more fascinating were the Mersey ferries, with labyrinths of stairs and passages, smoky dark saloons to explore below and breezy, railed promenade decks in the fresh air above with grand vistas of the docks and the waterfront.
>
> To get to Pier Head we had to change trains at Seaforth and Litherland, where we mounted a rickety tramlike apparition of two or three carriages which waited patiently on an adjacent platform. At first the ride was uneventful, with nothing but a depressing view into the tiny back yards of the terraced houses below the embankment. At Seaforth Sands there was no sign of the seaside, only railway sidings like the mysteriously named Sandhills station just before the Liverpool Exchange terminus. Soon the dockside cranes became visible, the train was running on an elevated platform over the road, and we could see that the cranes were busy with the job of loading and unloading great cargo ships. The noses of four small children pressed hard against the window and gasped in awe at the sheer size of the ships in the dock. Stations were frequent, with strange names like Huskisson, Canada and Nelson and when the train stopped we were sometimes unfortunate in that the view was obscured by a billboard, a waiting room or a warehouse. But when the train pulled away again a huge ship would be revealed with underside bared in a dry dock, showing its red-painted keel and giant propellers which were normally out of sight beneath the water. Workers on scaffolds sat high in the air repainting and repairing the underside of the vessel.
>
> Every ship had its name displayed across the stern in huge letters, with the name of the port to which it belonged written below. We read every name out loud; it was a romantic sight to see the great ships from every part of the world showing the colours of their country and flying the flags from the mast head. Some names we could not read, they were in Arabic or Chinese characters, but this merely added to the wonder and the world-wide flavour of the docks.
>
> Fussy little locomotives, dwarfed by the giant ships, puffed around below with long trains of wagons. Cargoes of all kinds were stacked on the dockside. Other vessels stood out in the river, some with long lines of

portholes and all with brightly painted funnels carrying the different emblems of their shipping lines. As we came near to the Pier Head passenger liners and ferries came into view and a maze of tramlines intersected the dock railway below. We alighted from our train and found our little party dwarfed below the gaze of the Liver Birds perched high on top of a building so tall that it seemed like a skyscraper. We knew we had only seen half of the dock system, and the next time we travelled to Pier Head we insisted on making the journey via Dingle.[2]

By the time Geoffrey Moorhouse came to write about Liverpool in the early 'sixties the Overhead was a thing of the past, and its passing was already greatly lamented.

Moorhouse was influenced by the journeys of J. B. Priestley and he tried to get at the heart of the city and the people. He admired the planning of the city centre; he stood on the terraces at both Goodison Park and the Kop to absorb the electric atmosphere of Liverpool football, and he visited Chinatown, as Priestley had done before him:

> Liverpool has an air which Manchester lacks. Not to say a swagger and a sense of adventure. It is in the nature of a seaport to be more dashing than any inland clearing house, of course. Once you have seen the Liverpool waterfront, looking from mid-Mersey like a scaled-down version of New York's, but scarcely less impressive, or (before some authorised vandal decided that it must come down) ridden the overhead railway the length of the docks, you start to look for something out of the ordinary in the Pool. You find it most obviously in its cosmopolitan touches, in the lascars shuffling gloomily along the wind-whipped Lime Street, and in the shops and restaurants of the Chinese community. But it comes in local penny packets too. To anyone accustomed to the confinement of the other Lancashire towns the gusty acre of St George's Square with the Hall dominating nothing but a wide open space is a bit of an eye-opener . . .

The inspired design of Liverpool R.C. Cathedral. Visible for miles, it is known in Liverpool variously as 'The Mersey Funnel' or 'Paddy's Wigwam'.

> Liverpool does not appear to have made any more progress than Manchester towards reconstructing its centre. But at least it has Shankland's spectacular plan on its drawing board. And at least one building which breaks away from stylized forms is going up – Frederick Gibberd's Roman Catholic Cathedral. When completed it may look too much like a circus big top for most tastes. Yet this seems to me to matter much less than the fact that here someone has been having a go at something different for a change . . .[3]

The Roman Catholic Cathedral was consecrated in 1967. The foundation stone had been laid as early as in 1933, but the final structure was a total departure from the original plans of Edwin Lutyens. The final design, affectionately and variously known as 'Paddy's Wigwam' or 'The Mersey Funnel', was that of a huge and impressive conical roof supporting a tower of coloured glass rising to a crown of thorns and throwing a pool of coloured light into the striking interior. It was an outstanding example of what could be achieved by modern architecture given favourable sites and circumstances.

Moorhouse was interested in the division between Catholics and Protestants which, although it did not cut as deep as in Ireland or in Glasgow, was still a very real division in Liverpool. He noted that the Protestants were identified with Toryism while the Catholics often embraced socialism, one of the main reasons, he thought, why it was not until 1955 that Liverpool had a Labour-controlled council.

Certainly, politics in the city have always had a very distinctive local flavour. On the one hand, religion played a major role. Orangeism, still a powerful force up to the Second World War, was strongly linked to Unionism and the Tory Party – even today in the St. Domingo and Breckfield area graffiti proclaiming '1689: No Surrender' and obscenities regarding the Pope can still be seen. Partly because of this connection, the city's socialists were seen to be linked to Catholicism.

On the other hand, trade unions and working-class solidarity were strong features of Liverpool life. Outside the docks, in particular, trade unions were well organised and quickly found a role in articulating the grievances of ordinary people. After the war the Labour Party was able to take advantage of the decline of the religious vote and the Tories suffered accordingly. Under the daunting and progressive leadership of politicians like the Braddocks, Labour finally took control of the city and ended several generations of Tory rule.

The street parties, remembered with nostalgia by all those who celebrated the end of the war, found a new life in the 1950s. At the time of the Coronation in 1953 the number of flags and the amount of bunting strung between the upper floors of the streets in the inner city were prodigious. The smaller and narrower the street the easier it was to decorate in a great show of patriotism, and the greatest displays of national pride were from the poorer quarters near the city centre. Few of these loyal subjects were able to afford the new television sets in

Bessie Braddock (1899-1970). Liverpool Exchange consistently returned a Conservative member before the war, but in the General Election of 1945 Mrs Braddock captured the seat for Labour with a majority of 665. Her forthright style and her fight for the rights of the underprivileged made her into a very popular and respected local figure. She retained her seat in Parliament until her death in 1970.

their own homes to watch the Coronation, but they were able to watch the events live in the cinemas and local schools where projection television sets were set up for the occasion.

Flags came out again in 1957, when the city celebrated its charter from King John, granted 750 years previously. The Queen Mother unveiled a plaque that commemorated the rebuilding of the central libraries, damaged during the war. The Royal Liverpool Philharmonic played at the Liverpool stadium; there was jazz at the Philharmonic Hall and organ recitals in St George's Hall. Open-air concerts featured every band, from the King's Liverpool Regiment to the Merseysippi Jazz Band. The people did not need to wait for special occasions for an excuse to celebrate – there were annual holidays like St. George's Day and especially Empire Day when children had a day off school and were given a penny each by the Council.

By the economic boom years of the 'fifties and 'sixties, however, a new breed of young people began to appear. They were a fortunate generation born during the wartime years – they were too young to remember much about the war itself and they knew nothing of the Depression of the 'thirties. Gangs of adolescents aimlessly roamed the streets in search of something to do and looking for a means by which to express themselves. In the mid 'fifties the times were right for a new popular teenage culture to take shape. 'The gang, between the periods 1954 and 1958, was not only a microcosm of society; it was relatively speaking the only society the adolescent knew and felt sure of', wrote Colin Fletcher in *New Society*. 'This was the situation when Rock and Roll arrived on Merseyside.'

When the film *Rock around the Clock* was first shown in Liverpool the reaction of the teenagers was immediate and spontaneous. In 1955, when Bill Haley appeared live on stage at the Odeon, a hundred and forty seats were wrecked and the police had to be rushed in to control the crowds. What the police found when they arrived was not a riot but a crowd of ecstatic teenagers dancing barefoot in the aisles. When some University students sold Bill Haley's bathwater to raise money for the rag, they admitted under pressure that he had only dipped his hands in it, but it was evident that the age of the rock and roll idol had arrived.

The movement was accompanied by the growth of the skiffle groups, where young people sang ballads to the strumming of a guitar and the simple accompaniments of combs and washboards. In Liverpool the explosion of popular music was something very vital. For reasons which cannot fully be identified but which will keep the social psychologists busy for many years, the movement was more basic and alive in Liverpool than in any other part of the country. There was, of course, a very ancient seaport tradition of sea shanties and sailors' ditties from all over the world which could still be found in some of the dockside pubs, but this seemed to be at the most only a minor factor in the entirely new and spontaneous form of popular music that was born before 1960.

The fact that many Merseyside youngsters went to sea and travelled the world was certainly an important ingredient, in that brothers and neighbours brought back the latest records from New York and Hamburg to play at the jive hives and the gatherings of Saturday night fever. There were other factors, too, which fuelled the movement, not the least of which was the inclusion of girls, who held a very limited place in the street gangs, but who were an essential part of the adolescent scene and were indeed the subject of many of the songs that dealt with basic adolescent problems of boy-meets-girl relationships.

In 1953 Liverpool singer Lita Roza became the first British girl to top the charts with a typical early 'fifties song about the price of the doggy in the window. In 1958 came Michael Holliday with *The Story of My Life* and when the 'sixties arrived it was the groups which began to make the charts. Gerry and the Pacemakers reached the top with *How do you do it* in 1963.

The number of singers and groups which appeared in Liverpool was unbelievable, far more than anywhere else in the country. As well as Gerry Marsden, there were Billy J. Kramer and the Dakotas, Derry Wilkie and the Pressmen, Deke Rivers and the Big Sound, The Swinging Blue Jeans, The Mike Taylor Combo, The Searchers, The Fourmost, The Merseybeats, The Nomads, The Escorts, a young lady called Priscilla White who changed her name to Black, and so many others groups that the total number was estimated to be over three hundred.

Special mention should be made of the Spinners, a more serious-minded group interested in the folk songs and sea shanties of Merseyside and who remained together long after the other groups had disbanded. The groups started life on a local circuit which took them around the youth clubs, jive hives, and the teenage gatherings of Merseyside. If they were good enough they ended up at the great mecca for the Mersey Beat which was the basement of a warehouse in Mathew Street, right in the heart of central Liverpool.

The entrance to the Cavern was daubed with crudely painted CND symbols and graffiti, and access was down a flight of steep wooden steps into a hot, thick atmosphere of dim lights and amplified sound. The room comprised three arches of a low barrel-vaulted ceiling, made from bare bricks and with condensation on the walls. About two hundred youngsters, most of them teenagers, crowded into the room. Boys wore suits and jackets with thin lapels and matching thin ties; their faces were for the most part clean shaven, hair was not long but the short back and sides of the 'fifties was quite definitely out of fashion. Girls had far more variety in their clothing. Most of them wore short skirts with tight sweaters or a short sleeveless dress. The most popular hairstyle was a deep fringe over the forehead, with hair sprayed and fixed around the head in a beehive style.

There were recesses in the walls where groups of youngsters sat and sipped at the cokes and pepsis they bought at an improvised bar; others stood in the middle of the floor moving spasmodically to the sound of the music; some in couples and others shifting individually with the rhythm of the song.

At one end, under the bright glare of a set of arc lamps, a group in leather jackets thumped out a tune with an astonishingly powerful beat. They strummed at guitars and grinned as they shouted the words of the song into a microphone and they quickly and easily worked up an atmosphere of great excitement. They were accompanied by a fantastic percussionist, totally absorbed in his music, who hammered away energetically at drums and cymbals. The noise was loud and the atmosphere was totally absorbing. The group had started life as the

The Beatles' shop at 31 Mathew Street, one example of the now extensive tourist industry centred around the 'Fab Four'. Note the statue above the doorway.

Below: *A statue to Eleanor Rigby on a bench near Mathew Street in Liverpool.*

Quarrymen in the 'fifties and had risen to become the most popular on Merseyside. The song was called *Love Me Do.* In 1962 John, George, Paul and Ringo had been playing together for two years and called themselves The Beatles.

For an amazing fifty-nine weeks from April 1963 until the middle of 1964 Liverpool entertainers held the number-one spot in the charts, with Herman's Hermits as the only outsiders to get as much as a look-in. Brian Epstein was the manager who recognised the potential and talent which had appeared in Liverpool and was responsible for promoting the groups. In 1964 the Beatles' records *A Hard Day's Night* and *I Want to Hold Your Hand* sold fifteen-million copies and the group were invited to appear at the Royal Command Performance. They had become the most popular group in Britain.

The music critic of *The Times* devoted a column to the Beatles' music. He detected chains of pandiatonic clusters and the submediant switches from C-major into A-flat-major. He even noticed an affinity with Mahler in some of their compositions. But there was no need to take the sound apart and analyse it. The youth of the world loved the rhythm and the beat, the simple messages in the songs and the exciting way in which they were performed.

Today the Cavern, tomorrow the world. Epstein took the fab four to America. Wildly excited teenagers followed the group across the United States wherever they went. Stadiums echoed to the amplified sound of drum and guitar, and the songs were hardly heard above the screams of the audience. Police held back the crowds as thousands of hysterical teenagers with tears streaming down their faces beat against the wire fences and struggled to get near their pop idols. Never before had the popular music industry been hit by such a phenonenon.

The Mersey Beat sounded throughout the world. It became the expression of the swinging 'sixties, of liberation and freedom, of long hair, miniskirts and psychedelic colours, an age of liberation and self-expression, when the world at last threw off the doldrums of the war years and began to take notice of the message of the young, with their call for unity and peace.

Chapter Fifteen

Recession and progress

N 1934 the Grand National was won by Golden Miller whose successes included the winning of the Cheltenham Gold Cup in five successive years. The next year Golden Miller was hot favourite to win the National again, but after successfully clearing Valentine's he refused at the next fence and threw his jockey very expertly over his head. The winner was Reynoldstown who ran a faultless race and came in a clear first at the post. When Reynoldstown won again the following year he became the most famous horse in the history of the race and it was not until the 'seventies that a more popular horse appeared at Aintree. He was the immortal, lovable and high spirited Red Rum, trained on the sands at Birkdale, who not only eclipsed Reynoldstown by winning the Grand National three times with apparent ease, but also earned two second places to add to his credit. Some Liverpudlians have had mixed feelings about the National after Mrs Topham, Aintree's owner, was widely quoted as disapproving of the large numbers of working-class racegoers from the city. Jump Sunday, however, was always popular and thousands would take the opportunity of inspecting the course and taking the measure of Becher's Brook for themselves.

Sporting success on Merseyside flourished with the boom of the 'sixties, which marked the start of a prolonged run of football successes. In the 'fifties the Liverpool clubs surprisingly won no major trophies, but in the next decade, under the inspired management of Bill Shankly, Liverpool won two league championships and carried off the FA cup for the first time in the club's history. The next year was Everton's turn to win at Wembley and their success was followed by a league title in 1970 to add to their previous title in 1963. In the 'seventies hardly a year went by without a major trophy coming to Liverpool, a success which continued into the 'eighties, and many youngsters will live to tell their grandchildren the highly improbable but true story of not one, but two FA Cup finals played between Everton and Liverpool.

Liverpool's soccer triumphs made the Anfield club into the finest and most respected team in Europe. Shanks was a god in Liverpool; he talked the people's language and dressed like them – usually an old coat and scarf – and was utterly dedicated to Liverpool. He painted his

Bill Shankly salutes an appreciative crowd. Under his inspired management, Liverpool FC added many cups and medals to the Anfield trophy room.

own house red and white and he endeared himself to thousands of fans, not only because of the constant run of successes he brought to the club, but because of the style in which he did it. He once said that football was more important than life or death and on another occasion quipped, much to the chagrin of devoted Evertonians, that there were only two teams in Liverpool – Liverpool and Liverpool Reserves. The whole of Merseyside mourned his passing.

In the years of high unemployment and depression the Liverpool and Everton Football Clubs between them did more to maintain the morale of the people than any other organisation in the city. It is all the more tragic, therefore, that the success of Liverpool FC was marred by two appalling disasters, one at the Heysel Stadium in Brussels and the other at Hillsborough. The two were of a quite different nature but both were terrible tragedies for the club, for its true supporters, and for the other clubs involved.

The disaster at the Heysel Stadium in Brussels, when thirty-nine Juventus supporters died in an outbreak of football violence, was, for any person with genuine feelings for Liverpool, one of the most shameful days in its history. A hundred years of goodwill, built up by sportsmen and supporters over generations, was destroyed in a few minutes by hooligans calling themselves Liverpool 'supporters'. The incident was filmed and seen on television before the eyes of the whole world.

The Hillsborough tragedy, in which ninety-five genuine Liverpool supporters died, was a quite different situation and one which raised searching questions of ground safety. It was a tragedy shared with Sheffield and Nottingham, but the shadows of sorrow were longest and deepest over Merseyside. The Taylor Report concluded that the police mistook the tragedy for a pitch invasion and lost much valuable time in reacting to the situation. It was the greatest disaster and loss of life in British sporting history. The strength of feeling on Merseyside was immense. The floral tributes that poured spontaneously into Anfield after the tragedy testified to the level of sorrow felt everywhere. A wet weekday afternoon six months after the tragedy could still witness a group of a dozen or so mourners outside the Shankly Gates laying wreaths or just standing in quiet tribute to those who died. Yet, mixed with sorrow, was anger. Anger at how the disaster had been allowed to happen – why after the experience of the previous year Liverpool had been allocated the smaller end of the ground; why the safety system had broken down so badly; and, most cruelly of all, why some tabloids had seized on the tragedy, without a shred of evidence, as further evidence of the hooliganism of Liverpool fans. There is still a boycott of *The Sun* in Liverpool for its shameful and unfounded reports of vandalism and looting from the dead.

For many also, the shadow cast by Heysel and Hillsborough was all the more cruel because it was so untypical of the spirit both of the game and the people of Liverpool. For years the most enduring feature of soccer in Liverpool has been not violence or hooliganism but good humour. Friendly banter and rivalry, not enmity, typify the Everton/ Liverpool relationship and the famed Scouse wit has always found eloquent expression on the Kop. That the 'Kop Choir' meets beforehand in a local pub to rehearse their repartee does nothing to lessen the spontaneity and sharpness of the performance. When some

The tributes to the fallen began the day after Hillsborough when this scene was captured by a photographer from the Echo, as mourners place wreaths and scarves around the Shankly Gates.

The Kop in full voice in the late 1950s. It is hard to imagine a sedentary Kop, but that appears to be the likely outcome of the Hillsborough tragedy.

years ago the Leeds United goalkeeper Gary Sprake had the misfortune to lose his balance while throwing the ball out, he spun round and threw the ball straight into his own net – the Kop burst immediately into a chorus of *Careless Hands*. The Taylor Report may result in a sedentary Kop, but it is hard to imagine that seating could quell the spirit that exists there.

The creation of the Metropolitan County of Merseyside in 1974 was welcomed in Liverpool, though it was not so popular in the more distant parts of the new county, where allegiance to Lancashire and Cheshire remained strong and where there was a fear of being swamped as part of an enlarged Liverpool. Of course, Liverpool had been an independent, self-governing entity for many years. The old Corporation was part of Lancashire but had been largely autonomous in terms of local government long before being elevated to the status of county borough in 1889. After 1974, Liverpool became part of the larger Merseyside and therefore actually lost some of this independence by becoming part of a larger whole. The situation was again reversed in 1986 when the Metropolitan County was abolished, leaving non-elected boards to manage several of the functions such as fire and waste that had traditionally been part of Liverpool's responsibility.

As far as commerce, local industry, new investment and jobs were concerned all these changes and instability certainly did not help. In the eighteenth and nineteenth centuries Liverpool was able to control its own destiny. The economy was managed by local people, by sugar, salt and timber and cotton merchants, by commerce and shipping lines largely developed by local enterprise and providing plenty of local employment. By the late-twentieth century this situation had changed completely. Successful businesses were bought up by huge consortiums controlled by international finance. When an international company needs to make cutbacks, the balance sheet is all that matters, the state of local employment is of purely secondary concern to the men on the board, and, if the Merseyside factory which they bought up a few years ago is not considered to be economical, then it is closed down. After the war another major factor was the retreat from Empire. It is difficult to assess how far Liverpool's decline in trade can be attributed to this, and in what ways, but it is certain that world economics as a whole did to Liverpool what the abolition of the slave trade and a ship canal were unable to do – it deprived the port of its shipping.

The obvious solution is to start up more local business and new enterprise, but a new business venture requires customers and people with money to spend. Only in areas which are already prosperous can such an undertaking hope to prosper quickly. Liverpool, with large areas of depressed and unattractive housing, was unlikely to attract workers from the prosperous south of England, or anywhere else for that matter. With woefully inadequate investment in the maintenance of property, many residential areas became ever more depressing and the downward spiral continued into the 'eighties, resulting in a net fall of population.

Unemployment was nothing new. Casual work on the docks and seemingly intractable problems of poverty and poor living conditions have always cast their shadow over the city. The recession of the early 1980s, however, was of a different magnitude. The port had been in decline for years, as had many of the city's manufacturing, import processing and service industries, but the recession cut particularly deeply. Besides the loss of jobs, there was a severe bout of Liverpool-bashing. Virtually everything emanating from government and sections of the media seemed to be critical. Local people looked on and listened as critics slated nearly every aspect of their city. Liverpudlians reacted strongly and it was no surprise when a political force whose principal rallying cry was anti-Thatcherism should begin to attract attention.

For years the Braddocks and others in the local Labour hierarchy had kept control of certain inner-city wards by keeping membership low and managing the local parties with an iron grip. One consequence was that by the time that control was lifted the local ward organisations had atrophied and were wide open to any concerted take-over. The Militants managed local parties in the time-honoured way and, by using the undemocratic caucus system, succeeded in controlling the Labour group of councillors despite never having a majority themselves.

By giving voice to anti-Thatcherism in such a powerful way, Militant helped to change the face of Liverpool politics. By 1986 Conservatives held only two seats on the 99-strong City Council and Militant claimed to have created or saved a thousand jobs and to have built three thousand new council homes. Disquiet was growing, however, with rumours and allegations of corruption and malpractice abounding. The crisis came in 1985 when forty-seven Labour councillors were surchaged and disqualified from office for refusing to set a rate. Out went prominent councillors like Tony Byrne and deputy leader Derek Hatton, to be replaced by a leadership which began to repair some of the damage done both to the city's finances and its image.

Meanwhile, into the breach caused by the decline of Conservative support and the abdication of the centre ground by the Labour Party, stepped the Liberal Party, later the Alliance. In 1974, buoyed by their strong support nationally and by their populist but effective brand of 'community politics', the Liberals won forty-eight seats out of ninety-nine and exerted a major influence on the Council until 1983.

The recession was accompanied by many evils. In 1981 Merseyside Police found themselves in a running battle with rioters, surging up and down Upper Parliament Street in combat with hundreds of youths. The Chief Constable authorised the first ever use of CS gas on the mainland; the Bishop of Liverpool helped to calm the situation but hundreds of windows were smashed and shops looted.

The reasons for the Toxteth riots are complex. They were not caused solely by unemployment, nor racism. Alienation, lack of hope in the future and what was seen as heavy-handed policing produced a tinder-box of resentment which was finally ignited by a police chase which resulted in a black youth coming off his motorcycle – a crowd formed to protect him and the police moved in. The crowd dispersed but re-formed later that night, setting off a train of events that are now well known, if as yet poorly understood.

People were shocked and concerned. Michael Heseltine came to Liverpool and seemed to understand at least some of the problems; many people thought he was the first government minister even to try. Lots of trees were planted, some imaginative schemes were introduced but all too little investment was forthcoming and other events in the city soon overshadowed the visits of the 'Minister for Merseyside'.

In 1983 Beryl Bainbridge, writing in the witty style of an era for which entertainment value was paramount, produced a piece of writing which is every bit as much a period piece as that of any of her predecessors. As a native of Liverpool, she was able to colour all the stories with outrageous and bitter-sweet anecdotes. Miss Bainbridge met the Rev David Sheppard, a talented cricketer who gave up the glamour of playing for England in exchange for a career in the Church and became a very popular and hard-working Bishop of Liverpool.

The bishop talked about the problems of the poor, the loss of the greater family unit, and the increased pressures on the one-parent families. He claimed that one third of his inner-city population lived in high-rise estates:

> He took me in his car to look at the infamous Netherly Estate. When it was completed the architect won a prize for the design. It would make a good prison complex. Twenty-thousand people originally lived here, shunted out of Liverpool in 1970 and left to rot by the Council, who had intended to build shops and a pub, but who forgot or else ran out of money. Eighty families remain, and Mrs Thatcher should visit it. If the Russians came over here and made it into the subject of a documentary film, the Eastern Bloc would send food parcels and donations. The concrete paths are overgrown with weeds and paved with broken glass and bricks. Those flats which aren't burnt out are boarded up with bits of rotting plywood. There's graffiti on the walls and old cookers in the matted grass. Worse, every now and then on the ground floors you see a little patio, a sort of open landing behind ornamental gates hung with nappies. Business as usual in the concentration camp. There aren't any children playing out. They stand behind the bars staring at the waste land.[1]

Beryl Bainbridge's healthy disgust for modern architecture, coupled with a nostalgic longing for an earlier Liverpool makes her account into a punchy and sharp critique of the times. 'It's as well the Liver

Birds are tied down with cables; otherwise they'd fly away in disgust', was her parting comment on the new Pierhead Concourse.

The heart of the city, its people, was ripped out. 'Overspill' towns and estates became fashionable – Kirkby, Skelmersdale and Winsford grew enormously as thousands of Liverpudlians were 'decanted' from the city centre. Planners and politicians were guilty of hideous mistakes. They built housing estates without shops; they threw up high-rise blocks without facilities and they destroyed whole communities without consultation. The whole idea of moving thousands of people out of their homes can now be seen for the mistake it was. Certainly the housing situation was bad and undoubtedly many homes were slums, but are these reasons to replace them with soulless, poorly constructed estates in green fields, without adequate transport provisions, without shops, cinemas, schools? One estate – Cantril Farm – was built without footpaths, the planners apparently blithely unaware that people may wish or need to walk about.

Again, Beryl Bainbridge's assessment is close to the root of the problem:

> When the grand scheme of redevelopment was started, the planners had enough cash to pull down all the buildings and make the motorways, and they hoped more would be found when the time came to erect houses. But they didn't find it. There isn't the money to buy any more concrete or to maintain what remains. Liverpool isn't the wealthy port it was when my father went as a cabin boy to America. It should have been obvious to a blind moggie, but it wasn't to the planners.
>
> If I were an historian I could chart the reasons for all this chaos: decline of trade, loss of Empire, aeroplanes instead of ships, cars instead of railways, synthetics instead of cotton, the trade unions, the rise of the Japanese. If I were a politician I could blame the Conservatives for greed, the Liberals for lack of confidence, the Socialists for naivety and jumping on the bandwagon of progress. But it hardly matters now. It's too late. Someone's murdered Liverpool and got away with it.[2]

Grandiose schemes multiplied. Kenneth Thompson, Tory MP for Toxteth and leader of the County Council, strongly supported what to us now is one of the most grotesque, a fourteen-lane ringroad around, or, rather, through the town centre. Thankfully, the huge public campaign against the proposals eventually won the day in this particular case.

It is easy to be critical with hindsight, to overstate the case against the planners and to overlook the good they did and the improvements that are still taking place. Many of the council houses built in recent years are of high quality. Cantril Farm is now Stockbridge Village, a partnership housing scheme set in motion after Heseltine's visit. A series of community housing initiatives have been established that are designed to give the estates back to the people. And it is significant that hundreds of 'ex-patriate' Liverpudlians regularly spend New Year's Eve back on the streets where they were brought up. Community links remain strong, despite all that has happened.

In many ways, the city's fortunes have been turned around in recent years. Hope and pride are returning and, though there is a long way to go, the image which outsiders have of Liverpool is rising; the media's portrayal is more sympathetic and realistic and many now see the city, if not actually on the road to complete recovery, then certainly at a

A modern view of the now re-developed Albert Dock looking towards the Anglican Cathedral on the hill in the distance. The project is very much in the 1980s' tradition of dockland redevelopment and has certainly proved popular with the tourists.

major crossroads on that road.

One of the first signs of revival was in 1984 when an estimated one million spectators turned out to see the great days of sail return for a brief spell as the Tall Ships Race came to Merseyside, and in the same year the International Garden Festival was one of the most positive events of the decade and, though temporary, another of the factors contributing to the birth of a new Liverpool. It provided an opportunity to reclaim the derelict land of the old Otterspool Promenade and people were actually able to walk again on the banks of the Mersey.

In recent years the Liverpool of which everybody despaired has done a great deal to help itself out of the recession. If Beryl Bainbridge had visited the Pier Head only a few years later her reaction would have been completely different. She would have found the rejuvenated Albert Dock complex, an inspired piece of renovation giving new life to Jesse Hartley's masterpiece. Television programmes broadcast from the dock, with the Liver Building standing tall and stately in the background, give a lively, refreshing and very imposing image of the famous Liverpool waterfront. Also on the waterfront is the new Maritime Museum and the Tate Gallery of Modern Art. The new complex draws millions of tourists every year. Some sceptics view the development as little more than a showpiece, diverting attention from very real problems elsewhere in the city, but there is no denying its popularity and the positive effect it has had on Liverpool's image.

It is very significant that the opening of part of the dock system to the public was such a success – though in retrospect it is not at all surprising. The popularity of the dock system with the tourists goes back to the time when Daniel Defoe admired the first wet dock, to Lord Erskine's eulogy of the waterfront at the end of the eighteenth century, to the descriptions of Herman Melville and John Masefield and to the popularity of the Overhead Railway.

A youthful and refreshing view of Liverpool is given by two sisters, Jane and Sarah Whiteley, both schoolgirls from Formby. Sarah describes her impressions of the new Tate Gallery:

When the Albert Dock was first renovated, it looked very different from old pictures. In 'George's Last Ride' – an episode from *Boys from the Blackstuff*, George Malone was shown being pushed around the dock in a wheelchair by Chrissie. The warehouses looked so bare. The place is very different now with its shops – but the iron pillars remain. On *Boys from the Blackstuff*, the pillars stood in front of the warehouses, but now they front the Tate Gallery and shops . . .

On my first visit to the Tate I was unsure of what to expect. I had heard lots about it, and I knew about the Rothkos and the glass of water. The first room we went into was full of surrealist art, and impressed me the most. It had various Dali pictures and the famous lobster telephone. I spent a long time looking at 'Autumnal Cannibalism', and discussing it with my sister.

We then went into the room with the Rothkos in. The massive red/burgundy pictures with the black lines were quite moving when you tried to appreciate them. It provoked lots of discussion among people, particularly old ladies, who completely disapproved of these being exhibited as art. The exhibition upstairs provoked the same response from the old ladies. The glass of water, which the artist was trying to 'fob off' as an oak tree, was also completely disapproved. Underneath it there was an interview with the artist. He was basically saying that, to him, it was an oak tree. When discussing that with my sister we decided that if he wanted to call it an oak tree he could, and either he believed it as an artist, and had strong beliefs in his work; or he was sitting at home laughing . . .

Jane's favourite spot was the Cavern Walks, which appealed to her age group because of its connections with the Beatles and the pop-music scene. Here, a new Liverpool comes together with that of a previous generation . . . and Jane was able to appreciate the attractions of both.

I remember my first visits to the Cavern Walks well. The first things you notice – and I remember being extremely impressed by this as a child – are the iron statues of the Beatles. They stand like idols as the centrepiece of the court. Steps spiral up to a second floor of glossy shops and as you look up you notice windows going up and up. These are flats – and very desirable ones too.

First walking into the Cavern Walks as a child is a bit like walking into the past. It was how I imagined shops would be in times gone by – except brighter and glossier. It's a mass of surprises. There is something new that you see every time you go. Sarah and I went recently and there was a giant chessboard in the centre, each square big enough to fit a human sized chess-piece on. In the middle was a large white globe lined with green fur and seated inside was a student! It was certainly a sight to puzzle at and we later discovered that it was connected with a celebration of the TV series *Prisoner* – which I've never watched. However, the juvenile eccentricities seemed to fit into the surroundings.

Each shop has a character of its own. There's a herb shop of exotic smells and pots of labelled liquids – rather like a store of potions and brews. There's a stark, trendy clothes shop, full of crude, bright colours and expensive garments. Everything is clean – almost a relief after the 'real world'. The brown tiled floor is unlittered – an unusual sight in Liverpool city centre. There are usually two or three carts selling jewellery and ice cream of all the colours and flavours you can imagine. The shops are a mixture of trendy, expensive clothes shops, novelty shops and specialist cuisine. There's a lovely little shop to explore that sells Japanese trinkets – the merchandise ranges from joss sticks to dressing gowns; everything is of Japanese origin and you can buy a beautiful fan or delicately painted chopsticks. Sarah and I once bought mum and dad a wonderful French cheese from a shop upstairs – every time you opened the fridge door its smell would fill the kitchen.

Whilst walking around the top floor you notice a child's ride, and what could be more appropriate than a yellow submarine! It is then that you notice the music playing. It's not the usual 'wallpaper' music – but a collection of Beatles' songs and, of course, you can sing along to them all. I find it interesting that I can walk around Cavern Walks and always hear someone's voice singing, with the correct accent, to the music. Mostly they are someone from my generation – who never knew the Beatles when they were having hits. Song after song is played and every one of them is familiar.

After looking around the extremely expensive Laura Ashley shop we noticed the lift for the first time. The only people who use the lift are the old, who can't manage the stairs, or the young and curious. As there are only two floors accessible for the public and both can be seen (the second is a balcony encircling the statues) everyone uses the stairs. However, when you see the lift, a feeling of excitement comes over you and you *have* to use it. It's made of glass and the experience is like travelling in a mechanical bubble from the balcony to the floor. Once you get inside you can see the people below going about their business. When you emerge at the bottom you realise that it is soundproofed and the bustle of the place hits you again.

The girls wished to explore beyond the traditional shopping areas. They quickly discovered other shops designed to appeal to a younger age group and when they explored the side streets they found that something of the traditional atmosphere of Liverpool still remained not far away from the smart, new shopping precincts.

The area around the Cavern Walks is the most exciting place for a student or young person to explore. The dark, dirty and loud shops that dominate the streets are fascinating to enter. They bring about a sense of fear for the newcomer – a fear of being too 'normal', for these areas are the height of all that is desirable and 'hip' for intelligent and outrageous youth. Hippies, Goths and Trends alike visit 'Probe', 'Backtrax' and 'Xtremes' to find out what is 'in'. The shops themselves don't resemble a 'shop' as we know it. The person behind the counter isn't at all polite, but shows some of the characteristic Liverpudlian aloofness. It's the type of shop that an average adult would be out of place in . . .

One hot Saturday afternoon Sarah and I were walking along a back street past one of the pubs. All the windows were open and from the dark tavern came the loud cheery tones of an Irish jig. Glasses clinked and beery men sang and laughed in the sweaty, grimy atmosphere. It was very amusing to listen to, and it took you away from the usual sulliness of the streets.

Away from the alcoholic smells and noises, the sadness sometimes becomes evident. Slogans insulting religion are daubed on walls. The words 'Thrash Buddhists' violently appear outside shops. Buddhism has been a religion for the young to turn to when Christianity seems to be too restricting and the ideas old-fashioned and inappropriate to real life. Elsewhere there is a political graffiti or simply a signature to show that part of this city belongs to someone. Around the graffiti are peeling posters advertising rock concerts, meetings or just giving a number to ring if you need help in any way – or if you just want to talk to someone.

I always feel as if I have never seen a part of the city inaccessible to some or simply uninteresting to some. I think it has made its impression on me and I always enjoy visiting the area when I'm in the city centre.

The Albert Dock complex and the Cavern Walks are just two of many projects which are worthy of mention and which show concern for the environment.

The Clayton Square shopping centre – of warm brick and slate, with terracotta carvings and with period plaster mouldings and attractive iron and glass arcades, where the ubiquitous motor traffic and the insipid concrete are relegated to their proper lowly status – is one of the most human-scale shopping precincts of its time in Britain.

The Canning Street restoration project, part of an effort to save some of Liverpool's two-thousand listed buildings, is a project which not only aims to save the city's heritage but also creates worthwhile and satisfying employment for local people. The restoration requires craftsman-orientated jobs needing skills in the working of metal and stone, jobs with an end product in which the worker can take some pride from the skill of his own hands – skills which seem today to be consistently undervalued, but which give a satisfaction which no kind of factory work or uncreative office job can ever match.

In Shaw Street are repairs to the peeling plasterwork, to broken windows and replacements for the corrugated iron doorways of a street which was once more famous than Rodney Street as an abode of medical practitioners. The development of the Merseyrail underground and overground transport system is an excellent and efficient piece of planning. There are many who remember St George's Hall, the Town Hall and all the civic buildings as black with the soot and grime of the Industrial Revolution. The natural colour of the stone has returned again, hopefully for ever.

Alexis de Tocqueville, writing in 1835, was probably the last outsider to call Liverpool beautiful, and it is difficult to convince outsiders that it ever was so or that it could ever have beauty again. The next and most daunting task facing the planners is to revitalise the housing in the inner city. Here the Eldonian Village housing co-operative has achieved what successive councils have failed to do. Families and pensioners have been rehoused from tower blocks into attractive, friendly and high-quality housing with a sense of community and belonging.

It is Liverpool's greatest challenge to provide a decent and friendly environment for people to live in, to provide jobs, trees and homes with front doors, to build recreation areas and create working local communities on land which is incredibly cheap compared to inner-

Top: The birthplace of W. E. Gladstone on Rodney Street, now near the heart of some excellent conservation work.

Bottom: *A hugely important addition to the twentieth-century Liverpool skyline, the Anglican Cathedral.*

city areas of more prosperous but less fascinating cities. In spite of its problems, Liverpool has a very strong sense of identity, and it has far more to offer as a city than any new town could ever hope to offer. It has a history.

Despite the problems of the last fifty years, Liverpudlians are intensely loyal to their city. Their outlook on life is very distinctive; their humour biting. They do not suffer pretension lightly and always have a stinging and usually witty put-down at the ready if they detect any falseness in others. This spontaneity of humour and strong attachment to the colourful phrase, rattled out as quick as a flash, is a Scouse hallmark evident to all visitors, most of whom are quickly captivated by the warmth and intense humanity of the people they meet there. One journalist with a national newspaper, finding himself in a Liverpool pub without anywhere to stay on his first visit to the city, ended up being offered the key to the landlord's own flat in town for the night – generosity and trust which, he claims, altered his view of the city for all time. More than any other place in the land, Liverpool's history is in its people.

By what name should we call them? The correct terminology for the Liverpool native will long remain a topic of conversation in public houses and other local gatherings. Some argue that the term 'Liverpolitan' is correct and that 'Liverpudlian' is clearly a later, debased term, generated no doubt by the inverted snobbery and down-to-earth philosophy of the natives. While 'Liverpolitan' is certainly the older form, 'Liverpudlian' was in use, by James Picton among others, as early as 1875. It was obviously in general use by that date, and is clearly now the only recognised form. Picton states that the term 'Dicky Sam' was derived from 'the familiar mode of address of the natives in older times' – there is a theory that Dicky Sam was a landlord called Richard Samuels who ran a pub on Mann Island, but the story seems to be apocryphal. The change of familiar terminology from 'Dicky Sam' to 'Scouser' belongs to the early-twentieth century, although scouse as a local dish is mentioned in connection with Liverpool from at least a century earlier. The subject is surrounded by a great deal of folklore and little factual evidence so that it becomes dangerous grounds for the historian – but it is evident that all these terms are clearly acceptable in the right context.

The familiar Liverpool accent, noticeably different from the dialect of the surrounding part of the country, is certainly not without interest and carries within it a fascinating piece of history. For language experts have been able to prove that it comprises a hybrid of Lancashire and Irish, a relict of the great influx of Irish into Liverpool in the 1840s. Liverpool has been a very cosmopolitan town for many generations, but going back to the time of Roscoe and earlier, it may be safely assumed that the Liverpool speech was a pure Lancashire dialect and was much closer to the neighbouring accents of Lancashire and Cheshire.

Liverpolitan, Liverpudlian, Dicky Sam or Scouser. For those who lived on the banks of the Mersey in times past their world was every atom as real as the world of today and the problems they faced were every bit as pressing. The youth of the world will always associate Liverpool with the Mersey sound of the 'sixties, which still reverberates around the world. But the history of Liverpool goes much deeper than pop music, comedians and football clubs.

Lesser ports have their ships and their ocean liners and some have an enviable history of sail, but it was Liverpool which developed the man-made dock system; it was Liverpool which became the main port of the abominable slave trade and it was Liverpool which became the centre of the emigration to America and further afield when the movement reached its peak in the nineteenth century.

It was Liverpool's position as the seaboard of the Industrial Revolution which gave it great importance in the history of transport – not simply in the development of the canals and the railways but also the sea transport and the long changeover from sailing ships to ocean-going vessels powered by steam and oil. In many cases the history of Liverpool is not only of national importance but touches on some of the great episodes in the history of the world.

It is the history and evolution of shipping from the fishing smacks to the *Mauretania* and to the container traffic of today. It is John Masefield captivated by the *Wanderer* in full sail tacking her way proudly out of the Mersey. It is William Rathbone writing to Florence Nightingale about his district nursing movement. It is the emigrant ships unfurling their sails on the Mersey to depart for a new world and a new life. It is Gladstone's childhood memories in Rodney Street. It is Fanny Kemble riding on the footplate of the *Rocket*. It is William Roscoe fighting for the abolition of the slave trade. It is the terrible disaster at St Nicholas' Church when the spire fell on that fateful Sunday morning.

Earlier still, it is the eighteenth-century shipping merchants with their telescopes trained on the horizon. It is Thomas Steers building the first wet dock which eventually evolved to eight miles of man-made waterfront. It is Edward Moore grumbling and belly-aching about his tenants. It is the euphoria which greeted the appearance of the long awaited *Antelope* over the horizon with her cargo of sugar cane from the West Indies. It is Jeremiah Horrox peering at the skies through his telescope and developing his theory of the lunar motion. It is the busy market town for the villages of Lancashire and Cheshire. It is a fishing village dominated by a great square castle with drawbridge and moat. It is a green, wooded riverbank with a medieval town field and a small natural harbour. It is all these things and much more.

'What it may grow to in time, I know not', said Defoe in 1708, and we could just as well ask the same question in 1990. Anybody who is prepared to take the trouble to study Liverpool could not help but arrive at the same conclusion as Daniel Defoe. 'Liverpoole is one of the wonders of Britain.'

THE END

Appendix

The streetnames of Liverpool

ANY of the street names mentioned in the early chapters no longer exist. This appendix will help the reader to identify certain obsolete street names and to includes items of interest on street names which still exist. The list is by no means complete and covers only the central area of the city, it is selected to include street names of local significance to help the local historian. As with any other town or city, many streets are named after national figures, battles and statesmen – these names are usually obvious and are therefore not generally included.

Atherton Street
This street ran eastwards from Pool Lane in the early eighteenth century. It was granted to the corporation by Peter Atherton who was bailiff in 1673.[1]

Banastre Street
Named after a local man, General Sir Banastre Tarleton MP, son of John Tarleton, who fought in the Amercian Civil War. He was born in a house at the corner of Fenwick Street and Water Street.

Bank Street
One of the original streets of King John's Liverpool. In the Middle Ages there was probably an earthen embankment at the river end of the street. It became Water Street in the sixteenth century.[2]

Bankhall Street
Bank Hall was the second home of the Moore family and was demolished in 1770.

Basnett Street
Laid out in the 1770s by the Basnett family. Christopher Basnett was the first minister of Key Street Chapel where the Protestant Dissenters met in 1707.[3]

Bath Street
A reminder of when Liverpool was frequented for sea bathing. The sea water baths were built on the river bank in 1765 and demolished in 1817 to make way for Princes's Dock.

Beloe Steeet
Charles Henry Beloe was a civil engineer who served for Abercromby Ward on the Liverpool Council in the 1890s.

Benson Street
After John Benson, a member of the Liverpool family of that name.

Berry Street
Henry Berry was the second of Liverpool's Dock Engineers.

Bixteth Street
Thomas Bixteth was mayor of Liverpool in 1701. He is reported to have paved the street in front of his house with his own hands.[3]

Bold Street
After Jonas Bold, who held the lease of the land when it was a ropery in the eighteenth century.

Bolton Street
John Bolton was a wealthy merchant who in 1803 raised and equipped a regiment of 800 men. He fought and won the last duel to be fought in Liverpool, on December 20th 1805.[3]

Bridge Alley
The alley ran from Castle Street to Fenwick Street in the seventeenth century. At one end was the Dry Bridge over the castle moat. At the other end lived Thomas Bridge – a 'drunken fellow' according to Edward Moore.[1]

Brodie Avenue
John Alexander Brodie of Aigburth Hall was Liverpool City Engineer from 1898 to 1925. He is credited with the invention of football goal nets and a type of concrete prefabricated house. He introduced the first reserved tracks for Liverpool tramcars.

Brooks Alley
Joseph Brook was an eighteenth-century merchant and ropemaker. The alley was laid through the ornamental garden of his house in Hanover Street.

Button Street
John Button was a leaseholder when the street was cut in 1722. He was still alive in 1784, claiming to have lived in the reigns of six monarchs.

Byrom Street
After George Byrom, a pavoir and builder, who had a yard nearby. It was formerly known as Towns End Lane or Dog Kennel Lane, as for a time the Corporation kept a pack of hounds there.[3]

Cable Street
Mentioned in the municipal records of 1701, originally a rope-making centre.

Campbell Street
Formerly Pot House Lane and the site of one of the Liverpool potteries. George Campbell was a slave dealer and a sugar merchant, he was Mayor in 1763.

Canning Place
The site of the Old Dock. It received its present name in 1832 in memory of George Canning MP, a benefactor of the new customs house which was built on the site.

Cases Street
After Thomas Case, early eighteenth century, brother-in-law of Sarah Clayton (see Clayton Square).

Castle Hill
Near the castle in what is now the Derby Square area; it had 18 houses in the rates assessment of 1705. Daniel Defoe lodged here, in Samuel Done's house, on one of his visits to Liverpool.[1]

Castle Street
One of the seven original streets of Liverpool, originating from the early thirteenth century. The castle stood on what is now Derby Square.

Catherine Street
The first house in Catherine Street was built by William Jones (1788-1876). He named the street after his mother.

Cazneau Street
After Joseph Cazneau, a merchant, who built the first house here in 1796.

Chapel Street
Another of the seven original streets of Liverpool. Although St. Nicholas Chapel stood at the seaward end from about 1355, the street was named after the older and smaller chapel of St. Mary del Key which existed in 1257.[2]

Christian Street
After Philip Christian, a potter who is reputed to have built a house on the corner of the street. The stone for his house was salvaged from a tower called Gibson's Folly which stood on the site of the Wellington Column.[3]

Church Street
St. Peter's Church was consecrated 'over the pool' in 1704 (Chap 4), a beautiful post-Renaissance church which served as the Pro-Cathedral from 1880 to 1922. St. Peter's was the oldest building in twentieth-century Liverpool, but it was inexplicably and thoughtlessly demolished as soon as the cathedral was consecrated.

Clayton Square
Named after Sarah Clayton who planned the original square circa 1745. She was the daughter of William Clayton MP. According to Gore, Mrs Isabel James and Madam Clayton were the only people in Liverpool to have closed carriages in the year 1741.[4]

Cleveland Square
John Cleveland (1661-1716) was Mayor of Liverpool in 1703 and MP from 1710 to 1713. He purchased the Manor of Birkenhead shortly before his decease.

Cockspur Street
The site of one of the Liverpool cockpits.

Colquitt Street
John Colquitt was a collector of customs. He lived in Hanover Street but his land also included Berry Street.

Cook Street
Mentioned as early as 1697, presumably a cook's premises.

Combermere Street
Lt. General Stapleton Cotton, 1st Viscount Combermere was awarded the freedom of the borough in 1821 for his wartime service and for his services as Governor of Barbados.[3]

Copperas Hill
The Copperas Works, shown in Buck's Prospect of 1728, produced copper parts for the shipping industry, and was situated outside the town at that time. The works were forced to move in 1756 because of the foul smell they emitted, but the name Copperas Hill remained.[2]

Cresswell Street
Justice Cresswell MP represented Liverpool in Parliament from 1837 to 1842.

Cropper Street
James Cropper was a Quaker shipping merchant. He was an abolitionist and a pacifist – his ships carried only dummy guns as a deterrent.

Crosshall Street
The site of the Cross family residence which stood on the site of the Municipal Buildings.

Cumberland Street
A memorial to the regiment of Liverpool Volunteers in the 'forty-five' rebellion. The Duke of Cumberland defended Carlisle against the rebels with the aid of the Liverpool regiment.

Cunliffe Street
Foster Cunliffe became Mayor in 1716, 1729 and 1735. His epitaph described him as 'a merchant whose sagacity, honesty and diligence procured wealth and credit to himself and his country, a magistrate who administered justice with discernment, candour and impartiality, a Christian devout and exemplary' – it omitted to mention the fact that he was a slave trader![3]

Customhouse Lane
A narrow lane which led to the site of Liverpool's third customs house near the Old Dock.

Dale Street
One of the seven original streets of Liverpool and for several centuries the most populous. In the Middle Ages the Dale was in the neighbourhood of St. John's Gardens.

Dawson Street
Pudsey Dawson was Colonel of the Royal Liverpool Volunteers and became Mayor in 1799. A humane man and a social worker, he is remembered as the founder of the School for the Blind (See Pudsey Street and references 4 and 5).

Deane Street
Richard Deane owned a ropery on the site of this street.

Denison Street
William Dennison was a successful privateer who made a profit of £7,000 from his first three enterprises.[3]

Derby Square
Named after the Earls of Derby, this is the site of Liverpool Castle.

Dorans Lane
Felix Doran was an Irish merchant who lived in Lord Street. He was part owner of a slaver called *Bloom* which made a profit of £28,123 from the sale of 307 slaves on one voyage alone.[3]

Edmund Street
Formerly Mill House Lane. Renamed in the early eighteenth century by Sir Cleave Moore in honour of his bride Ann, daughter of Joseph Edmund.

Fenwick Alley
Phenwyck Alley (1708). Ran from Fenwick Street to Castle Street. Laid out in 1668 by Edward Moore.[1]

Fenwick Street
Phenwyck Street (1708). Laid out in 1668 by Edward Moore, named after the family of his first wife Dorothy Fenwick. (see Chapter Three).

Gildart Street
Richard Gildart was Mayor in 1714 and 1736. He later became an MP for Liverpool.

Gore Street
Commemorates John Gore who compiled the first directory of Liverpool in 1766 and published Gore's *Liverpool Advertiser.*

Goree
The Goree Piazzas, dating from 1793 but reconstructed after a fire in 1802, were

once almost as famous as the Liver Buildings on the Liverpool waterfront-they were destroyed in 1941 during the Blitz. Goree was supposed to be a bare rock off the Cape Verde Islands where slaves were assembled for shipment to the plantations.

Grayson Street
Edward Grayson was a shipwright who was killed in a duel in the year 1804.

Great Howard Street
John Howard was a reformer and a philanthropist. He was involved with the building of the Borough Gaol here in 1786.

Great Newton Street
The Newton commemorated here is John Newton, a former Liverpool slaving captain who became an active abolitionist. Later in life he was completely reformed and wrote several well-loved hymns including 'Amazing Grace' and 'How Sweet the Name of Jesus Sounds'.

Hackin's Hey
John Hacking was a tenant of Edward Moore and lived in a 'pretty croft' on the site. He was described as a 'very honest man' – this was praise indeed from Edward Moore.[1]

Hall Street
Medieval, see Mill Street and Bank Street. Moore Old Hall was built here and by 1633 it had become known as Old Hall Street.

Hardman Street
Named after the wife of John Hardman of Allerton Hall who owned the land where the street was made.

Hardy Street
After Thomas Masterman Hardy, Captain of Nelson's flagship at Trafalgar.

Harrington Street
Originally known as Castle Hey, it was built on land owned by the Harrington family, circa 1700.

Heyworth Street
James Heyworth was a landowner in this neighbourhood and built the first villa in the street.

High Street
See Juggler Street. It ran through the site of the Town Hall and Exchange Flags.[2]

Hockenhall Street
Edward Moore in the seventeenth century refers to his cousin Henry Hockenhall of Tranmere. The Hockenhalls presumably had property here. It was formerly known as Molyneux Weint.[3]

Hope Street
William Hope was a merchant who built the first house in the street at the corner of Hardman Street, on the site occupied by the Philharmonic Hall.

Hunter Street
Rowland Hunter was a retired tax collector and tradesman who previously lived in Cable Street.

Hurst Street
Thomas Hurst was a shipwright who was granted a lease in part of the Strand in 1710.

Huskisson Street
William Huskisson, MP for Liverpool, was killed on the opening day of the Liverpool and Manchester Railway. (see text).

James Street
Originally called Saint James Street, it was cut through Tarleton's fields in 1676. Incorrectly attributed to Roger James, a seventeenth-century ship's carpenter (but not a saint!) who died in 1694.[1]

Juggler Street
The original main street of Liverpool. Thought to be the place where jugglers, acrobats and street entertainers performed in the thirteenth century. It ran from Castle Street to Old Hall Street, and became known as High Street in the eighteenth century. The Town Hall stands on the site.

Kent Street
Richard Kent was a merchant and shipowner. In 1768 he built a house at the corner of Kent Street and Duke Street.

Knight Street
Laid out by the brothers John and James Knight circa 1785.

Leather Lane
The leather market stood here until 1833, when it was moved to Gill Street.

Leece Street
William Leece was an eighteenth-century merchant, who had lived in Water Street.

Leeds Street
Formerly known as Maiden's Green, this was the original terminus of the Leeds and Liverpool Canal.

Leigh Street
Early eighteenth-century. Elizabeth Leigh was the mother of Sarah Clayton (see Clayton Square).

Lime Street
Named after the lime kilns which stood on the site of the railway station until about 1806. It was formerly known as Lime Kiln Lane.

Lister Drive
James Lister was a cotton broker who became chairman of the West Derby Local Board.

Lord Street
Originally Lord Molyneux's Street, it was laid out in 1668. In 1671 it was extended to bridge over the Old Pool.

Lancelot's Hey
Seventeenth-century, it ran through the croft of Thomas Lancelot whom Edward Moore called 'a drunken idle fellow'.[1]

Lydia Anne Street
Lydia Anne was the wife of George Perry who managed the Phoenix Foundry at the end of the street.

Manesty's Lane
Joseph Manesty was a merchant who lived on the corner. His garden was famous for its lavendar.

Mann Island
John Mann was an oil-stone dealer who died in 1784. Formerly known as Mersey Island, it was an artificial island created by the docks at the Pier Head. It ceased to be an island when George's Dock was filled, but the name is still in use.

Mill Street
One of the original streets of Liverpool. Also known as Whiteacre Street, it became Hall Street in about 1620 and then Old Hall Street. The site of the Old Hall built by Thomas Moore in 1388-9.[2]

Moor Street (Medieval)
Thirteenth-century, it is named after the Moore family. It ran into Tythebarne Street where Lord Molyneux built his tithebarn, and eventually became known as Tithebarn Street.

Moor Street (17th-century)
An alley off Fenwick Street, laid out by Edward Moore in 1665.

Moorfields
Formerly fields on the estates of the Moor family. First mentioned in 1697.

New Bird Street
Alderman Joseph Bird was a slave trader who became Mayor in 1746. There was an older Bird Street between James Street and Redcross Street.[3]

North John Street
Seventeenth-century, see Saint John Street

Oil Street
The firm of Earles and Carter produced oil on this site by a seed-crushing process.

Old Hall Street
The site of the original Moore Hall, it became the Old Hall when they built a new residence at Bank Hall. (See Hall Street and Mill Street).

Old Haymarket
The site of the Hay Market until 1841.

Old Ropery
Goes back to the seventeenth century, when William Bushell had a rope works on the site.

Paradise Street
Named in about 1710 by Thomas Steers, the engineer of the Old Dock and so called because he once lived in Paradise Street, Rotherhithe, London. Formerly known as Common Shore, it follows the line of the Old Pool very closely.[3]

Pickop Street
Pickop and Miles was a firm of brewers whose premises were in the street.

Pilgrim Street
Formerly Jamieson Street. The *Pilgrim* was a Liverpool privateer which brought a prize ship into Barbados and sold it for a handsome profit.

Pool Lane
The continuation of Castle Street, it ran down to the old Pool of Liverpool in the seventeenth century. [1] and [2]

Porter Street
Thomas Colley Porter was elected Mayor in 1827 and laid the foundation stone of the Customs House in 1828. A scandal followed when it was discovered that his election had been fixed.[3]

Preeson's Row
A row of houses running from James Street to Red Cross Street, originally built on the edge of the castle moat by Alderman Thomas Preeson circa 1660.[1]

Price Street
The Price family were Lords of the Manor

of Birkenhead, and were related to the Clevelands of Liverpool.

Pudsey Street
This street seems to be the second street to be named after Pudsey Dawson. It is unusual, but not unique, to find a forename used. (see Dawson Street).

Quakers Alley
The site of the original Friends' meeting house, which became a school in 1796 when the Quakers left for Hunter Street.

Queen Street
Named after Queen Anne. The centre of the Welsh immigrant community.

Rainford Gardens and Square
Peter Rainford was Mayor in 1740. He ran a market garden in 1697, on land which bordered on the Old Pool.

Ranelagh Street
The Ranelagh Gardens were in Chelsea, London. The Liverpool Ranelagh Tea Gardens were named after them and stood on the site of the Adelphi Hotel.

Rathbone Street
After the Rathbone family (see text).

Renshaw Street
In the eighteenth century the brothers John and Edward Renshaw owned a ropery on the site.

Red Cross Street
Very old, and mentioned in 1677. The name is a mystery. The pillory stood at the east end of the street but there is no reference to a cross in the area.[1]

Richmond Street
The Richmonds were a very old Liverpool family. Silvester Richmond was mayor in 1672. He was the son of Doctor Silvestor Richmond, a celebrated Liverpool physician who built some almhouses for sailor's widows.[1]

Rodney Street
No compendium of Liverpool would be complete without a reference to Gladstone's birthplace and the Harley Street of the North. Baron Rodney (1719-92) won great renown with his victory over the French in 1782.

Roe Street
William Roe was a merchant who lived at the north end of Queen Square. He had a fountain in his garden fed by piped water from the old Fall Well. His house became the Stork Hotel.[3]

Roscoe Street
Hardly known outside Liverpool, William Roscoe (1753-1831) is often referred to as 'Liverpool's greatest son' and enjoys a local status even greater than that of Gladstone.

Rose Mary Lane
The original name of Fazakerly Street, (before 1706). Rose Mary cannot be identified.[2]

St. James' Street
Derived from St. James', Toxteth, but James Street was once known by this name.

St. John Street
Now North John Street and South John Street. So called because the land belonged to a chantry in the name of St. John in the church of St. Nicholas. St. John's Gardens are named after the church of St. John which stood there until 1898.[1]

School Lane
The charity school which was founded by Bryan Blundell originally occupied a site on the south side of School Lane until 1718; it was then transferred to the purpose-built Blue Coat School, close to the original site.

Seel Street
Thomas Seel was a merchant who lived in Hanover Street. Seel Street was built through his extensive garden.

Sir Thomas Street
Sir Thomas Johnson MP (1654-1728) was mayor in 1715, but died in London in poverty.

Slater Street
Gill Slater was a Captain of the Liverpool Volunteers in 1766.

South John Street
Formerly Trafford's Wient after Henry Trafford who was Mayor in 1740. Formerly part of John Street (see John Street and North John Street).

Sparling Street
John Sparling was Mayor in 1790. He proposed the building of Queens Dock and began construction at his own expense before selling it to the Corporation.

Strand
Formerly called New Street. It was laid out in 1740 and before that time it was a strip of sand between high and low water.

Sweeting Street
Alderman Sweeting was Mayor in 1698. The street was formerly called Elbow Lane.

Tabley Street
Built on the land of William Pownall who was mayor in 1767. He came from Tabley in Cheshire.

Thomas Street
Early eighteenth-century. Built on land owned by Thomas Lurting, it was one of the streets running eastwards off Pool Lane.

Tithebarn Street
Tyth Barn Street (1708). Here Lord Molyneux built his barn to store the tithes. It was formerly known as Moor Street.[2]

Union Street
Commemorates the union of England and Scotland in 1717.

Vandries Street
Vandries was a Dutchman who ran the Vandries House Hotel on the North Shore. It was a place for sea bathing in Regency Liverpool (see text).

Water Street
Originally Bank Street but the name Water Street was used from about 1540. It ran down to the waters of the Mersey.

Waterside
Extended from Red Cross Street to Pool Bridge in the early-eighteenth century.

Whiteacre Street
One of the original streets from the thirteenth century, became Hall Street and then Old Hall Street (see Mill Street).[2]

William Brown Street
Formerly known as Shaw's Brow. William Brown was a wealthy Victorian benefactor who gave Liverpool its first museum and public library.

Wolstenholme Square
The Wolstenholme family owned the land on which this square was built. It was supposedly the first enclosed garden to be constructed in Liverpool.

References:
Where a reference is given, more information on the particular street or individual will be found in the numbered publication. Picton's work is also a valuable general reference, plus the many maps and plans in the Liverpool Records Office:

1. Henry Peet, 'Liverpool in the Reign of Queen Anne', (1908). *THSL&C* Vol 59 (NS Vol 23).
2. Merseyside Archealogical Society, *The Changing Face of Liverpool* (1981).
3. Thomas Lloyd-James, *Liverpool Street Names* (1981).
4. Gore, *Annals of Liverpool* (1895 etc.).

Notes on the text

MANY previous histories of Liverpool exist. They are full of interest and some have value today. The main reference works are listed here in chronological order. Other references will be found in the various chapters, usually dealing with specialised subjects covered in that chapter. This bibliography does not, of course, pretend to be complete. There is a vast amount of literature on Liverpool and its history, with more appearing all the time, and this is not the place to list it exhaustively. If readers wish to read more about Liverpool, there is an excellent collection of primary, printed and secondary sources in Liverpool's Library and Record Office, the Maritime Record Centre and, for the earlier period in particular, the Lancashire Record Office in Preston.

W. Enfield, *An Essay towards the History of Liverpool* (1773).

T. Troughton, *The History of Liverpool . . .* (1810).

J. Touzeau, *The Rise and Progress of Liverpool from 1551 to 1835* (1835).

T. Baines, *History of Liverpool* (1852).

J. A. Picton, *City of Liverpool Municipal Archives* (2 volumes, 1883 and 1886).

W. F. Irvine, *Liverpool in Charles I's Time* (1899).

R. Muir and E. M. Platt, *A History of Municipal Government in Liverpool* (1906).

W. Farrer and J. Brownbill, *The Victoria History of the Counties of England, Lancashire*, vol. 2 (1908).

H. Peet, *Liverpool in the Reign of Queen Anne* (1908).

W. Farrer and J. Brownbill, *The Victoria History of the Counties of England, Lancashire*, vol. 4 (1911).

H. S. and H. E. Young, *Bygone Liverpool* (1913).

J. A. Twemlow, *Liverpool Town Books*, vol. 1. (1918), vol. 2 (1935).

G. Chandler, *Liverpool* (1957).

G. Chandler and E. B. Saxton, *Liverpool under James I* (1960).

G. Chandler and E. K. Wilson, *Liverpool under Charles I* (1965).

W. C. M. Jackson, *Herdman's Liverpool* (1968).

F. E. Hyde, *Liverpool and the Mersey* (1971).

E. Midwinter, *Old Liverpool* (1971).

Abbreviations

IN the notes on the text the following abbreviations have been used:

THSL&C	*Transactions of the Historic Society of Lancashire and Cheshire*
RS	*Record Society of Lancashire and Cheshire*
CS	*Chetham Society*
VCH	*Victoria County Histories.*
Liv. RO	Liverpool Record Office.

References in the following notes are also abbreviated by using the surnames only of the authors of the various general histories listed above. Picton refers to his *Memorials of Liverpool*. Chandler refers to his *Liverpool*.

Notes on the text

Chapter One

1. King John's Charter, Liv. RO.
2. Chandler.
3. Poll Tax, 3 Richard II (1379), Public Record Office.

Chapter Two

1. Dodsworth MSS, lxxxvii, p39, Bodleian Library.
2. 'Scottish Fielde', CS, xxxvii.
3. Special Collections (1414), Ancient Petitions file 122, no. 6091, Public Record Office.
4. Twemlow, ii, p53.
5. Ibid.
6. John Leland, *Itinerary.*
7. R. Gladstone, 'A Report on Liverpool Castle', THSL&C, lix.
8. Twemlow, i, p292.

Chapter Three

1. A. B. Whatton, *Memoir of Jeremiah Horrox* (1859).
2. E. M. Platt, 'Liverpool during the Civil War', THSL&C, lxi (n.s. xxv).
3. Adam Martindale, 'Autobiography of Adam Martindale, CS, iv.
4. Platt.
5. Edward Moore, 'Moore Rental', CS, xii.

Chapter Four

1. Celia Fiennes, *The Journeys of Celia Fiennes.*
2. Ibid.
3. CS, xii.
4. Daniel Defoe, *A Tour Through England and Wales.*
5. Ibid.
6. Henry Peet, 'Liverpool in the Reign of Queen Anne, THSL&C, n.s. xxiii.
7. Ibid.
8. Defoe, op cit.

Chapter Five

1. Nicholas Blundell, 'The Great Diurnal of Nicholas Blundell, RS, cx, cxii, cxiv.
2. P. Aughton, *North Meols and Southport* (1988).
3. Defoe, op cit.

4. E. Baines, *History of the County Palatine of Lancaster,* vol 1.
5. S. &. N. Buck, 'The South-West Prospect of Liverpoole', (1728), copy in Liv. RO.
6. John Wesley, *Journal of John Wesley.*
7. Baines, op cit.
8. Samuel Derrick, *Letter from Liverpoole to the Earl of Corke,* (2 August, 1760).
9. John Gore, *The Liverpool Directory for the year 1766,* copy in Liv. RO.
10. John Eyes' 'Plan of Liverpool' (1765).
11. George Perry's 'Plan of the Town and Port of Liverpool (1769).

Chapter Six

1. G. Williams, *History of the Liverpool Privateers* (1897).
2. Gore's *Directory*: 'Annals of Liverpool' (1895).
3. VCH, iv.
4. W. Roscoe, *The Wrongs of Africa.*
5. Chandler.
6. Roscoe, op cit.
7. J. Newton, *Thoughts Upon the African Slave Trade* (1788).
8. R. Anstey and P. E. H. Hair, *Liverpool, the African Slave Trade and Abolition* (1976).
9. F. E. Sanderson, *The Liverpool Abolitionists* (chapter of Ref 7).
10. T. Clarkson, *History of . . . the Abolition of the Slave Trade* (1808).
11. G. Chandler, *William Roscoe of Liverpool* (1953).
12. VCH, iv.

Chapter Seven

1. W. E. Gladstone, *Autobiography* (1880).
2. Enfield.
3. Ibid.
4. Compiled from Gore, Baines and Troughton.
5. *Lancs. & Cheshire Antiquarian Society,* xliv.
6. Picton.
7. Baines.
8. Original from a broadsheet by Harkness of Preston.
9. Picton.
10. Baines and Picton.

Chapter Eight

1. Thomas Creevey, *The Creevey Papers* (ed. John Gore, 1903 and 1948).
2. Ellen Weeton, *Journal of a Governess* (2nd Edition, 1969).
3. R. Syers, *History of Everton*.
4. Picton.
5. Alexis de Tocqueville, *Journeys to England and Ireland* (1835). De Tocqueville here is falling prey to the popular misconception that slavery and cotton were the twin pillars of Liverpool's dramatic eighteenth-century growth. In fact, overseas trade in other goods laid the basis of expansion. Cotton did become very important, of course, but slavery was never a major component of the town's overall trade.

Chapter Nine

1. L. T. C. Holt, *George and Robert Stephenson* (1961).
2. T. Creevey, op cit.
3. F. A. Kemble, *Record of a Girlhood* (1878).
4. *Wheeler's Manchester Chronicle*.
5. *Liverpool Courier*.

Chapter Ten

1. *Liverpool Courier,* 5 July 1815.
2. A. C. Wardle, 'Early Steamships on Merseyside, THSL&C, xcii.
3. *Liverpool Mercury* 23 July 1819.
4. Lawrence Hill, 'Glimpses of Liverpool during the reign of George IV' THSL&C, xcii.
5. *Liverpool Courier*, June 1819.
6. Herman Melville, *Redburn*.
7. Ibid.
8. Ibid.

Chapter Eleven

1. E. Baines, *Directory of Lancashire* (1824).
2. Ibid.
3. Chandler.
4. H. Melville, op cit.
5. Midwinter.
6. Nathaniel Hawthorne, *English Notebooks* (ed. Randall Stewart, 1941)/
7. Cecil Woodham-Smith, *Florence Nightingale*.
8. Ibid.

Chapter Twelve

1. Liverpool Heritage Bureau, *Buildings of Liverpool* (1978).
2. Gore, 'Annals of Liverpool' (1895).
3. VCH, iv.
4. Masefield to W. B. Yeats, correspondence.
5. Franklin D. Roosevelt, correspondence.
6. John Masefield, *Ships*.

Chapter Thirteen

1. Scouse Press, *An Everyday History of Liverpool*, ii.
2. J. B. Priestley, *English Journey* (1934).
3. H. Forrester, *Twopence to Cross the Mersey* (1974).
4. J. B. Priestley, op cit.
5. Richard Whittington-Egan, *The Great Liverpool Blitz* (1987).
6. F. J. Williams, 'The Blues and the Reds', THSL&C, cxxxiv.
7. Midwinter.

Chapter Fourteen

1. Author's memoirs.
2. Ibid.
3. Geoffrey Moorhouse, *The Other England* (1964).

Chapter Fifteen

1. Beryl Bainbridge, *English Journey* (1986).
2. Ibid.

Acknowledgements

THE author and publisher wish to acknowledge the help and assistance of many people. In particular, all of the staff of the Liverpool Record Office who helped greatly in tracking down many of the illustrations for this book and the Library Authorities for their permission to reproduce them; the staff of the Merseyside Maritime Record Centre for their invaluable assistance; also the staffs of the Lancashire Record Office, of the Walker Art Gallery and of Liverpool City Libraries. Without the help of these institutions the book would have been much the poorer. Thanks also to the *Liverpool Echo* for several of the more recent photographs. Particular thanks go to Rob Philpott and the Merseyside Archaeological Society for permission to reproduce some of the maps from their excellent book, *The Changing Face of Liverpool, 1207-1727*, published jointly with the University of Liverpool, Merseyside County Council and Merseyside County Museum in 1981.

Many individuals have contributed items to the book, including the late Joe Bagley of Liverpool University, one of the first to convince me of the fascination of Liverpool's history; the Liverpool and District Family History Society, a truly world-wide society and already a great Liverpool institution; Bryan Kernaghan of Southport, Dr Alan Crosby who did a great deal of excellent picture research; Tony Bolt of Bristol for help with the clock photographs; my nieces Jane and Sarah Whiteley of Formby.

Several people have very kindly read the text, commented upon it and suggested improvements. In particular I would like to thank John Woods, whose excellent new book *Growin' Up* has recently added a most refreshing view of Liverpool in the 1920s and '30s; Tony Goddard, Frank Nicholson and Peter Rainford also helped greatly.

Note on the illustrations

MOST of the illustrations in this book have been taken from the superb collection of local photographs in Liverpool Record Office. The Walker Art Gallery supplied many of the portraits and photographs of the paintings: those reproduced on pages 48, of Vicountess Molyneux on page 49, 61, 67, 80, 81, 85 (2), 86 (centre and bottom), 88 (2), 89, 93 (bottom), 96-7, 100, 103, 104 (2), 107, 112 (top), 118 (2), 119 (2), 120 (top), 134 (2), 147 (centre), 149, 161, 162, 164 (bottom), and 165 are from their collection. The Merseyside Maritime Record Centre at the Albert Dock provided many of the photographs with a nautical theme: those on pages 84, 139 (top), 146, 147 (bottom), 170 (2), 171 (bottom), 177 (2), 178 (top) and 196 (bottom) are from their collection. *The Liverpool Echo* kindly provided the illustrations on pages 193, 199, 204, 205 and 206. The Lancashire Record Office in Preston kindly allowed us to reproduce the following illustrations from their archives: on pages 33 (DP 175), 56 (DDX 99/5), 57 (DDX 99/6) and 82 (DDX 99/8). The fold-out map (DP 175) is also reproduced by kind permission of the Lancashire Record Office. Four maps of Liverpool, on pages 12, 22, 39 and 53, are taken from *The Changing Face of Liverpool*. All other hand-drawn maps are by Alistair Hodge. The coats of arms were drawn by the author.

Index

Note:
* – denotes multiple reference on one page.
P – refers to pictures and illustrations.